Published by Robert Kennedy Publishing
5775 McLaughlin Road
Mississauga, ON
L5R 3P7 Canada

Design by Gabriella Caruso
Edited by Wendy Morley

National Library of Canada Cataloguing in Publication

Kennedy, Robert, 1938-
        1001 musclebuilding tips / Robert Kennedy.

ISBN-13: 978-1-55210-040-0
ISBN-10: 1-55210-040-5

        1. Bodybuilding. I. Title. II. Title: One thousand one
musclebuilding tips.

GV546.5.K459 2006   613.7'13   C2006-906645-0

10 9 8 7 6 5 4 3 2

Distributed in Canada by
NBN (National Book Network)
67 Mowat Avenue, Suite 241
Toronto, ON
M6K 3E3

Distributed in USA by
NBN (National Book Network)
15200 NBN Way
Blue Ridge Sumitt, PA
17214

Printed in Canada

1001
MUSCLEBUILDING
TIPS

ROBERT KENNEDY
PUBLISHER OF MUSCLEMAG INTERNATIONAL

RKP ROBERT KENNEDY PUBLISHING

PREFACE

The late Vince Gironda, the cantankerous owner of Vince's Gym in North Hollywood, was probably the world's greatest trainer in his time (1950s – 1990s).

Vince never told an individual how to train; he always showed him by grabbing a weight and actually performing. Almost every time I visited his Ventura Boulevard establishment, Vince would be in the middle of the gym floor, demonstrating a technique and growling instructions. *"All they want is information,"* said Vince, *"I tell them something; show them an exercise, offer information on nutrition, and the next day they're back again asking the same type of questions. They never get enough!"*

Most aspiring bodybuilders seem to believe that there is some hidden secret to musclebuilding success. I guess it's human nature.

This **1001 Musclebuilding Tips** collection is a compendium of information that could be construed as enormously important, but if any of the thousand-plus items are secret, then with the publishing of this book the secret is out!

You don't have to read this whole book at one go. Keep it in your gym bag and glance at a few tips when you feel the need for revitalizing your database of musclebuilding knowledge. One thing's for sure, these 1001 tips are published to help you build a better body. There has never been a similar publication in the history of the Iron Game. **The 1001 MuscleBuilding Tips** are yours for a lifetime to read in the gym, on a break at school, college or work, or even as toilet enlightenment. And who was it that inspired me to put these thousand-plus tips together? Who else? The cantankerous old geezer himself, smiling down from that big gym in the sky – *Vince Gironda.*

THE LATE VINCE GIRONDA, AGE 50.

> ## "KNOWING IS NOT ENOUGH. YOU HAVE TO PUT WHAT YOU KNOW INTO PRACTICE."
> **–VINCE GIRONDA**

CONTENTS

CONTENTS

Preface   **3**

Contents   **5**

CHAPTER 1 First Principles   **9**

CHAPTER 2 Equipment: Your Own and the Gym's   **23**

CHAPTER 3 Safety   **29**

CHAPTER 4 Warming up and Record Keeping   **39**

CHAPTER 5 Training Partners   **47**

CHAPTER 6 Beginning Strategies   **51**

CHAPTER 7 Beginning Exercises   **55**

CHAPTER 8 The Big Four -   **69**

        Tips for Improving your Bench Press

        Tips for Improving your Deadlift

        Tips for Improving your Squat

        Tips for Improving your Barbell Curl

CHAPTER 9 Bodybuilding Etiquette   **79**

CHAPTER 10 Nutrition   **85**

CHAPTER 11 Supplements   **101**

CHAPTER 12 Cardio Training   **109**

CHAPTER 13 Intermediate Exercises and Strategies   **121**

CHAPTER 14 Symmetry and Proportion   **137**

CHAPTER 15 Injuries   **141**

CHAPTER 16 Advanced Training Techniques   **147**

CHAPTER 17 Overcoming Sticking Points   **161**

CHAPTER 18 Coming Back After a Layoff   **169**

CHAPTER 19 Relaxation and Recovery   **173**

CONTENTS

This book is not intended as medical advice, nor is it offered for use in the diagnosis of any health condition or as a substitue for medical treatment and/or counsel. Its purpose is to explore advanced topics on exercise and sports nutrition. The primary aim is the sculpting of the physique in the natural training style. All data are for information only. Use of any of the programs within this book is solely at the risk and choice of the reader.

STAN MCQUAY

CHAPTER 20 Bodybuilding on the Road   **179**

CHAPTER 21 Circuit Training   **185**

CHAPTER 22 Competitive Bodybuilding-   **189**

Why Compete?

Your First Contest

CHAPTER 23 The Four Rounds   **195**

CHAPTER 24 Designing Your Posing Routine   **201**

CHAPTER 25 Bodybuilding Photography   **207**

CHAPTER 26 Precontest Dieting   **211**

CHAPTER 27 Precontest Training   **217**

CHAPTER 28 Shaving: Looking your best on stage   **221**

CHAPTER 29 Tanning   **227**

CHAPTER 30 Hairstyle   **233**

CHAPTER 31 Stretch Marks   **237**

CHAPTER 32 Posing Trunks   **241**

CHAPTER 33 Striking Oil   **245**

CHAPTER 34 Showtime   **249**

CHAPTER 35 Post Prejudging   **255**

CHAPTER 36 Communication Skills   **259**

CHAPTER 37 The Business of Bodybuilding   **263**

CHAPTER 38 Contest Promotion   **269**

CHAPTER 39 Acting   **275**

CHAPTER 40 The Gym Business   **279**

CHAPTER 41 Final Thoughts   **285**

Credits   **289**

FIRST PRINCIPLES

1. Reps and sets
2. How many reps?
3. Rep ranges
4. Beginner reps
5. Never too young!
6. Never too old!
7. Don't worry about genetics
8. Write down your goals
9. Strict versus loose reps
10. Concentration is the key
11. Throw them out
12. Patience is a virtue
13. The ups and downs
14. 10 for 1
15. Forced reps
16. How many sets
17. A guide for too many sets
18. The final set
19. Don't burn them out or fade them away
20. Develop a balanced workout
21. The strongest may survive but the weakest need extra work!
22. Bring a friend
23. Don't go catabolic
24. Training to failure
25. One-rep maximums
26. Classical vs heavy duty
27. Keep it simple for ectomorphs
28. Go at your own pace
29. Time between sets
30. Straight sets
31. Pyramiding – the Egyptians had it right
32. Half-Pyramids
33. Perform full range of motion
34. How much weight?
35. Progressive overload

36. Keep it big
37. Ground yourself
38. Conflicting goals
39. Exercise speed
40. Breathing
41. Time between workouts
42. Sleep
43. Warm milk – Mom was right!
44. Power napping
45. Dispelling an urban myth
46. Training at home
47. Buying home equipment
48. Don't fall for the late-night TV ads
49. Commercial gyms
50. Types of gyms
51. Selecting a gym
52. How much?
53. Buyer beware
54. At work!
55. The great outdoors
56. Protection
57. Water
58. Dizziness
59. Training morning, noon, & night
60. Training frequency
61. Workout duration
62. Missing workouts
63. Training during the flu
64. Visualization
65. Photo inspiration

1

FIRST PRINCIPLES

1. REPS AND SETS

The most basic term in bodybuilding is the rep. Rep is short for repetition and simply means performing one complete movement of a given exercise. For example if you were doing a flat barbell bench press it would mean lifting the bar off the rack, slowly lowering it to mid-chest and then pushing it back up to arm's length. Performing a group of continuous reps is called a set. Most bodybuilders perform 8 to 12 reps per set.

2. HOW MANY REPS?

There are three broad categories of rep ranges – one for building maximum muscle size, one for maximum strength, and one for general conditioning. There is no one rep range that will maximize all three categories at once. You must decide what your primary goal is. Generally speaking, for maximum strength 3 to 6 reps seems to work best. Bodybuilders trying to gain muscle mass find sets in the 8 to 12 range most effective. For general conditioning, 12 to 20 reps is normal.

3. REP RANGES

Even though most people may respond best to a given rep range, everyone is different. Over time, experiment with different rep ranges to see what works best for you. Don't stick with a given rep range if it doesn't give you the results you desire.

4. BEGINNER REPS

When starting an exercise program, perform higher reps. The higher reps will force you to use lighter weight. This means you can concentrate on mastering your technique. You will achieve better results and there is less chance of injury.

5. NEVER TOO YOUNG!

For those younger readers (or those who have young teens), be reassured that you are never too young to benefit from a regular weight-training program. Regular exercise improves physical fitness and strength, promotes a healthy lifestyle, and boosts self-esteem. The old myth of weight training stunting growth is just that – a myth! There is no evidence to support this old belief.

6. NEVER TOO OLD!

The fastest growing demographic segment of society is the baby boomer generation (anyone born between the years 1946 and 1964). Unlike their counterparts from 30 or 40 years ago, most baby boomers are not content to grow old. They want to stop the clock. Weight training is one of the best forms of exercise to combat the decline in physical health brought about by age. Unlike cardio, which can be stressful on older joints, weight training can be tailored to the individual's fitness level. In addition, only weight training can slow down the problems associated with bone loss due to osteoporosis. So, you baby-boomer readers, get up off the coach and hit the gym!

7. DON'T WORRY ABOUT GENETICS.

The bad news is that your genetic makeup is the primary limiting factor in your training. That's the bad news. The good news is that no one has ever utilized his or her full genetic potential. Although unfavorable genetics have made thousands of bodybuilders' ultimate achievements difficult, no individual has ever been completely hindered by them. So get to it!

8. WRITE DOWN YOUR GOALS

Just as you wouldn't haphazardly drive around hoping by accident to reach your destination, so too should you have a "road map" to follow when bodybuilding. Grab a piece of paper and write down exactly what you want to change about your body. Is it an extra inch or two on your arms? How about a 225-pound bench press? Or perhaps you want to see your abs again! Next, give yourself a timeline to follow and try to stick to it. This will keep you honest and less likely to skip workouts.

9. STRICT VERSUS LOOSE REPS

Bodybuilders perform two types of reps – strict and loose. As the names imply, strict reps are those that are performed in almost flawless fashion. There is no cheating or jerking the weight up. Loose reps are those for which some body momentum is used to assist the target muscles in lifting the weight. There is an argument to be made that reps should always be performed in strict style. This is especially true at the beginner level, but advanced bodybuilders frequently use a loose training style.

10. CONCENTRATION IS THE KEY

Always concentrate and focus on the muscles you are trying to stimulate when exercising. Try to make a lighter weight feel like a heavier weight. In his prime Arnold Schwarzenegger used 60 to 70 pounds to work his biceps while others were flinging up 80- or 100-pounders. Arnold made those 60's feel like 80's and built two of the greatest biceps in bodybuilding history.

11. THROW THEM OUT

Unless you are hundreds of pounds overweight, throw your scales out the window. Body weight is not always a good measurement of fitness and health. You could gain 10 pounds of muscle and lose 10 pounds of fat. Your weight will not have changed, yet you've improved yourself considerably by losing fat and adding muscle.

12. PATIENCE IS A VIRTUE

Don't expect results in a few weeks. It takes an average of two to four months before you'll see significant changes in strength and muscle size. Even then you might not see them, but they are occurring just the same. Some things are worth waiting for. Stay dedicated and be persistent.

13. THE UPS AND DOWNS

There will be days when there won't be enough weight in the gym for you. Conversely there will be days when the warm-up will feel heavy. There is no way you will be able to max out on every workout. Let the body be your guide. On the days when it says: "go at 75 percent," listen.

14. 10 FOR 1

On average you'll need to gain 10 pounds of bodyweight for every inch of arm size. For most people who train consistently this means that in a five-year period they'll increase their bodyweight by 50 pounds and add five inches to their arms.

15. FORCED REPS

After you have a few months of training under your belt you can try a few advanced training techniques. One of the easiest to learn is forced reps. A forced rep is a rep performed after you can no longer lift the weight on your own. Let's say you complete 10 reps on the bench press and cannot do number 11. Have a partner place his hands under the bar and provide just enough lift to help you complete a couple of additional, or "forced" reps. In gym jargon your partner is giving you "a spot."

16. HOW MANY SETS

As with the number of reps in a set, there is no magic number of sets to perform in a workout. In time most bodybuilders discover what works best for them. Perform too many and you run the risk of overtraining and burnout. Perform too few and you won't adequately stimulate the muscles. Our advice is to start off by performing 6 to 8 sets total for bigger muscles like chest, back and legs, and 4 to 6 sets for smaller muscles like biceps and triceps.

17. A GUIDE FOR TOO MANY SETS

One of the best guides for determining when to stop training a particular muscle is to go by "the pump." As soon as a muscle is subjected to exercise it begins to fill up with blood, giving it a tighter and fuller feeling. Bodybuilders have discovered a point when doing extra sets not only doesn't increase the pump, the pump can actually drain away. It is at this point that you should stop training the muscle and move on to the next body part.

18. THE FINAL SET

As you exercise a muscle, waste products such as lactic acid begin to build up. It is these metabolic by-products of exercise that play a major role in fatiguing the muscle. One way to help flush these "exercise limiters" out is by performing a lighter/higher-rep set at the end. High reps flush the area with blood, speeding up waste removal.

19. DON'T BURN THEM OUT OR FADE THEM AWAY

Even though they are the "showy" muscles of the body, the biceps are one of the easiest muscles to overtrain. Your biceps receive a good workout just by being used in your back workouts. Don't make the mistake of training them three or four times a week for 15 to 20 sets. Try 6 to 8 sets in total, once or twice a week.

20. DEVELOP A BALANCED WORKOUT

Don't overemphasize one part of the body, like the chest or biceps. Get an expert to help you design a smart, comprehensive program that works all muscle groups. Do at least one exercise for each of the major muscle groups or you can end up with a muscular imbalance. Not only does that look funny, it causes a greater risk of injury.

21. THE STRONGEST MAY SURVIVE BUT THE WEAKEST NEED EXTRA WORK!

Closely related to the previous tip is the fact that many bodybuilders fall victim to the trap of working their largest and strongest muscles more than their weakest. The temptation is strong to give into the quick gratification of working the muscles that respond the quickest. The last thing you want is your gym buddies saying things behind your back like "he's all arms", or "pity he has no legs." Keep a close eye on each muscle's progress and adjust your training accordingly.

22. BRING A FRIEND

Unless you are passionate about training, you'll have days when going to the gym is the last thing on your mind. Studies have shown that over 60 percent of people new to weightlifting will stick with it for at least six months if they have a friend or spouse training with them. So as soon as you decide to take up exercising, try to recruit a training partner.

23. DON'T GO CATABOLIC

One of the biggest detriments to gaining size and strength is performing too many sets for a muscle group. Try to stick with 6 to 8 sets for smaller muscles and 10 to 12 for bigger muscle groups.

24. TRAINING TO FAILURE

Training to failure means terminating a set when you can no longer lift the weight. If you were doing 10 reps in a set, you would pick a weight that does not allow you 11 reps. We don't recommend training to failure at the beginner level. Doing so is very taxing on your recovery system. Instead terminate the set one or two reps from failure (i.e. use a weight that you would fail at 12 reps but only perform 10).

25. ONE-REP MAXIMUMS

If you decide to see how strong you are on a few of the exercises (squats and bench presses usually being the guilty parties), limit the testing to once a

1 Rep

FIRST PRINCIPLES

month. One-rep maximums place a lot of stress on the soft connective tissues such as ligaments and cartilage. They also tend to stress out the muscles and tendons. Make sure you have a trusted spotter behind you in case you miss the lift attempt.

26. CLASSICAL VS HEAVY DUTY

The classical system of sets consists of starting out doing 1 to 3 sets per bodypart and adding a couple of sets and exercises every month or two. It's not uncommon after a couple of years for advanced bodybuilders to be performing 15 to 20 sets per bodypart. The heavy-duty style of training was popularized by Dr Arthur Jones and the late Mike Mentzer. Both argued that 1 to 3 all-out sets to failure was more productive and less draining on the recovery system than 15 to 20 sets performed in moderate style. Experiment with both styles and see what works best for you. Virtually all the top bodybuilding champions use the classical system of training.

27. KEEP IT SIMPLE FOR ECTOMORPHS

If you have an ectomorph-type body (tall, lean, little muscle mass), keep your training simple and infrequent. Perform basic exercises for low sets and reps. Train only two or three times per week. Keep your protein intake high (at least one gram per pound of bodyweight), and limit your cardio to two to three 20-minute sessions per week.

28. GO AT YOUR OWN PACE

Keeping up with the Joneses may be fine in the suburbs, but it's not a good idea in the gym. Don't let someone else's workout influence your training. It's fine to feed off others' intensity, but don't try to lift too-heavy weights just to keep up. Train at your own pace and strength level. You'll make better progress and have less chance of suffering a severe injury.

29. TIME BETWEEN SETS

You want to wait long enough between sets to recover your breath but not long enough to cool down before the next set. For most muscles this works out to about a minute. For a larger muscle like legs you may have to wait 90 seconds to two minutes. You may get by on 30 seconds' rest for a small muscle like biceps.

30. STRAIGHT SETS

When you begin weight training, perform all your sets as straight sets. This means performing a given exercise with a chosen weight for a given number of reps. The straight-sets style of training is the most common training method used by bodybuilders.

31. PYRAMIDING – THE EGYPTIANS HAD IT RIGHT

After a few months of training with straight sets, try pyramiding your reps and weight. Pyramiding involves starting with a light weight for higher  reps and then increasing the weight and decreasing the reps with each successive set. The top of the pyramid would be the point at which you are using your maximum weight. You then start decreasing the weight and increasing the reps. Generally speaking the lighter sets are performed for 15 to 20 reps and the heavier sets for 6 to 8 reps.

32. HALF-PYRAMIDS

Because a muscle tires with each successive set, many bodybuilders feel they should start their training with their heaviest weight. If they perform too many high-rep, light-weight sets they'll never be able to reach their heaviest weight. To get around this they do one or two very light sets and then put their heaviest weight on the bar or machine. The weight is then decreased and reps are increased with each successive set. In effect they are working down the backside of the pyramid.

33. PERFORM FULL RANGE OF MOTION

With the exception of a few advanced training techniques discussed later, perform all your exercises through a full range of motion. This means fully stretching and contracting the muscle and moving the limb or limbs through their entire possible distance. Half movements will only build strength in the part of the muscle being worked when the movement is taking place.

34. HOW MUCH WEIGHT?

As much as we would like to, there is no way to know specifically how much weight to use on each exercise. Everyone is different. First decide how many reps you want to complete in a given set. Then pick a weight that limits you to that number. There will be

days when you'll have to use less weight to achieve the same number of reps. On other days you'll need more weight.

35. PROGRESSIVE OVERLOAD

Although there will be the odd day when you will need to use less weight, the primary method for increasing muscle size is progressive overload. That is, as soon as a muscle adapts to a given weight, you must increase the weight to keep the muscle growing. With few exceptions, the biggest bodybuilders are also the strongest.

36. KEEP IT BIG

During your first few months of training, focus on exercises for the large muscle groups of the body (i.e. quads, hamstrings, calves, chest, back, shoulders, biceps, triceps). Don't worry about the smaller muscles like the serratus, teres, and rhomboids. These muscles will get a good workout just by training the bigger muscles.

37. GROUND YOURSELF

As soon as you begin working out, take a lesson from your parents and "ground" yourself. Place both feet securely on the ground and keep them there. At the end of your set your feet should not have moved so much as an inch. If they have it probably means you've used your legs to cheat!

38. CONFLICTING GOALS

One of the biggest mistakes you can make when you start training is trying to lose fat and gain muscle at the same time. Unless you are that one-in-a-million, genetically gifted freak, you won't be able to do both simultaneously. If you are 20 pounds or more overweight, your first priority is losing the body fat. If you are very lean but lacking in muscle size, focus on gaining some good muscular bodyweight. Don't attempt to stay lean while trying to get big. You can't have it both ways.

39. EXERCISE SPEED

Exercise speed is another name for tempo. Our advice is to use a 2-2 exercise tempo when starting out. This means take two seconds to raise the weight and two seconds to lower it again. With time you can experiment with ultra-fast reps (explosive training) and ultra-slow reps (10 seconds or more).

40. BREATHING

When exercising intensely, the body needs enormous amounts of oxygen. If you hold your breath while training you run the risk of passing out. Try breathing on each rep of the exercise. Most bodybuilders inhale on the lowering part of the rep and exhale on the upward part. In effect you are "blowing" the weight up.

41. TIME BETWEEN WORKOUTS

You don't grow in the gym. Training only stimulates muscle growth. You must rest long enough between workouts to recover. For most bodybuilders a minimum of 48 to 72 hours is needed between muscle groups. Hitting the same muscle two days in a row will only leave you in a constant state of overtraining. If in doubt take an extra day off.

42. SLEEP

Get a minimum of 6 to 8 hours of sleep each night. One late night out partying probably won't set your training back too much, but making a habit of surviving on three or four hours sleep a night will prevent you from achieving the success you desire. It's that simple.

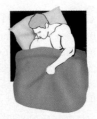

43. WARM MILK – MOM WAS RIGHT!

If you have trouble sleeping, try drinking a small glass of warm milk just before bed. Warming the milk activates the amino acid tryptophan, which has been shown to be a natural sleeping aid.

44. POWER NAPPING

If circumstances prevent you from getting 6 to 8 hours of sleep a night, try napping once or twice during the day. A 30- to 60-minute nap in the middle of the day produces wonders in terms of mental and physical acuity. Even a couple of 15-minute naps spread over the day can boost your energy reserves and recovery abilities.

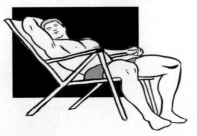

45. DISPELLING AN URBAN MYTH

Don't worry about training before bed. The old belief was that exercise interfered with sleep patterns by increasing adrenaline levels. Recent studies have shown that those who exercise a shortly before bed sleep just as well as those who exercise earlier in the day.

46. TRAINING AT HOME

Training at home has numerous advantages. You don't have to fight for a parking space and you don't have to wait for equipment. You can also train at your convenience. The disadvantages are limited equipment, distractions, and no one around for motivation.

47. BUYING HOME EQUIPMENT

You can spend more than $1000 on the latest TV home-gym setup, or $50 at a flea market for a few weights. Millions of home-gym setups are bought, but few are used. Before blowing hundreds or thousands of dollars, check around with friends and relatives. Basement flea markets are also a good bet for buying exercise equipment for your home. Anyone who has had teenage males in the house probably has an old York or Weider barbell set kicking around.

48. DON'T FALL FOR THE LATE-NIGHT TV ADS

You've seen the ads: "Just five minutes a day will develop a six-pack!" Save your money and invest it in either a gym membership or a piece of legitimate training equipment. Most of those crazy TV gizmos are useless and designed to cash in on most people's quick-fix mentality. In most cases you are wasting your money. Not to mention that many of those contraptions are potentially dangerous.

49. COMMERCIAL GYMS

The primary disadvantages to training at home are the advantages to working out at a gym. You'll have access to the latest training gear. There will be lots of advanced bodybuilders around for inspiration. Finally, such distractions as the phone, TV, and fridge are nonexistent.

50. TYPES OF GYMS

Gyms can be divided into three types: hardcore, middle of the road, and spas. Our advice is to avoid spas. The equipment tends to be more glitz than practical, and the owners don't really want people who train seriously there anyway. Stick with either a good middle-of-the-road gym or a hardcore bodybuilding gym.

51. SELECTING A GYM

When selecting a gym, make sure to take into consideration such issues as cost, location (are you or your car safe?), equipment selection, quality of staff, hours of operation, change-room facilities, crowds during peak times, and atmosphere. Most gyms offer day passes to try out their facilities. Before plunking down a year's membership try out a few gyms to get a feel for the place. It is well worth the $5 or $10 day-pass fee.

52. HOW MUCH?

Most middle-of-the-road gyms will cost $35 to $50 a month to work out at. If $600 a year sounds expensive, keep in mind that this works out to just $1.65 a day! That's a trivial amount of money to be investing in improving your energy, health and physique. If taking the money out of your wallet each month is difficult, arrange for a direct bank account withdrawal. Many gyms will also do a payroll deduction. Either way you may never miss the money.

53. BUYER BEWARE

When joining a gym, beware of fly-by-night operations. Numerous gym chains have reputations for hitting town with much flash and fanfare. After a couple of hundred people take out a "lifetime" membership, the gym is gone! Our advice is to only join for a month or so. If you do decide to commit to a year, pay by post-dated checks or some other means that allows you to stop payment if the shady characters leave town. Never agree to have your credit card charged each month.

54. AT WORK!

One of the more popular trends is for employers to set up fitness rooms for their employees. Although a few are doing it as a generous fringe benefit for staff, the primary reason is that insurance companies will give companies better rates if their employees are healthy and working out. If your company doesn't have a gym yet, talk to the owner (or the appropriate person in the chain of command) and see if they'll explore the

option of setting one up. You may be the one voted to do the job.

55. THE GREAT OUTDOORS

For a change of pace try training outdoors. The fresh air will do you wonders and the openness is a welcome change from the sometimes stuffy confines

of a gym. Venice Beach in California is famous the world over for its outdoor training pit. A word of caution for those who live in larger cities. Pay attention to smog alerts.

Gulping in huge amounts of toxic air will not do your health any good. In fact doing so may only shorten it. On those days stick to an air-conditioned facility.

56. PROTECTION

If you decide to train outdoors, always use a good sunblock. Two or three hours training in the sun can play havoc with your skin. Time passes very quickly while you're training and before you know it you have second- or third-degree burns. You may also want to avoid training outside in the 11 am to 3 pm time slot, as this is when the sun is most dangerous.

57. WATER

The human body is about 70 percent water. While we have water conservation systems, at times our hydration levels fall dangerously low. Always consume copious amounts of water when training. You can use the gym's fountain, but then so will almost everyone else. That's a lot of potential germs. Buy a water bottle and keep it filled. Rather than gulping large amounts, try sipping it throughout your workout.

58. DIZZINESS

If at any time during your workout you feel dizzy, immediately stop what you are doing and sit down. Try tilting your head slightly forward to

increase blood flow to the brain. Dizziness is one of the first signs of lack of oxygen to the brain. It is also the body's way of saying you will faint if you don't do something about the situation. If you find yourself getting dizzy on a regular basis, consult your physician.

59. TRAINING MORNING, NOON & NIGHT

Although the most popular time to train is between 4 and 8 pm (that's when most people get off work and school), there is no best time to train. For some, 6 am works best. For others training at that time would be nauseating. Likewise, many like to finish work and head straight to the gym to unwind. The best time to train is whatever time works best for you.

60. TRAINING FREQUENCY

Even if your primary goals are maximum size and strength, it's not recommended you start out with an advanced four- or six-day split routine. You'll get great results by training the full body every second day for a total of 3 or 4 days per week.

61. WORKOUT DURATION

How long you spend in the gym ultimately depends on the type of program you are following. There is no need to be dragging your training session out for two or three hours. In fact if you are still training after three hours your intensity level is probably too low to be effective. Try putting everything you've got into a 60-minute workout.

62. MISSING WORKOUTS

No matter how dedicated you are to your training, sooner or later you'll miss the occasional workout. As long as you are fairly consistent, don't worry about it. One or two extra days off a month will not set you back. In fact it may help you, as many people are in a chronic state of overtraining. You'll find that after an extra day off your energy and strength levels are often much higher.

63. TRAINING DURING THE FLU

Although some people swear that exercising will somehow "sweat out" the flu virus, our advice is to give training a pass when you're under the weather. The common cold, while not life-threatening, is still weakening your overall recovery system. One of the warning signs of overtraining is an increased

frequency of colds. Let the body deal with the virus before subjecting it to another grueling workout.

64. VISUALIZATION

The great Arnold Schwarzenegger used to imagine his biceps were mountains when he trained them. Numerous studies have shown that those people who visualize where they want to be down the road get there more quickly than those who don't visualize. Set small strength and size goals and then visualize obtaining these goals.

65. PHOTO INSPIRATION

Flip through a copy of MuscleMag International and find a large picture of your favorite bodybuilder. Cut it out and paste it on the fridge, bathroom wall, or some other place you see every day. Use the photo for motivation and inspiration. Every time you look at the photo imagine what it would be like to look like that bodybuilder. Then go into the gym and train your butt off.

EQUIPMENT:
YOUR OWN & THE GYM'S

66. Gloves

67. Sponges

68. Wraps

69. Belts

70. Bench press shirts

71. Straps

72. Wrist protection

73. Hi-tech vs low-tech straps

74. Head straps

75. Headbands

76. Chalk

77. Barbells

78. Dumbells

79. Benches

80. Arm Blasters for strictness

81. Cables and pulleys

82. Machines

2

66. GLOVES

Unless you are used to manual labor, you'll notice after your first few training sessions that your hands will develop blisters. The way to prevent this is to wear gloves. You can use gloves specifically made for weightlifting or you can substitute golf gloves. Keep in mind that once you start wearing gloves you are committed to them. Your hands will never get a chance to toughen up and callous over. Forget your gloves just once and it's back to the blisters. Unless you need soft hands for your job or hobby (i.e. musician or surgeon), our advice is to give the gloves a pass.

67. SPONGES

Sponges are a cheaper way to protect the hands during a workout. Go to the kitchen section of any store and for a buck or two pick up a package of sponges. They come in different shapes and sizes but the 4 X 6 X 1/2-inch variety will probably work best. Place a sponge in each hand and grab the bar, dumbell, or machine handle. The sponge will protect the skin on your hands from blistering.

68. WRAPS

No matter how diligent you are with proper technique, your joints will be subjected to a tremendous amount of stress. The soft tissues at the joints will occasionally start letting you know that maybe you should take some sort of preventive measure. Many bodybuilders find that by wrapping the common

trouble areas such as the knees, wrists, and elbows, they can reduce the chances of injury to the joint. Wraps come in many shapes and sizes. Some are elastic in nature and have a pre-set tension. Others are nothing more than simple first-aid elastic bandages that allow you to adjust the tension. While we don't recommend wrapping yourself up like an Egyptian mummy, you may want to experiment with wraps on such exercises as squats, deadlifts, and bench presses.

69. BELTS

The most popular piece of weightlifting equipment is the lifting belt. However, wearing a belt at all times never allows the lower back muscles to strengthen. We suggest that you use one only if you really need it. Our advice is to only wear a belt for lower back protection on such exercises as squats, deadlifts, barbell rows and overhead standing presses, and only when using heavy weight.

70. BENCH PRESS SHIRTS

If you decide to test your ego on the bench press, you might want to invest in a bench press shirt. These specially made shirts are usually made of polyester and about two or three sizes too small! By compressing the arms, shoulders, and chest muscles, the upper body is put into a better leverage situation, enabling you to lift more. Some powerlifters will add 50 to 100 pounds to their bench press with the aid of a bench shirt.

71. STRAPS

Straps are short (one and a half to two feet) pieces of woven cloth that you wrap around a barbell, handle on a machine, or horizontal bar to give you a better grip. You'll quickly discover that on such exercises as deadlifts, shrugs, rows, chins and pulldowns, your forearm grip will be the weakest link. Straps allow you to handle more weight in these exercises. As with weight belts, don't get too dependent on straps. It's better to allow the forearms to strengthen than assisting them all the time with straps.

72. WRIST PROTECTION

If you decide to use straps, a word of caution. Many bodybuilders place the straps directly over the bony extrusion located between the lower forearm and hand. This bump is really the meeting place for the ends of the radius and ulna (two bones that make up the forearm). These small bones were not designed to have hundreds of pounds placed on them, and this is the weight you'll be using down the road on exercises such as shrugs. The solution is to place the wrist straps above this area. If the straps cover any part of the wrist or hand, they are too low.

73. HI-TECH VS LOW-TECH STRAPS

You can purchase a set of fancy wrist straps for $15 or $20, or you can make your own for mere pennies. If you decide to make your own, use a strong piece of material. Martial arts belts, car seat belts and woven nylon are three dependable choices for making wrist straps. There are two styles of wrist straps. Some are straight at both ends. Others have a loop at one end that you feed the other end through. Neither style is better than the other. It comes down to personal preference.

74. HEAD STRAPS

This is nothing more than a special harness that fits over the head, allowing you to attach a weight to the

other end. By moving the head in various directions (forward and back, side to side) you can strengthen the neck muscles. Be careful, as the neck muscles are very easy to strain. You'll probably get enough indirect neck stimulation from the other exercises you'll be performing, such as upright rows, shrugs, etc., but if you participate in sports where a strong neck is vital (judo, wrestling, football), you may want to consider direct neck training.

75. HEADBANDS

Also called sweatbands, headbands are another simple piece of equipment that will make a big difference to your workouts. Nothing is as irritating as getting sweat in your eyes. The problem is compounded if you are wearing contacts. Even those who train in an air-conditioned gym are not immune to having beads of sweat rolling down their forehead. For a few dollars (or mere pennies if you want to make your own) invest in a headband to soak up the moisture before it starts giving you a severe case of redeye.

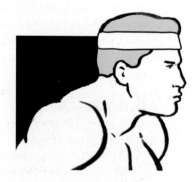

76. CHALK

The body's primary cooling mechanism is to release water to the skin surface in the form of sweat. While sweat does wonders for cooling the body, it plays havoc with gripping sports. The next time you watch a gymnastics competition take a close look at the hands of the athletes. They are virtually white with chalk. Weightlifting is like gymnastics in that a firm grip is an absolute must on all the exercises. Chalk is cheap ($2 to $3 for a six-inch block) and makes an excellent training aid for drying sweat and giving you a better grip. Just check with your gym's policy on chalk before buying. Some gyms don't allow chalk as it messes the floor.

77. BARBELLS

It's probably safe to say that no weightlifting machine will ever replace the good old-fashioned barbell. Barbells come in an assortment of sizes and shapes. Olympic bars are the largest at seven feet long and 45 pounds. You'll use these on such exercises as bench presses, squats, deadlifts, and barbell rows. Shorter bars are more convenient for various biceps and triceps exercises. Finally, EZ-curl bars have a series of s-shaped curves that allow a more natural grip. Many people find straight bars hard on the wrist and elbow joints and opt for the curved EZ-curl bar. You should try to use all types of barbells in your training program.

78. DUMBELLS

Dumbells are the baby brothers of barbells. Instead of holding one long bar in two hands, you hold a shorter one in each hand. Dumbells range in size from one

pound up to over 150 pounds. You will use dumbells on such exercises as biceps curls, flyes, presses, and side raises.

79. BENCHES

To provide support and target different areas of the body try using different bench angles in your workout. If you are training chest you can shift the stress from the lower chest to the upper by using a tilted or incline bench. Likewise the lower and outer chest can be stressed by using a decline bench.

80. ARM BLASTERS FOR STRICTNESS

No matter how hard you try to prevent it, the body will always attempt to cheat when exercising. We are inherently lazy creatures. With standing barbell curls the lazy way out is to start rocking the body and lifting the elbows forward from the torso as the bar is lifted upwards. One way to reduce this is to use an Arm Blaster. This two-foot long, six-inch wide piece of curved metal fits around the waist and allows you to place your elbows firmly against it. Locking the arms in this position makes it much more difficult to cheat. The cover photos of Arnold Schwarzenegger using the Arm Blaster back in the 1970s are nothing short of inspirational.

81. CABLES AND PULLEYS

For added variety in your training nothing beats pulleys. As the name suggests, pulley exercises are those where the weight is attached to the handles by a long cable running through one or more pulleys. Although biceps curls (cable curls) cable crossovers (for the chest) and triceps pushdowns are the most popular pulley exercises, you can use pulleys to train just about every muscle.

82. MACHINES

It probably started with Universal back in the 1960s. Now there are dozens of strength-machine manufacturers. Strength machines are clean, convenient, and safe. Machine exercises are easier to learn than barbell or dumbell exercises, especially when you begin resistance training.

DEREK FARNSWORTH

SAFETY

83. Warm up
84. The stronger you are the longer the warm-up
85. Use a spotter
86. Never perform potentially dangerous exercises alone in your house or apartment
87. Buy or use a power cage
88. Use collars on all barbells
89. When never to use collars
90. Use a weight-lifting belt on heavy exercises such as squats, deadlifts & barbell rows
91. Put your weights away when finished
92. If you are unsure of exercise technique – ask!
93. Rotations for preventative medicine
94. Try to perform all exercises in good style
95. 90 degrees is best
96. Keep them to the front
97. Never lock out
98. Never bounce
99. Never hyperextend
100. When stiff should never be stiff
101. Putting the hook on injuries with S-hooks
102. Correct height on the stationary bicycle
103. Where applicable, use weight racks
104. Dress appropriately
105. Footwear for support
106. Footwear for protection
107. Have a medical check-up before beginning any intense weight lifting (or any form of intense exercise) program.
108. Keep long hair secure
109. Watch your time
110. Use the mirror
111. Let your shoulders be your guide
112. Good pain, bad pain
113. Reducing neck pain
114. What you lie on
115. Experiment with grips
116. Knowledge is power

83. WARM UP

Always warm up before training. Most injuries are the result of jumping to heavy poundages too quickly. A warm muscle is much more flexible and pliable than a cold one. A warm up takes only a few minutes but it can save you a lifetime of pain.

84. THE STRONGER YOU ARE THE LONGER THE WARM-UP

As you progress in your bodybuilding you'll find that you'll be hoisting some serious poundages in your workouts. What this means is that your muscles, tendons, and ligaments will be subjected to much more stress than when you started training. It's a fact that the stronger you get the more likely you are to incur an injury. To reduce the chances of this happening, increase your warm-up time proportionally. One or two light sets may be fine for a 100-pound bench press, but when you get up to 300+ pounds you'll need to do three or four light and medium warm-up sets to adequately prepare the muscles.

85. USE A SPOTTER

Whenever possible have someone stand behind you (called a spotter) to lend assistance on potentially

dangerous exercises like squats and bench presses. Besides safety, a spotter can help you complete a few extra forced reps.

86. NEVER PERFORM POTENTIALLY DANGEROUS EXERCISES ALONE IN YOUR HOUSE OR APARTMENT

A small number of bodybuilders have been found dead in their basements. In most cases they had tried that extra rep on a set of bench presses and failed. The result was a heavy barbell crashing down on their neck.

87. BUY OR USE A POWER CAGE

If you must train at home, consider buying a power cage. A power cage allows you to set catch-bars at any height. By setting them an inch or two below your maximum depth, you have a backup if something goes wrong. Even on the bench press you could manage to wiggle out from under the bar if you can't return it to the supports.

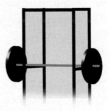

88. USE COLLARS ON ALL BARBELLS

Even with the best of techniques the odds of lifting a barbell perfectly even are remote. If the plates are not locked on with a collar it's possible that they could slip off the lower side. This in turn causes the side with the plates left on to drop suddenly. This violent wrenching motion can tear muscles, tendons, and ligaments. Always use collars.

89. WHEN NEVER TO USE COLLARS

This is going to contradict a previous tip, but there is one occasion when you shouldn't lock the plates on with collars. Even though you should never perform barbell bench presses alone, some readers will still go ahead and do so. If you do this and don't have access to a powercage or Smith machine, leave the collars off. This way if you get the bar stuck across your chest you have an out. Simply force one side of the bar upwards to cause the plates to slip off the other side. Now the side with the plates still on is heavier and will drop, thus spilling those plates on the floor. You've now got an empty bar on your chest. Place it back on the rack and promise yourself you'll never do it again! Needless to say, dropping heavy weights could ruin your floor.

90. USE A WEIGHT-LIFTING BELT ON HEAVY EXERCISES SUCH AS SQUATS, DEADLIFTS & BARBELL ROWS

The human spine is a marvel of engineering but it was not meant to have hundreds of pounds suddenly placed on it. Wearing a thick leather belt provides support by securing the ligaments and muscles of the lower back.

91. PUT YOUR WEIGHTS AWAY WHEN FINISHED

Although gym staff will enforce this rule, please take the initiative yourself. Weights left all over the floor are a safety hazard. Sooner or later someone will trip and fall. Return your weights to the proper location when finished. This prevents injuries and makes it easier for the next person to find the weights they want.

92. IF YOU ARE UNSURE OF EXERCISE TECHNIQUE — ASK!

Most gym instructors are knowledgeable and only too willing to help out. Weightlifting exercises are probably not the best activities for experimenting with when learning.

93. ROTATIONS FOR PREVENTATIVE MEDICINE

If you were to rank the body's joints in terms of how prone they are to injury, the shoulders would probably place third behind the lower back and knees. In fact the shoulders may move up to the number one position in those who regularly lift weights. Years of heavy pressing movements (both for chest and shoulder  training) can play havoc with the shoulder joints. In many cases the problem is not the large, outer deltoid muscle, but the smaller, underlying rotator muscles. These small muscles located on the scapula (shoulder blade) are prone to injury from repeated heavy pressing movements. Two ways to reduce the risk of damaging the rotators is to train them from day one, and to warm them up before doing any heavy pressing exercises.

94. TRY TO PERFORM ALL EXERCISES IN GOOD STYLE

Unless you are employing the cheating principle, try to execute all exercises with good biomechanical technique. This means no bouncing, jerking, or heaving the weight up. Proper technique not only prevents injuries but also ensures that the muscles are getting maximum stimulation.

95. 90 DEGREES IS BEST

The goal on a set of leg presses is to bend your knees low enough to stimulate your quads without going too low and damaging the knees. For most people this means having a 90-degree angle between your upper and lower legs when the knees are bent. If you have no knee problems and have good flexibility, then lowering to 75 or 80 degrees is fine, but don't make the mistake that some individuals do and try bouncing your knees off your chest.

96. KEEP THEM TO THE FRONT

Even though many bodybuilders swear by them, behind-the-neck pulldowns and shoulder presses can destroy your small rotator muscles (the small muscles and tendons located on the shoulder blades collectively called the rotator cuff). Unless you've been doing them for years and have experienced no problems, we suggest that you not include them in your workouts. Front presses and pulldowns will work the same muscles without placing the same degree of stress on the rotators.

97. NEVER LOCK OUT

Although they are marvels of engineering, human joints can only take so much abuse. You should never lock out completely on any exercise (with the possible exception of triceps exercises). Locking out places tremendous stress on the joints, particularly

the soft tissues that surround the joints. If locking out can be compared to making a 180 degree angle between two lines, then stop at about 170 to 175 degrees.

98. NEVER BOUNCE

It's amazing that some people ever walk out of a gym. One of the most abused machines in any fitness facility is the leg extension. People load the thing up with more weight than they can lift in good style, and then bounce it up and down using body momentum. The amount of stress this places on the knees at the top of the exercise is enormous. It's bad enough if you stop just short of locking out, but many people

actually hyperextend at the knee joint when they do leg extensions. Next to the lower back, the knee is the easiest joint to damage. Always treat knees with kindness!

99. NEVER HYPEREXTEND

They are commonly called hyperextensions but in reality you should never hyperextend. One of the best exercises for the lower back muscles is to lie face down on a ball or back extension machine and then gently raise the torso upwards. You should only rise up until your upper body is in line with your lower, or just slightly beyond. Do not try to arch as high as you can. This places tremendous stress on the lower back ligaments. You can still call the exercise hyperextensions, but please don't hyperextend.

100. WHEN STIFF SHOULD NEVER BE STIFF

Although they are called stiff-leg deadlifts, you should not do them with the legs completely locked out straight. Always keep the knees slightly bent. The same holds true for every other exercise that calls for a "straight" leg (leg raises for example). Always keep the knees slightly bent to reduce the pressure on the lower back.

101. PUTTING THE HOOK ON INJURIES WITH S-HOOKS

As you've probably discovered by now, most cable-machine attachments are hooked on to the end of the pulley with an S-shaped metal hook. While providing security and ease of use, S-hooks do have one big disadvantage; they don't lock the attachment in place. At least once a day at some gym, an attachment will pop off after being accidentally struck or pulled on. For example on some cable machines as soon as you pull on the low pulley the top attachment is automatically pulled backwards (it's the same cable). When this happens it's quite easy for an attachment to be bounced off. Always beware of overhead pulley attachments when working out. You may even want to suggest to the gym's owner to invest in climbing hooks, or  carabiners. They are the same size and strength as S-hooks, but they lock the attachment in place so it can't pop off. And they are ultra strong.

102. CORRECT HEIGHT ON THE STATIONARY BICYCLE

If you decide to use the stationary bike, adjust the seat so you can't completely lock out your legs. If the chair is too high you run the risk of hyperextending the knee joint when your legs are in the outstretched position.

103. WHERE APPLICABLE, USE WEIGHT RACKS

It will only be a matter of time before you are using hundreds of pounds on your squat and pressing movements. Even a strong spotter will be hard pressed to prevent that amount of weight from landing on you. To stop the barbell before it crashes down on you, use a weight rack. Many squat racks have a set of pins that you can set just below your maximum squatting depth. If you fail on one of the reps, simply let the weight drop to the safety pins and walk away.

104. DRESS APPROPRIATELY

If it's mid-summer, don't strut around in three layers of sweatshirts just so you'll look bigger. This will only lead to severe dehydration. Conversely, a T-shirt and shorts will probably not cut it in mid-winter, especially if you're the type who likes to wear his gym clothes to and from the gym.

105. FOOTWEAR FOR SUPPORT

With the possible exception of during calf raises and some yoga or stretching exercises on a mat, wear some sort of footwear at all times. Many leg exercises place tremendous stress on the supporting soft tissues of the foot region. A good sturdy sneaker (crosstrainers will offer more support than runners) will offer a great deal of support to this region. Even on exercises such as bench presses you'll be using your feet for stability. The last thing you want is for your foot to slip along the floor during a set of flat barbell presses.

106. FOOTWEAR FOR PROTECTION

A less obvious but equally important function of footwear is protection from wayward plates and dumbells. You'll be handling dozens if not hundreds of weight plates during a typical workout. Sooner or later you'll drop one. A 45-pound plate can do wonders to an unprotected foot. A sneaker will at least cushion the blow somewhat.

107. HAVE A MEDICAL CHECK-UP BEFORE BEGINNING ANY INTENSE WEIGHT-LIFTING PROGRAM (OR ANY FORM OF INTENSE EXERCISE).

Granted, if you are a healthy, athletic 18-year-old, a medical check-up is probably not necessary. But for anyone who hasn't lifted anything heavier than a cold beer over the last 10 or 20 years, we strongly urge you to consult your physician before trying to relive your high-school days. Ask your doctor for a physical stress test to ascertain your ability to recover from strenuous exercise.

108. KEEP LONG HAIR SECURE

A modern gym is filled with hundreds of moving parts. The last thing you want is to become intimately acquainted with one of these moving structures.

Although it's possible to get your hands or clothing stuck, more times than not, it's long hair that causes problems. If you sport long hair, keep it in a ponytail or secure it in some other fashion. Even tucked up under a baseball hat will lessen the chance of its getting caught by a pulley or cable.

109. WATCH YOUR TIME

The days of three and four-hour workouts are over. Most bodybuilders nowadays try to get in and out of the gym in 60 to 90 minutes. After about 90 minutes the body's energy reserves are all but depleted. Not only are you coasting (and possibly overtraining) after this point, your thought processes are probably muddled from the high levels of endorphins circulating in your system. It's at this point that you are very susceptible to an injury. Try to split up your workouts so that they take no longer than 90 minutes.

110. USE THE MIRROR

While some people use them strictly for vanity, and the owners use them to make the place look larger than it really is, mirrors do serve a useful purpose. On many exercises, particularly dumbell exercises, you'll discover that trying to coordinate both arms is difficult. Things will get easier with time, but during the learning phase you should use the mirrors as much as possible to ensure your technique is sound. In addition, during some exercises such as rows a mirror can be a helpful ally in keeping your back straight and not hunched over.

111. LET YOUR SHOULDERS BE YOUR GUIDE

When in doubt, position your feet shoulder width apart, or lower the bar (dumbells or machine handles) to shoulder height. The natural and most stable stance for most people is with the feet about shoulder width apart. This tends to place the least amount of stress on the joints (ankles, knees, lower back). Likewise the finished position of many exercises is shoulder height. For example on dumbell presses for shoulders or incline presses for chest, the dumbells will be approximately in line with your shoulders at the bottom of the exercise. Although it doesn't apply to all exercises, there are numerous examples for which the shoulders are a useful guide.

112. GOOD PAIN, BAD PAIN

As you progress in your bodybuilding career, always pay close attention to your body's signals. You have to learn to differentiate between pain that is signaling

an impending injury and pain that is nothing more than the normal soreness associated with an exercised muscle. If the pain seems to be localized to the muscle and disappears after a few days, odds are it's normal post-exercise muscle soreness. On the other hand if the pain is more severe, includes the joints, or lasts longer than a couple of days (or gets worse with each successive day). Then we urge you to stop training that area and seek medical advice from a knowledgeable sports doctor.

LARRY VINETTE

113. REDUCING NECK PAIN

Most of those home-exercise gizmos you see on TV are a waste of time and money. Surprisingly, some have their advantages. One example is the abdominal machine. They go by different names, and claim to take inches off your waist in "as little as five minutes per day." While these claims are outlandish, you may want to try one if you have neck problems. Many individuals find abdominal exercises stressful on the neck. Most of the ab machines have a headrest to support the head, thus reducing neck strain. Don't make the mistake of pushing with the arms. This only reduces the amount of abdominal stimulation.

114. WHAT YOU LIE ON

Make sure that the mattress on your bed is firm enough to support your body weight. If not, it won't keep your body in proper alignment. One of the primary causes of sore or "bad" backs is a mattress that is too soft. Treat your bed mattress like your footwear – update it regularly.

115. EXPERIMENT WITH GRIPS

Although most exercises should be performed with a shoulder-width grip, this is not etched in stone. Many people find a shoulder-width grip places too much stress on the triceps and shoulders when doing barbell presses for the chest. Likewise a shoulder-width grip may bring too much of the biceps into play on chins and pulldowns. When performing the various exercises, start out by using the recommended grip, but if you start getting joint problems or you don't seem to be hitting the targeted muscle, try widening or narrowing the grip. A few inches either way could be all it takes to reach success.

116. KNOWLEDGE IS POWER

Learn everything you can about bodybuilding. Buying and reading this book is a good start. Bodybuilding is (or should be) a lifelong pursuit. Read plenty of bodybuilding books, and magazines such as MuscleMag International. The more you learn and apply, the less chance of serious injury and the more success you'll get out of your training. Popular proven books include MuscleMag's Encyclopedia of Bodybuilding.

WARMING UP & RECORD KEEPING

117. Whole-body warm-up

118. Training journal

119. Workout information

120. Time

121. What you ate

122. Which supplements

123. Sleep

124. Cardio type and duration

125. How do you feel?

126. Stretching to perfection

127. Static stretching

128. Dynamic stretching

129. Ease into it

130. Be conscious of foot position

131. Heel drops (calves)

132. Seated straddle (hamstrings)

133. Flyaway (chest)

134. Back stretch (back)

135. Reach behind and pull (biceps and trapezius)

136. Straight-arm across (rear deltoid)

137. Upper scoop (back)

138. Elbow bend and push (triceps)

139. Roll on the ball (abdominals)

140. Lying glute and hip stretch (glutes, hips)

141. Lying quad stretch (quads)

142. Toe touch (hamstrings, lower back)

143. Overhead stretch (back, chest,)

144. Specific muscle warm-up

145. Increase your warm-up in proportion to your strength

146. Constant evaluation

147. Photographs

148. Taking measurements

117. WHOLE-BODY WARM-UP

Even though it may be chest day or leg day, keep in mind that your heart and lungs are going to play an integral part. Always perform five to ten minutes of general cardio to bring the heart and lungs up to speed. This ensures full circulation and oxygen delivery to the muscles when you hit the weights. Popular cardio machines for warm-ups include the treadmill, rowers, stationary cycle, and, in recent years, the elliptical or crosstrainer.

118. TRAINING JOURNAL

One of the best ways to know where you are going is to know where you've been! For just a few dollars, pick up a spiral-bound notebook to record all your training information. Every couple of weeks, examine the information to see if there are patterns. For example are there days when your eating or sleeping habits impacted your workouts? Write down any information relevant to your training and recovery. A perfect book for record keeping is MuscleMag's Hardcore Training Journal.

119. WORKOUT INFORMATION

The most basic information to include in your journal is which exercises you performed. Also write down the number of sets, reps, and the weight you used on each exercise. Include the day, month and year – looking back at a journal after a period of years can be fun.

120. TIME

Write down the length of time it took to do your workout. You can use this information later to determine if there is a correlation between your workout intensity and workout duration.

121. WHAT YOU ATE

Keep a detailed log of everything you eat on a daily basis. For example, don't just write down cereal; write the kind of cereal. Also include what you put on it, i.e. milk (and what type), type of sweetener, fruit, etc. Also record when you had your meals. Every couple of weeks, check to see if there is a pattern between meal timing and workout intensity. Record your weight regularly.

122. WHICH SUPPLEMENTS

As with food, keep detailed notes of your supplement consumption. What protein supplement did you use? How much? When? Any fat burners? Again, when and how much? Are you on the loading or maintenance phase of your creatine supplementation?

123. SLEEP

Sleep is one of the simplest things to record, but also one of the most important. Check to see if there is a correlation between your workouts and sleep patterns. Compare the data from both angles. Do your workouts influence your sleeping duration, and does the amount of sleep you receive each night impact your workouts?

124. CARDIO TYPE AND DURATION

You may be a bodybuilder at heart but you still need to do cardio. This is especially true during the precontest season. Write down the type of cardio you performed (machine or aerobics class), duration, and intensity level. This information will be invaluable the next time you compete or need to get ready for a photo session.

125. HOW DO YOU FEEL?

Even though it's very subjective, don't be afraid to jot down how you feel each day. Are you in a positive or negative mood? Do you have enough energy for all your daily activities and your workout? Are you still motivated to hit the gym, or would you just as soon do something else? The answers to these questions are often a good way to determine if there is a problem with your training or eating.

126. STRETCHING TO PERFECTION

It's ironic how many people spend thousands of hours contracting (shortening) their muscle by weight lifting, and yet devote little or no time to lengthening the muscles. Stretching is nothing more than the opposite movement to weightlifting. Stretching lengthens the muscles, plays a major role in warming the muscles, and research shows that stretching can also indirectly stimulate muscle growth. For maximum effect, spend 10 to 15 minutes each day stretching, and hold each stretch for 15 to 25 seconds.

127. STATIC STRETCHING

Static stretching involves moving into a designated position slowly and holding for 15 to 25 seconds. Holding for less time than this will not affect the muscle enough to cause a physiological change in length. Holding for more time than this can actually cause muscle tearing and injury. Static stretching is best performed at the end of your workout.

128. DYNAMIC STRETCHING

Dynamic stretching involves actively stretching muscles through movements that will mimic the training activity to follow. Forward lunges and leg swings and good examples. You are better served performing dynamic stretches during your pre-cardio routine in order to increase body coordination and circulation in joints and muscles.

129. EASE INTO IT

To fully stretch a muscle or joint you must slowly ease into it. Take 30 to 40 seconds to move slowly into a stretch. The maximum point to stretch to is the point at which you just begin to feel pain in the stretched muscle. Many experts call this the "pain edge." With time your "pain edge" will move further and further along as you gain flexibility.

130. BE CONSCIOUS OF FOOT POSITION

One of the first things you'll notice when you begin stretching is that the position of your feet can make a big difference to the stretch. For most leg stretches try to keep your feet dorsi-flexed (the foot and lower leg make a 90-degree angle) rather than pointed. This is especially true for hamstring stretches.

131. HEEL DROPS (CALVES)

Stand on a step riser, your feet shoulder width apart and your heels hanging off the back so that only your toes are on the edge. Slowly drop one heel down until you feel the stretch in your calf. Don't force the stretch. If your heels touch the floor you will need a higher step. Hold the stretch for 20 seconds and return to the starting position. Switch legs and repeat many times.

132. SEATED STRADDLE (HAMSTRINGS)

Sit up straight on a mat with your legs open as wide as possible. Gently lean forward over one leg as far as you can until you feel the hamstrings become tight. Push your shoulder to your knee as you lean forward. Hold for a few seconds and then lean more into the stretch. Hold again, and then return to the starting position. Switch legs.

133. FLYAWAY (CHEST)

Stand straight with your feet shoulder width apart. Lift your arms out to the side of your body at shoulder height, palms facing down. Reach behind as far as comfortably possible and hold.

134. BACK STRETCH (BACK)

This is an excellent exercise both for stretching the lower back muscles and reducing the stress on the lower back ligaments and discs. Lie on your back. With the knees bent, draw your legs towards your chest. Hold this position for 15 to 20 seconds and then relax.

135. REACH BEHIND AND PULL (BICEPS AND TRAPEZIUS)

Stand straight with your feet shoulder width apart. Bring one arm straight out behind you, palm facing down. Reach your other hand behind your back and with an underhand grip, gently tug on the wrist of the extended arm. Hold and then repeat on the other arm.

136. STRAIGHT ARM ACROSS (REAR DELTOID)

 Stand straight with your feet together. Grab your right elbow with your left hand and pull it across your chest toward the opposite side. Hold, and then switch arms to stretch the other shoulder.

137. UPPER SCOOP (BACK)

Sit on a mat with your legs extended straight in front of you. Collapse the upper body until you can reach the back of your calves. Exhale and hold while trying to reach as far as possible, stretching the back.

138. ELBOW BEND AND PUSH (TRICEPS)

Stand straight with your feet together. Bend one arm behind your head, reaching down until your palm hits the middle of your shoulder blades. Use your free hand to grasp your elevated elbow and pull it toward the back of your head. Hold, and then switch arms.

139. ROLL ON THE BALL (ABDOMINALS)

Lie on an exercise ball so that it's situated in the middle of your back. Drop your glutes down and bend your legs. Place your hands behind your head, which should be lying back over the ball. For a bigger stretch, you can extend your arms as far down as possible until you are touching or nearly touching the floor. Hold, then release.

140. LYING GLUTE AND HIP STRETCH (GLUTES, HIPS)

Lie on a mat with your back flat on the floor. Cross your left leg over your right so your left heel is touching your right knee. Lift your upper body so you can hug your right knee and gently pull it toward you. Exhale and hold, then switch and repeat on the other side.

141. LYING QUAD STRETCH (QUADS)

Lay facedown on a mat, and then raise your upper body to support yourself on your forearms. Reach behind you with your left hand to grab your left foot and pull until your heel touches your glutes. Hold the position and switch legs.

142. TOE TOUCH (HAMSTRINGS, LOWER BACK)

Sooner or later someone will say to you "can you touch your toes?" Besides being a test of flexibility,

touching your toes is a great way to stretch your hamstrings and lower back – even calves. Make sure you don't overstretch when first doing this exercise, as it can be stressful on the lower back. For the same reason don't bounce at the bottom.

143. OVERHEAD STRETCH (BACK, CHEST)

This is a very simple movement that can be performed every day. Stand up and raise your hands above your head. Clasp your hands together and push as high as you can, trying to touch the ceiling.

144. SPECIFIC MUSCLE WARM-UP

Don't walk into a gym and immediately throw your top weight on the barbell. Many a pec-delt tie-in has been torn that way (the area where the chest and front shoulder muscles join together). Always perform a couple of light-to-medium, high-rep sets before putting your maximum weight on the bar.

145. INCREASE YOUR WARM-UP IN PROPORTION TO YOUR STRENGTH

As the muscles get stronger the need for a warm-up becomes greater. A beginner may get by on a quick five-minute warm-up but once you start using hundreds of pounds on your exercises you'll need to adequately prepare the muscles. You may save time by skipping your warm-up, but at what cost? A torn pec or biceps muscle will set you back many months of training. A lower back injury could be a lifelong menace.

146. CONSTANT EVALUATION

If you are training hard, eating well and getting sufficient rest, yet you are not making gains, then something is amiss. You have to find out where you're going wrong. Don't continue training in the exact same manner hoping the problem may solve itself. You have to sit down and re-evaluate your whole approach. The best way to do this is to refer to your training logs and records.

147. PHOTOGRAPHS

Taking a set of photos when you begin training is a good way to evaluate your physique. We should warn you that the first set of photos you take will probably depress you, as you will no doubt compare them to the bodybuilding superstars in MuscleMag International. But over time as you make progress your physique (and photographs) will start looking like more and more the ones you see in the bodybuilding magazines. In fact Robert Kennedy may even approach you to do a photo shoot!

148. TAKING MEASUREMENTS

Opinion is split on taking measurements. Unless you are one of those genetically gifted types, you probably won't see a rapid change. For example, it takes on average about 10 pounds of muscular bodyweight to add a single inch to the arm. Coincidently, this

is about the amount of weight the average person can expect to gain in the first year of training. On the bright side, in four or five years you'll be sporting 20-inch arms.

A lower back injury could be a lifelong menace.

TRAINING
PARTNERS

149. When two heads are better than one
150. Friendly competition
151. Brutally honest
152. The right time
153. The right attitude
154. The right consistency
155. Is strength important?
156. The stronger sex?
157. Double the knowledge

5

149. WHEN TWO HEADS ARE BETTER THAN ONE

Few people achieve success without help from others. Even something as individualistic as weight training has room for doubling up. A training partner provides numerous advantages. For starters you won't have to keep bothering other people for a spot. Another benefit is motivation. On days when you don't feel like training (or training with enough intensity), your training partner can encourage you. You can then reciprocate on his or her lazy days.

150. FRIENDLY COMPETITION

Another benefit of a training partner is that you and your training partner can engage in little competitions. If he gets 10 reps, you try to do 11. This back and forth will do wonders for your progress.

151. BRUTALLY HONEST

A good training partner can be honest. You may think your physique is flawless, but your partner can quickly bring you back to reality. This brutal honesty will help you immensely if you decide to compete in a bodybuilding contest down the road.

152. THE RIGHT TIME

The most basic thing to keep in mind when choosing a training partner is what time you both like to work out. If you're a morning person and he or she prefers late evening, odds are you two will never mesh. Try to pick someone who works out around the same time of day as you do.

153. THE RIGHT ATTITUDE

Nothing derails a good workout like negativity. If you're training with someone who is always complaining and constantly seeing the downside to everything – get rid of him! You want someone who will motivate you to train harder, not get you thinking about changing sports. It doesn't matter if your training partner can bench press as much as you can. What's more important is his or her mental approach to training.

154. THE RIGHT CONSISTENCY

One of the main benefits of a good training partner is that he can motivate you to strive for higher goals. He will not be able to motivate you if he's only making every second or third workout. His inconsistency is telling you that working out is very low on his priority scale. Drop him and look for someone else.

155. IS STRENGTH IMPORTANT?

Although not as important as attitude and consistency, it does make sense to train with someone who is in the same strength range as you. It won't make any difference on most machine and dumbell exercises, but a huge difference in your bench press weights will mean a lot of loading and unloading the bar. Of course a slight difference in strength might be a benefit. You can push yourself to catch up on your partner's stronger exercises, and he can try to match you on exercises in which you are stronger.

156. THE STRONGER SEX?

Does your training partner have to be of the same sex? Absolutely not. Some of the best training partnerships consist of a couple. Knowing that there is a female watching you will bring out the best in you, and most women who train with weights want to show the guys that they belong in the weightroom.

Unless there are major differences between the two of you with regards to some of the other more important traits already discussed (you can find a way around the strength differences), try training with someone of the opposite sex.

157. DOUBLE THE KNOWLEDGE

The best scenario is if your training partner has an equal but different range of knowledge and experience as you do. You can alternate back and forth, drawing on one another's suggestions.

THE BEST SCENARIO IS IF YOUR TRAINING **PARTNER** HAS AN EQUAL BUT **DIFFERENT RANGE** OF KNOWLEDGE AND **EXPERIENCE** AS YOU DO.

BEGINNING
STRATEGIES

158. What do I want?

159. Keep it simple

160. Compound exercises

161. To bulk or not to bulk

162. Ribcage expansion

163. Beware of the boxy look

6

158. WHAT DO I WANT?

One of the most fundamental questions you should ask yourself before you pick up that first dumbell is "what do I want to achieve from bodybuilding?" For some, losing a few pounds and perhaps some general conditioning is all they are after. Building a 50-inch chest is the furthest thing from their minds. For others, nothing short of elbowing the current Mr. Olympia off the stage will suffice. Keep in mind that even if your goal is dethroning the current Mr. Olympia, you don't start training at the Mr. Olympia level. Start out slowly and gradually progress to the next level.

159. KEEP IT SIMPLE

The primary goal at the beginning level is to learn how to train – nothing fancy, just basic sets and reps.

For the first few months follow a full-body three-times-a-week training routine. Pay strict attention to form and increase the weight only when the muscles are capable of handling it.

160. COMPOUND EXERCISES

When beginning bodybuilding, virtually all your exercises should be compound. Compound exercises are those in which more than one joint is involved and more than one muscle group is utilized. Compound exercises are the ones that allow you to use the most weight, and hence they are the best for gaining mass. Examples of compound exercises are bench presses, squats, deadlifts, barbell rows, barbell curls, chin-ups, and shoulder presses.

161. TO BULK OR NOT TO BULK

Bulking up was a popular term back in the '60s and '70s. It basically means eating as much as possible and training as heavy as possible to gain as much bodyweight as possible. The reason bulking up has fallen out of favor is that much of the weight gained is fat, which has to be lost if you want to compete (or even just look good). Today many bodybuilders try to keep their off-season weight to within 20 pounds of their competitive weight (as opposed to the 40 to 50 pounds of years ago). Unless you are very skinny and have a hard time gaining muscular body weight, we don't recommend bulking up.

162. RIBCAGE EXPANSION

Although the chest muscles receive all the glory, it is the underlying ribcage that makes up most of the chest measurement. While you can't enlarge the ribs, it is possible to slightly lengthen the cartilage and ligaments connecting the ribs to the sternum (center rib bone). We should add that by your early 20s these soft connective tissues have hardened, so the techniques for expanding the rib cage won't have much effect. Ribcage expansion works best in the teenage years. The two best exercises for expanding the ribcage are breathing squats and cross-bench pullovers.

163. BEWARE OF THE BOXY LOOK

Although ribcage expansion may be desirable for some, for others it should be avoided. Those with a narrow shoulder structure should probably avoid trying to expand the ribcage, as it will only leave you looking like a "box." By this we mean you'll be nearly as thick as wide. Those with boxy physiques tend to look fat in clothes.

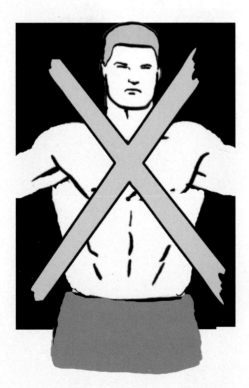

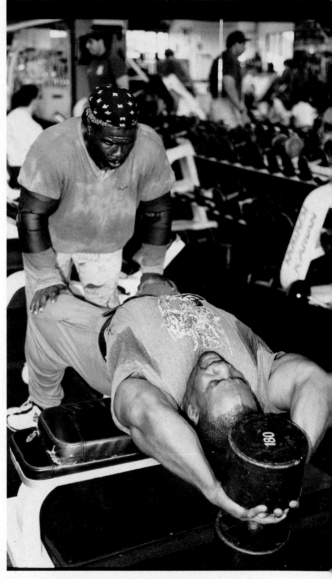

ROBBIE ROBINSON SPOTS CHRIS CORMIER ON HIS CROSS-BENCH PULLOVERS.

BEGINNING EXERCISES

164. Crunches – torso and leg position
165. Crunches – arm position
166. Crunches – watch the neck
167. Crunches – don't lock the feet
168. Suck it in
169. Vacuum
170. Back extensions
171. Leave them till last
172. Lying leg raises
173. Leg raises - leave your butt alone!
174. Barbell squats
175. Smith-machine squats
176. Leg presses
177. Horizontal or 45-degrees?
178. Lying leg curls
179. Leg curls- don't hyperextend
180. Flat barbell presses
181. Incline barbell presses
182. It's all in the angle
183. Supine dumbell presses
184. Dumbell presses – 90 degrees is safest
185. Incline dumbell presses
186. The weakest link
187. Your knees – a helping hand!
188. Dips
189. Parallel or V?
190. Dips: thick or thin?
191. Assisted dips
192. Chin-ups
193. Hanging around for width
194. Assisted chins
195. Lat pulldowns
196. Think of them as hooks
197. Bent-over barbell rows
198. Keep the natural arch
199. Bench barbell rows
200. Reverse-grip barbell rows
201. T-Bar rows
202. T-bar machine rows
203. Seated rows

204. One-arm dumbell row
205. Use the mirror
206. Rotations
207. Front barbell press
208. To the front only
209. Dumbell presses
210. A slight tilt
211. Lateral raises (also called side raises)
212. Triceps pushdowns
213. French presses
214. Lying EZ-bar extension
215. Incline or decline EZ-bar extensions
216. Dumbell extensions
217. Bench dips
218. Dip, not rock!
219. Narrow presses
220. Straight or EZ-bar?
221. Standing barbell curl
222. Standing dumbell curls
223. Do the twist
224. Preacher curls
225. Incline curls
226. Thumbless?
227. Standing calf raises
228. Calf-induced shoulder rash?
229. Toe presses on leg press
230. Experiment with foot stance and width
231. Calf stretching
232. For all to see

7

164. CRUNCHES – TORSO AND LEG POSITION

When performing crunches always keep your knees bent and feet flat on the floor. Performing any exercise with the legs locked out straight, particularly abdominal exercises, adds excessive pressure on the lower back. Also, raise the shoulders only 8 to 10 inches off the floor. Raising all the way up to your knees doesn't work your abs harder, it just brings the hip flexor muscles into play.

165. CRUNCHES – ARM POSITION

When you start performing crunches, keep your arms across the middle of the chest. This makes the exercise easier by "reducing" the weight of the arms. As you get stronger you can move the arms farther away from your abdominals – first to behind your head, and finally to a fully stretched-out position above your head.

166. CRUNCHES – WATCH THE NECK

One of the big mistakes people make when performing crunches with the hands behind the head is to push the back of the head with the arms. This

not only takes some of the pressure off the abdominals, it also puts stress on the neck. Try to keep your elbows pointed outwards at all times and keep your head stationary by locking your eyes on a point on the ceiling.

167. CRUNCHES – DON'T LOCK THE FEET

Another mistake many bodybuilders make when performing crunches is to lock their feet. The primary culprits for this are abdominal boards with rollers. Locking the feet will place

excessive stress on the lower back as you crunch forward, in addition to working the hip flexors excessively.

168. SUCK IT IN

Well the military was right: regularly sucking in your gut and puffing out your chest does work. Before you hit the sack every night (and/or first thing in the morning) practice pulling in your abdominal muscles. Count to 10 and then release. Doing 3 or 4 "sets" of this simple exercise will make your waist appear smaller.

169. VACUUM

Vacuums are a variation of the suck-it-in tip discussed earlier. Suck in your stomach, puff out your chest, and

then blow all the air out of your lungs. Hold for 10 seconds. Three-time Mr. Olympia Frank Zane was a master of this technique.

170. BACK EXTENSIONS

Most muscles work in pairs and the abdominals are no exception. In this case the opposing muscles are the spinal erector (lower back) muscles, and you should train them regularly. One of the simplest exercises to work the lower back is to lie face down on the floor and gently raise the torso

upwards. Don't excessively arch (hyperextend) the lower back. You must strike a balance between working the lower back muscles and placing too much stress on the lower back ligaments.

171. LEAVE THEM TILL LAST

As the abdominals and lower back muscles are used for stabilizing on most of the exercises for the legs and torso muscles, you should train them after these larger muscle groups. Fatiguing them early, will interfere with the execution of these exercises and could lead to an injury of the lower back.

172. LYING LEG RAISES

As with crunches, never perform the exercise with totally straight legs. Always keep a slight bend at the knees. Start with the incline board at the lowest level and gradually increase the angle over the weeks and months to make the exercise more difficult.

173. LEG RAISES - LEAVE YOUR BUTT ALONE!

Some people rest their hands under their butt when doing lying leg raises. This adds extra stress to the lower back and tends to shift the stress from the lower to the upper abs.

IMPORTANT!

LEAVE YOUR BUTT ALONE!

174. BARBELL SQUATS

Squats are considered the best quad exercise. They'll also stimulate muscle growth over your entire body.

With the barbell resting across the shoulders, slowly squat down until your thighs are at least parallel to the floor. Return to the starting position. Do not bounce at the bottom of the movement. Try to keep the torso perpendicular to the floor. Don't let the body start leaning forward – doing so could lead to a lower back injury.

175. SMITH-MACHINE SQUATS

Even though barbell squats are king when it comes to building the legs, there are a few occasions when you may want to use the Smith machine. Those with

poor flexibility in their Achilles' tendon may find it difficult to keep their balance when doing regular barbell squats (the old "up on the toes" syndrome). The Smith machine will allow you to keep your feet slightly forward or back in your stance, enabling you to keep your feet flat on the ground. Also, those with injured lower backs or knees may find the Smith machine less stressful on these areas.

176. LEG PRESSES

Leg presses are a close second to squats in terms of effectiveness and have the advantage of letting you use hundreds of pounds of weight in relative safety. As you lower the platform by bending your knees, don't bounce at the bottom of the movement. You run the

risk of damaging your knees or ribs. Likewise don't lock the legs completely straight at the top as you could hyperextend and tear the knee ligaments or cartilage.

177. HORIZONTAL OR 45-DEGREES?

If your gym has both the 45-degree and horizontal leg press, try both to see which one feels more comfortable or gives you the best leg workout. If you find both equally effective, try alternating them on different leg days.

178. LYING LEG CURLS

This exercise is one of the best for developing the hamstring muscles. As you raise the lower legs toward your butt, don't let your butt lift off the bench in an attempt to move the weight. There should be no jerking or bouncing as you lift the weight up.

179. LEG CURLS – DON'T HYPEREXTEND

Many of the older leg extension machines allow you to extend the legs past the locked-out position. In other words you can hyperextend at the knee joint. While you may be giving the hamstring muscles a better stretch, you are also forcing the knee joint through a greater range of motion than it was designed for. Try to keep your legs from locking out completely on leg-curl exercises.

180. FLAT BARBELL PRESSES

Like squats, barbell presses are considered one of the best for stimulating muscles, in this case your chest, shoulders, and triceps. With a slightly wider than shoulder-width grip, lift the bar off the rack and slowly lower it to your mid-chest. Push it back up to arm's length. Don't bounce the bar off your chest. Likewise don't arch your lower back excessively when lifting. For a few extra pounds of weight you run the risk of lower back injury.

181. INCLINE BARBELL PRESSES

Incline presses are performed the same way as flat presses except you are lying back on a tilted or  inclined bench. This shifts the stress from the lower and outer chest to the upper chest. Instead of lowering the bar to your mid-chest, try lowering it to your collarbone. Keep your elbows back throughout the movement.

182. IT'S ALL IN THE ANGLE

As you perform incline barbell presses, experiment with different angles on the bench to see which angle hits the upper chest most effectively. Too high and it's more a shoulder exercise. Too low and you are virtually doing a flat bench press.

183. SUPINE DUMBELL PRESSES

This exercise is very similar to supine barbell presses except that you use two dumbells instead of one barbell.

Try to keep your upper arm at 90 degrees to your torso as you lower the dumbells to just below chest level. Push them back up until they just touch at the top. Dumbells allow you to get a greater stretch at the bottom of the exercise than a barbell.

184. DUMBELL PRESSES – 90 DEGREES IS SAFEST

Ironically one of the primary advantages of dumbell presses is also one of the disadvantages. Dumbells allow you to lower the arms past the shoulders' natural range of movement. The barbell will come in contact with your chest before this happens. For safety considerations lower the dumbells only until your upper arms are parallel to the floor or just slightly below.

185. INCLINE DUMBELL PRESSES

Most everything we said about incline barbell and supine dumbell presses also applies here. Experiment with different angles and don't let the upper arm go far below shoulder height.

186. THE WEAKEST LINK

The primary disadvantage of incline dumbell presses is that you will reach a point at which your chest and shoulders are capable of lifting more weight than you can hoist off the floor and into position. When this happens have two spotters pass the dumbells to you at arms' length. Lowering the dumbells to the floor at the conclusion of the exercise is not usually a problem.

187. YOUR KNEES – A HELPING HAND!

As we just stated in the previous tip, it won't be long before your chest is capable of lifting heavier dumbells than your arms are capable of hoisting into position on an incline press. When this happens and no one is around to help, try using your knees to position the dumbells. Hoist the dumbells from the floor and lay them on your knees in a vertical position. As you lean back towards the bench force one and then the other dumbell upwards by rapidly pushing upwards with your knees.

188. DIPS

Dips are another great exercise for packing muscle mass on the chest, shoulders, and triceps. The late Vince Gironda was the most vocal spokesperson for dips, an excellent exercise for developing the clean line that separates the chest from the ribcage. Grab the bars with both hands and with the torso leaning forward and chin tucked down on your chest, slowly lower your body between the bars to a comfortable stretch (for most this will mean your shoulders are in line with or just slightly above the bars). Return to the starting point by straightening the arms. As with dumbell presses, avoid bouncing at the bottom of the movement.

189. PARALLEL OR V?

Dipping bars come in many shapes and sizes. In some, the bars are parallel to one another. Others start wide and join together at one end, forming a "V." If you're lucky enough to work out at a gym that has a couple of different styles of dipping bars, experiment. The advantage of the V-shaped bars is that they allow you to take different grip widths. Generally you'll find the wider the grip the more the outer chest is worked, while narrow grips bring in more triceps and shoulders.

190. DIPS: THICK OR THIN?

Besides shape, dipping bars may be thick or thin. Again, if your gym has an assortment of dipping bars to choose from, experiment to see which feels most comfortable and effective for your chest and shoulders. Most trainers prefer thicker bars for dips and thinner bars for chins.

191. ASSISTED DIPS

For those who have trouble lifting their bodyweight on regular dips, try the assisted machine. The machine works by providing an upward force as you perform the exercise. In simple terms the machine is making you lighter. Your goal on assisted dips is to use less and less weight (not more weight as with most exercises). With time you should be able to lift your full bodyweight and you'll be able to use the parallel bars. Eventually you may be strong enough to add weight with the use of a dipping belt.

192. CHIN-UPS

Chin-ups are one of the best exercises for adding width to the back. They'll give you that much sought-after V-shaped look. You will need access to your gym's overhead bar to perform this exercise. With a slightly wider

than shoulder-width grip, pull yourself up until your eyes are in line with the bar. Slowly lower your body back down until your arms are just short of lockout.

193. HANGING AROUND FOR WIDTH

If you are still in your teens you have another method for increasing your back and shoulder width. Simply hanging from a chin-up bar can spread the scapulae (shoulder blades). After you complete your regular chin-up sets, hang from the bar for as long as possible and let your shoulder blades stretch out as far as possible.

194. ASSISTED CHINS

Chins are great but unfortunately not everyone can do them. From day one you'll have to lift your entire bodyweight. If you can't lift your bodyweight, try an assisted chin-up machine. This apparatus is usually part of the same machine that allows assisted dips. You kneel or stand on a platform that provides upward pressure as you lift yourself up. Just as with the assisted dips, you use less and less weight (assistance) as you get stronger.

195. LAT PULLDOWNS

Can't do chin-ups and don't have access to an assisted chin-up machine? Lat pulldowns are a close second. Instead of having to pull your entire bodyweight up to a stationary bar, you pull the bar down towards you. We strongly urge you to pull the bar toward your collarbone or chin. Some people pull the bar down behind the head to their neck. Pulling behind the head puts extra pressure on the rotator cuff (the collection of small muscles and tendons that attach to the shoulder blade). Every time you move the bar up and down there is repeated chafing of the rotator cuff. With time it could become inflamed or worse, torn. There is virtually no difference in terms of effectiveness. Pull the bar to the front.

196. THINK OF THEM AS HOOKS

When performing lat pulldowns, try to think of the hands as merely hooks. The more you squeeze and grip with your hands the more biceps and forearm involvement you bring in. Since these smaller muscles fatigue before your larger back muscles, your back will not get enough work.

197. BENT-OVER BARBELL ROWS

Another basic back exercise, barbell rows add strength and mass to the central back region. Bend forward and grab a barbell with a slightly wider than shoulder-width grip. The torso should be held at approximately 30 degrees to the floor. Pull the bar toward the lower rib cage. Lower the bar to just short of arm lockout.

198. KEEP THE NATURAL ARCH

Even though you'll routinely hear instructors say, "keep your back straight," the human spine is in fact not straight, but slightly curved. Try to keep the natural arch in the lower back when you perform barbell rows. If you let the back round (i.e. if you reduce the natural curve), the lower back muscles relax, placing most of the stress on the ligaments.

199. BENCH BARBELL ROWS

If you find standard barbell rows stressful on the lower back, try performing the exercise on a flat bench. Simply lie face down on a high bench and have the bar placed directly underneath. If you have long arms you may need to bridge the bench up on blocks of wood or milk crates to get a good stretch.

200. REVERSE-GRIP BARBELL ROWS

To target the lower and central lats more, try reverse-grip barbell rows. The main differences from a regular row are that you use a narrower grip (about shoulder width) and you hold the bar with a reverse grip (palms facing forward instead of backward). Because

reverse-grip barbell rows bring more of the biceps into play, you'll find that you can use more weight. Former Mr. Olympia, Dorian Yates, would use over 400 pounds in this exercise!

201. T-BAR ROWS

A close variation of the barbell row, the T-bar row is another great back-thickening exercise. Most gyms have a special T-shaped apparatus for this exercise, but a regular barbell (and the V-shaped attachment used on the seated row exercise) will suffice as long as you find a way to keep one end anchored to the floor (either have a training partner hold it down with

his foot or stick the bar in a corner and place a few heavy dumbells or plates on top). Grab the handles or V-shaped apparatus and pull the bar towards the torso. As with barbell rows, try to keep the torso at about a 30-degree angle to the floor and the lower back slightly arched. Return the bar to just short of a locked-out position.

202. T-BAR MACHINE ROWS

Even with perfect technique many people find T-bar rows stressful on the lower back. Equipment manufacturers have responded to this by offering a version of the T-bar that has an angled pad to rest the torso on. If you find regular T-bar rows stressful on the lower back and your gym has such a T-bar, try incorporating it into your workouts.

203. SEATED ROWS

Seated rows are like barbell and T-bar rows in that they are great for hitting the muscles in the center of the back. You will need a cable machine to perform this exercise. Grab the V-shaped pulley attachment and sit down on the floor or on the machine's seating pad. With your legs slightly bent, pull the handle into the lower ribcage. Slowly stretch forward until your arms are fully stretched.

As you pull the handle towards the torso, try to squeeze the shoulder blades together. This will fully stretch the chest muscles and contract the back muscles. Don't let the torso go past 90 degrees as you pull the handles towards the torso.

204. ONE-ARM DUMBELL ROW

If your gym doesn't have a T-bar or seated row and you find barbell rows stressful on the lower back, one-arm dumbell rows are a good substitute. Place one knee and hand on a flat bench. Lean your weight onto your arm and keep your back arched. With the free hand, grab a dumbell and pull it upwards in a sawing motion. At the top of the exercise your upper arm should be parallel with the floor. One-arm rows

place less stress on the lower back because you are braced on the bench. Be sure to reach right down to the floor each rep – stretch those lats.

205. USE THE MIRROR

If you find your coordination lacking while doing dumbell rows, try placing the bench parallel to the mirror. This allows you to adjust your torso and arm position as you execute the exercise. At the conclusion of a set, allow the arm to stretch down stressing the lats. Hold this straight arm position for 8 seconds and feel the burn.

206. ROTATIONS

One of the few disadvantages of repeated pressing movements is stress on the small rotator muscles located at the

shoulder on the scapula. Most people start doing rotations only after they've incurred a rotator cuff problem. Try to strengthen the rotators from day one, and be sure to warm them up before doing any chest or shoulder pressing movements. Grab a light dumbell or weight plate. Hold your upper arm tight to the body and, with your elbows at a 90-degree angle, slowly rotate your lower arms in toward each other and out from the body.

207. FRONT BARBELL PRESS

This exercise is one of the best for adding size to the shoulder muscles, particularly the front and side shoulders (anterior and medial deltoids). Sit down in the shoulder press rack (preferably one with a vertical back support). Reach back and grab the barbell with a slightly wider than shoulder-width grip. Lift the bar up and out so that it's positioned above your head. Slowly lower the bar to your upper chest or collarbone and then press

back up to arms' length. Don't bounce the bar off your collarbone at the bottom of the exercise.

208. TO THE FRONT ONLY

Although some bodybuilders prefer to lower the bar behind the head when doing barbell presses, we advise against doing this. As with behind-the-head pulldowns, there is considerable stress placed on the small rotator muscles when doing this.

209. DUMBELL PRESSES

As with flat barbell and dumbell presses for chest, you can substitute dumbells for a barbell when working

shoulders. Sit down in a chair with some sort of back support and raise a pair of dumbells to shoulder height so that the palms are facing forward. Press the dumbells upwards and inwards so that they touch above the forehead. For variety you can alternate pressing the

dumbells. As with front barbell presses, dumbell presses primarily target the front and side shoulders.

210. A SLIGHT TILT

To reduce the pressure on the rotator cuff when doing dumbell presses, set the angle of the adjustable bench at about 80 degrees. If you don't have access to an adjustable bench, keep your butt slightly forward on the vertical bench and lean slightly backwards.

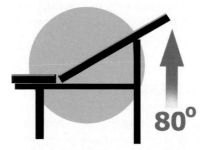

80°

211. LATERAL RAISES (ALSO CALLED SIDE RAISES)

Side raises are probably the best exercise for widening the shoulders because they add size to the medial (side) shoulder. With both the elbows and knees slightly bent, raise a set of dumbells outwards and upwards, until the arms are parallel with the floor. Slowly lower the dumbells down so that they meet in front of the body. The palms should be facing together at the bottom of the exercise. Resist the urge to swing the body as you lift the dumbells. This adds stress to the lower back and lessens the effectiveness of the exercise.

212. TRICEPS PUSHDOWNS

Pushdowns are one of the best exercises for targeting

the triceps muscles. You will need to use your gym's cable pushdown for this exercise. Grab the attachment with the palms facing downwards, hands about shoulder width apart. With the elbows held firmly against the torso, push downwards until the arms are locked out. Slowly raise the attachment back up to about chest level. For variety you can

use different attachments. They probably won't make much difference to your triceps but there may be a big difference on your wrist.

213. FRENCH PRESSES

One of the best exercises for adding mass to the triceps, French presses have been performed successfully by bodybuilders for years. Although you can use just about any type of bar, most bodybuilders find the EZ-bar less stressful on the wrists and elbows. The key to this exercise is to keep the upper arms locked in position and elbows pointing at the ceiling. The only thing that should be moving is your forearms.

214. LYING EZ-BAR EXTENSION

This exercise is another great one for adding mass to the triceps muscles. With an EZ-curl bar placed on the edge of a bench, lie back and grab the bar with a narrow (10 to 12 inches) grip. Raise the bar above your forehead, and with the upper arm locked vertical with the floor, lower the bar to the forehead by bending at the elbows.

There should be little or no upper-arm movement. The popular nickname for this exercise is skullcrushers, but we strongly urge you to avoid doing this!

215. INCLINE OR DECLINE EZ-BAR EXTENSIONS

For variety try doing your EZ-bar extensions on a decline or incline bench. You'll find that decline

extensions target more of the upper triceps, while inclines bring in more of the lower triceps.

216. DUMBELL EXTENSIONS

While sitting on a flat bench (or better still, one that has some sort of vertical back support), grab a dumbell and lower it behind the head, trying to keep the elbow pointed at the ceiling. You may need to reach across the front of the body with the free hand for balance and support. Some bodybuilders prefer to do this exercise with both hands at once. In this case grab the dumbell as if you were about to volley a volleyball (i.e. the fingers

pointing backwards and the palms facing the ceiling). The advantages of using two hands at once are that it saves time and it keeps you balanced (as opposed to one-arm extensions, for which you hold a weight on one side).

217. BENCH DIPS

While dips are usually performed as a chest exercise, with modification they can be an excellent triceps exercise. Instead of performing the movement on dipping bars, arrange two benches so that they are about four feet apart and parallel to one another. Position yourself between the benches so that your heels are barely resting on one bench and your hands are resting on the other (fingers facing forward). With the knees slightly bent, slowly lower your body between the benches until your butt is about a foot

off the floor (your upper arms will be approximately parallel with the floor at this point). Return to the starting position by straightening the arms. Resist the urge to bounce at the bottom of the exercise, as this places tremendous stress on the elbow, wrist, and shoulder joints. Need more weight? You can rest a plate or two on your lap, or hold a dumbell between your legs.

218. DIP, NOT ROCK!

When performing bench dips, make sure the benches you are resting your feet and hands on are stable. Either use benches with a wide base, or place some weight plates or dumbells on the base ends. Even though it rarely happens, there is the risk of one of the benches tipping over in the middle of your set. You can probably guess the damage this will cause

if you are dipping with two or three plates resting on your lap.

219. NARROW PRESSES

Narrow presses are another staple exercise for packing mass and strength onto the triceps. The exercise is performed much like standard barbell presses for the chest, with the exception that the grip is much narrower – only about 10 to 12 inches apart. As you press the bar upwards, concentrate on pushing with the triceps and not the chest and shoulders.

220. STRAIGHT OR EZ-BAR?

For variety, try experimenting with straight and EZ-curl bars when doing narrow presses. Many bodybuilders find straight bars stressful on the wrists. On the other hand others have discovered that straight bars seem

to target the triceps more effectively. See which one is least stressful and most effective for you.

221. STANDING BARBELL CURL

Considered one of, if not the best biceps exercises, barbell curls are also one of the easiest to perform. Grab a short straight bar with a shoulder-width or slightly wider grip. Slowly curl the bar up until the forearms are at about a 45-degree angle with the horizontal (about 8-10 inches from the shoulders). Lower the bar back down to within a couple of inches of your thighs. Don't swing the body in an attempt to lift a few extra pounds. The only thing moving should be your forearms. Experiment with the EZ-curl bar as well. You probably won't find much difference to your biceps but there may be a big difference on your wrists.

222. STANDING DUMBELL CURLS

This exercise is virtually identical to the previous except you use two dumbells. Using dumbells gives you the option of raising them in alternate fashion (as one dumbell is rising the other is lowering). Curling with dumbells also assures that each arm is subjected to the same degree of resistance.

223. DO THE TWIST

The biceps perform three functions. In addition to the familiar raising of the forearm and as a secondary muscle in raising the arm from the shoulder, biceps also rotate the forearm. You can make alternate dumbell curls more effective by twisting the dumbells from an inward to outward position as you raise them. Twisting the dumbells as you lift and lower (called supination) stimulates the biceps over their full range of motion.

224. PREACHER CURLS

Preacher curls (also called Scott curls after bodybuilding's first Mr Olympia, Larry Scott) are another basic biceps builder. They are especially effective at working the lower biceps and filling in the gap between the upper forearms and lower biceps. Start by sitting on the stool or bench attached

to the preacher board (a padded board angled at approximately 45 degrees). Raise or lower the seat so the preacher board fits snug under your armpits. Reach forward and

lift the barbell off the rack (most preacher benches have an attached barbell rack) or have a training partner pass you the barbell. Curl the bar up until your forearms are parallel with the floor. Slowly lower back down until your arms are just short of locked out. Do not bounce at the bottom of the exercise. Many bodybuilders have torn their biceps tendon doing just that. Once you tear a biceps tendon your only option is surgery, and 100 percent correction is unlikely.

225. INCLINE CURLS

As far as the biceps are concerned, incline curls are the opposite of preacher curls. Instead of working the lower biceps to a greater degree, they target the upper biceps. As the name suggests, you perform this exercise on an incline bench. Grab two dumbells and sit down on the bench (between 45 and 60 degrees will work best). Curl the dumbells

upward until your forearms are almost vertical with the floor. Slowly lower back down until your arms are just short of a lockout.

226. THUMBLESS?

As you try out the various biceps exercises, experiment with keeping the thumbs on the same side of the bar (or dumbell) as the fingers – this is called a thumbless grip or a false grip – or on the opposite side to the fingers. You may discover that one grip feels more comfortable than the other and may give you better biceps stimulation.

227. STANDING CALF RAISES

You will need access to a standing calf machine to do this exercise. Step up onto the machine's foot support and rest the pads atop the shoulders. With your legs locked, lift yourself up on your tiptoes as far as possible. Lower back down, trying to drop your heels as low as possible at the bottom. We have to warn you that out of all the muscles you will train, the calves hurt the most! A couple of sets will leave them burning with pain.

228. CALF-INDUCED SHOULDER RASH?

Don't be alarmed if you discover a slight rash on each shoulder the day after you do standing calf raises. In simple terms, the combination of pressure and thinness of the skin in the shoulder region causes the breakage of tiny blood vessels called capillaries. It will clear up within a day or two. Adding two sponge rubber pads under the pad may help you avoid this problem.

229. TOE PRESSES ON LEG PRESS

This exercise is an example of using a machine for an exercise other than the one it was designed for. Sit down in the leg press machine and place your toes on the bottom edge of the pressing platform. Instead of moving the platform by bending at the knees and using your thighs, you flex at the ankle and use your calves. As with standing calf raises, go for the maximum stretch at the top and bottom of the exercise. The primary advantage of this exercise is that you don't have hundreds of pounds placed across your shoulders as you do with the standing calf raise.

230. EXPERIMENT WITH FOOT STANCE AND WIDTH

As you perform toe presses, try experimenting with different stances. Try both wider and narrower than shoulder width. Try toes turned in, forward, and out. Each different angle hits a different part of the calf. When the toes are pointing out at "ten to two" the inside of the calf is worked. The outside is stressed when the toes are pointing in.

231. CALF STRETCHING

Calf training is as much about stretching as it is about lifting weights. Perhaps no other muscle group relies as much on extending its range of motion as the calf. As you are resting between sets, stand on a high block of wood (or the calf machine's foot block) and practice stretching your heels as far down as possible. The more flexible your calf and associated  Achilles' tendon, the greater your range of motion when you perform calf raises. The end result is greater calf development.

232. FOR ALL TO SEE

If your calves are weak and you need incentive to train them, try a tip from seven-time Mr. Olympia Arnold Schwarzenegger. Early in his career Arnold had weak calves and a lazy attitude about training them. To kick himself in the ass, he cut the lower legs off his sweat pants so his calves were always on display. Because of negative comments from others and his own dissatisfaction with how they looked, Arnold made calf training a priority.

THE BIG
FOUR

TIPS FOR IMPROVING YOUR BENCH PRESS

233. Plant your feet firmly on the floor

234. Lock your body tightly to the bench

235. Use a secure grip

236. Keep your wrists locked and straight

237. Keep the forearms vertical

238. Hold your breath

239. Pause at the bottom

240. Maintain control of the bar

241. Focus on lifting with the chest

242. Drive the bar up explosively

243. Have a spotter

244. Check the bar for warps

245. Retract your shoulder blades

TIPS FOR IMPROVING YOUR DEADLIFT

246. Starting position

247. Stance

248. Glued to your shins

249. Legs first

250. Don't jerk like a jerk!

251. Never rounded

252. Neck alignment

253. Hip thrust

254. Just hooks

255. Lower under control

256. Get a grip

TIPS FOR IMPROVING YOUR SQUAT

257. Experiment with your stance

258. Rack it or cage it

259. Break from the hips first

260. Not too high

261. Hold your breath

262. Head up

263. Increase your flexibility

264. The 2 x 4 – a temporary fix

265. Don't bounce

266. Elbows under hands

267. Stick your butt out!

268. To the floor – if you can.

269. Don't lock out

270. Racking the bar

271. Recruit a spotter

272. Proper spotting

273. The belt issue

TIPS FOR IMPROVING YOUR BARBELL CURL

274. Different grips for different heads

275. Bend the knees

276. Don't swing excessively

277. Lower slowly

278. Try an EZ-curl bar

279. Try "cheating."

280. To 45 degrees only

281. All the way down

282. Don't do a wrist curl

8

TIPS FOR IMPROVING YOUR BENCH PRESS

233. PLANT YOUR FEET FIRMLY ON THE FLOOR

Even though the bench press is primarily targeting the upper body, the legs play a major role in stabilizing. If you don't believe this, try benching with your legs up in the air. Both your coordination and strength suffer considerably. When benching try to keep your feet pressed into the floor. Try not to let them move, slip, or rise.

234. LOCK YOUR BODY TIGHTLY TO THE BENCH

What the floor is for your feet, the bench is for your torso – a platform for stability. When you lie on the bench, try to become part of it. Try to lock your back, glutes, and shoulders as tightly to the bench as possible.

LOCK IT!

235. USE A SECURE GRIP

Perhaps redundant to say, but you'd be surprised the number of guys who haphazardly grab the bar when benching. As soon as you grab the bar, lock both your fingers and thumb tightly around it. Never use a false (thumbless) grip when bench pressing.

236. KEEP YOUR WRISTS LOCKED AND STRAIGHT

To reduce the amount of stress on your wrist ligaments, keep your hands and forearms lined up while benching. Don't make the mistake of allowing the hand to flip back towards the back of the forearm.

237. KEEP THE FOREARMS VERTICAL

Although there are exceptions, the correct grip width on the bench press is the one that keeps your forearms vertical throughout the full range of motion. This will allow you to generate the most power as you push upward. Any wider or narrower is wasting energy, as your body will be trying to keep your forearms from sliding inwards or outwards.

238. HOLD YOUR BREATH

The bench press is another of those exceptions to the breathe-on-every-rep rule. As soon as you exhale your intrathoracic pressure drops. This not only puts you at risk for injury, but also diminishes your power base. Take your breaths at the top of the exercise when your arms are locked out.

239. PAUSE AT THE BOTTOM

If you plan on entering powerlifting competitions you will need to practice pausing the bar at the bottom of the exercise. The pause doesn't have to be a long one – about a second – but it will be required in competition to get a pass from the judges. Another reason for pausing is that it eliminates any bouncing. Bouncing the bar off the chest is a great way to break the sternum, a rib or tear a rotator – any of which can set your training back months if not years.

240. MAINTAIN CONTROL OF THE BAR

When benching you should be controlling the bar, not the other way around. Don't let the bar wander sideways or backwards towards the neck. This is not only dangerous but shifts more of the stress to the triceps. Find your groove and stay there.

241. FOCUS ON LIFTING WITH THE CHEST

Of the three primary muscles involved in bench pressing (chest, shoulders, triceps), the chest muscles are by far the most powerful. Many people place too much effort on pressing with the shoulders and arms when benching. Try to squeeze the chest on every single rep.

242. DRIVE THE BAR UP EXPLOSIVELY

When it comes to benching, speed is king (on the way up). For safety and official regulations you have to lower the bar down slowly and pause at the bottom. But if you want to move some meaningful poundages on the bench press, you must force the weight back up as explosively as possible. Forget the slow and controlled approach. Give it everything you've got as you push upward.

243. HAVE A SPOTTER

Having a spotter behind you is like an insurance agent – he or she is there if something goes wrong. You have enough on your mind without having to worry about what you'll do if you can't lift the weight. This worry will prevent you from testing your limits. Knowing that someone is there watching you will allow you to put all your focus on pressing the weight.

244. CHECK THE BAR FOR WARPS

They may be called straight bars but sometimes they're not. Like other metal objects, bars can bend

with repeated usage. This is especially true if your gym has a number of powerlifters and strong bodybuilders regularly working out with 500+ pounds on the bars. Place the bar on a rack and revolve it in your hands while looking at the ends. If there appears to be any warp, replace it and grab another bar. If the warp is severe, notify management. A bent bar can flop during your lift, breaking your wrist or worse, your neck.

245. RETRACT YOUR SHOULDER BLADES

As soon as you lie back on the bench, pull your shoulder blades together. This not only provides a more stable surface from which to push the bar, but also expands your chest and shortens the distance you have to press the bar. The shorter the distance, the better your chances of lifting the weight.

JASON GALLANT & MARKUS REINHARDT

TIPS FOR IMPROVING YOUR DEADLIFT

246. STARTING POSITION

The starting position for the deadlift is much the same as Olympic lifters use for the clean and jerk. Your shoulders, bar, and ankles should form a vertical, straight line. This set-up will generate the most power in the safest means possible. Your back should be flat throughout.

247. STANCE

The stance for deadlifts is similar to squats; that is, your feet are just slightly wider than shoulder width apart.

248. GLUED TO YOUR SHINS

When you start the deadlift try to keep the bar as tight to your shins as possible. As you start pulling up the bar can move out a wee bit, but it should be tight at the bottom of the lift.

249. LEGS FIRST

The first muscles to engage on the deadlift should be your legs. But don't straighten them out too early. This will limit the amount of weight you can lift and place undue stress on the lower back.

250. DON'T JERK LIKE A JERK!

As common sense should tell you, don't make a sudden yank at the beginning of the exercise. This is how most people injury their back on this exercise. Start the lift slowly.

251. NEVER ROUNDED

Always keep a slight curve, or arch, in the lower back when lifting. As soon as the back rounds, the lower-back muscles relax, placing tremendous stress on their ligaments.

252. NECK ALIGNMENT

When you deadlift, the neck has an important controlling function. It should stay in line with the trunk throughout the movement. If your neck is held too far back excessive stress will be placed on the back extensors. Too far forward and the back will round.

253. HIP THRUST

Once the bar reaches the mid-thigh position, concentrate on thrusting the hips forward and rolling your shoulders back while sticking your chest out as you lock the legs.

254. JUST HOOKS

Again, try to visualize your arms as nothing but hooks attached to the bar. They should remain straight at all times. Don't try lifting the weight with your biceps. The biceps' assistance will be minimal and you will run the risk of tearing a biceps tendon.

255. LOWER UNDER CONTROL

Once you lock out the bar, don't simply let it drop to the floor. Deadlifts are like every other exercise in that the lowering is at least as important as the raising.

256. GET A GRIP

There are three grips you can use for deadlifting are: pronated (palms facing you), supinated (palms facing forward), and mixed (one hand pronated and the other supinated). Most competitive powerlifters use the mixed grip as they find it gives them better control. Keep in mind that a supinated hand position will place tremendous stress on the biceps and associated tendons. For long-term safety and progress we suggest you use the pronated grip or the mixed grip.

TIPS FOR IMPROVING YOUR SQUAT

257. EXPERIMENT WITH YOUR STANCE

In general terms, the wider your foot stance, the more glute and inner thigh stimulation. Conversely, narrower stances tend to hit more of the center and outer thigh. When you begin squatting, try both to feel where each stance hits.

258. RACK IT OR CAGE IT

Unless your will for survival is sadly lacking, always perform your squats in a squat rack or powercage. No matter how well executed your technique is, sooner or later you will run into problems while squatting. The last thing you want is to crash to the floor with a few hundred pounds on your shoulders. Squat racks and powercages are designed to catch the bar before it could drive you into the floor. Put the ego aside and always use a rack.

259. BREAK FROM THE HIPS FIRST

The two main joints being used in the squat are the hips and knees. Try to begin the movement by breaking (bending) at the hips first and not the knees. The joint that comes into play first will be subjected to the full weight of the bar for a split second. The hips being larger and stronger can tolerate this while the knees probably can't.

260. NOT TOO HIGH

Try to rest the bar across your shoulder and upper traps and not your neck. It won't be long before you'll be using hundreds of pounds in this exercise. You don't want that kind of pressure resting on your neck vertebrae. Resting the bar high also forces your torso forward, which places additional stress on your lower back.

261. HOLD YOUR BREATH

Unlike most exercises for which you should try to inhale and exhale on each rep, you should hold your breath during your squat reps. Because of the weight involved you want as much intrathoracic pressure as possible when doing squats. Exhaling relaxes the small muscles surrounding the ribcage, thus decreasing the strength of your upper body. You want the upper body to be a strong and stable supporting platform.

262. HEAD UP

The body generally follows the position of the head. If you are walking along and turn your head to the right, your body will follow. The same is true for squats.

Always keep your head up and in good alignment with the rest of your body. If you start looking down, your body will tend to lean forward. This will change your center of gravity and place excessive stress on the lower back.

263. INCREASE YOUR FLEXIBILITY

If you have been giving stretching exercises the short-shift lately, now is the time to change your habits. Safe and effective squatting requires good flexibility in the hip, knee, and ankle joints. For example if you find that you come up on your toes as you squat down, you need to increase the flexibility of your Achilles' tendon. (See 231)

264. THE 2 X 4 – A TEMPORARY FIX.

While you are working on improving your Achilles' flexibility, you can maintain your balance by placing your heels on a 2 x 4. Keep in mind that elevating your heels will shift more of the stress to the front of your thighs, and perhaps more important, to the knee region. The sooner you can squat flat-footed the better.

265. DON'T BOUNCE

If you want to keep squatting for years to come, don't use your knees as elastic bands. Bouncing out of the lower position may give you a few extra reps or enable you to lift more weight, but at what cost? The supporting tissues of the knee region (ligaments, tendons, and cartilage) were not designed to be suddenly subjected to hundreds of pounds of weight. Always perform the exercise in a slow and controlled manner.

266. ELBOWS UNDER HANDS

Even though there are exceptions, most people will find holding the bar with a medium grip width will work best. This means your elbows are situated directly below your hands. If you hold too wide you'll rotate your shoulders inward and hunch forward. Too close together and you'll feel cramped.

267. STICK YOUR BUTT OUT!

As mentioned (251) the human spine is not perfectly straight, but has a slight S-shape to it. To reduce the stress on your lower back ligaments, try to keep the natural concave curve in your lower back. The easiest way to do this is to keep your butt stuck out as you descend into the full squat position. When you let the back round the lower back muscles relax, forcing the lower back ligaments to pick up the extra stress.

268. TO THE FLOOR – IF YOU CAN.

Unless flexibility or injury issues dictate otherwise, squat down until your quads go below parallel with the floor. You don't need to touch your butt on the floor, but to exercise the quads through their full range of motion the angle between the upper and lower leg should be 90 degrees or less. Keep in mind that safety comes first. If you start losing your alignment before you reach the full squat position, stop the exercise at this point. Don't squat lower than your unique bone structure comfortably allows.

269. DON'T LOCK OUT

One of the biggest mistakes many bodybuilders make when squatting is to forcibly lock the legs out at the top of the exercise. This practice is not recommended. Not only are you giving the quads a rest after each rep, you also run the risk of hyperextending at the knee joint. Terminate the rep just short of locking the legs out straight.

270. RACKING THE BAR

When placing the bar back on the rack, make sure it is secure on both sides of the rack before stepping out from under it. A good rule of thumb is to follow military procedure and "Visually acquire the target." Place the bar on one side of the rack and then look at the other side while you do the same. You now know that the bar is safely secure on both sides of the rack.

271. RECRUIT A SPOTTER

Even though a squat rack or powercage will enable you to perform squats in safety, for that extra security have a spotter standing behind you. A spotter can not only check your form, but also give you assistance if you have trouble completing a rep. Finally, you'll discover that simply knowing someone is watching you will result in a couple of extra reps! A good spotter can also verbally encourage you through a difficult set.

272. PROPER SPOTTING

Unlike most exercises where you or your spotter can provide assistance by lifting with your hands, the weight and positioning of the barbell on squats makes this all but impossible. The human body is not that strong when trying to push upwards from the waist to shoulder height. To safely spot on squats, you have to squat down with the person while keeping your arms loosely around the person's waist. If they get in trouble you can lock your entire arms around the torso and use your legs to help lift upwards. Don't worry about how "things" look. Safety takes precedence over appearance.

273. THE BELT ISSUE

Because of the weight you will be using, you may want to consider wearing a weightlifting belt while squatting. We say, "may," as it's a personal choice. There are no hard rules. Squatting does place some stress on the lower back but not as much as the anti-squat people would have us believe. Many people squat for years and never use a weightlifting belt. Conversely others need a belt for the extra security. Our suggestion is to first try squatting without a belt. As you increase the amount of weight you are using pay close attention to any signals your lower back may be giving off. If there seems to be extra lower-back stress, try wearing a belt. Tighten the belt before you set. Loosen or remove it immediately afterwards.

TIPS FOR IMPROVING YOUR BARBELL CURL

274. DIFFERENT GRIPS FOR DIFFERENT HEADS

If you go "by the book" the recommended width grip on barbell curls is shoulder-width. Don't, however, be afraid to experiment. Going slightly wider will target the inner head of the biceps while a narrow grip will stimulate more of the outer head. Trainers with elbow injuries often prefer a wider grip.

275. BEND THE KNEES

Always keep a slight bend at the knees when performing standing barbell curls. Locking the legs out straight will only add extra stress to the lower back.

276. DON'T SWING EXCESSIVELY

The biggest mistake bodybuilders make when curling is to rock back and forth with their upper body. Not only does this reduce the effectiveness of the exercise, it also stresses the lower-back ligaments.

277. LOWER SLOWLY

Fifty percent of a barbell curl's effectiveness is the negative, or lowering, phase. Always lower the bar in a slow and controlled manner. This not only provides better stimulation for the biceps, it places less stress on the biceps tendons.

278. TRY AN EZ-CURL BAR

If you find straight barbell curls stressful on the wrists, try switching to an EZ-curl bar. The bend on the EZ-curl bar will allow you to rotate the palms slightly inward, thus placing less stress on the small wrist ligaments.

279. TRY "CHEATING."

Cheat curls have probably built more biceps than any other exercise. We don't mean cheating from the first rep, however. Try to get 6 to 8 reps on your own, and then, add just enough body momentum to keep the bar moving for a couple of extra reps. Arnold Schwarzenegger used cheat curls to make his arms grow from 13 to 20 inches.

280. TO 45 DEGREES ONLY

You'll notice as you curl the bar up that a point will be reached where the exercise starts feeling easier. For most this point is where the forearm is at about a 45-degree angle with the torso. Try not to let the forearms go above this point (i.e. don't curl all the way to your shoulders).

281. ALL THE WAY DOWN

If swinging the body is the number one mistake bodybuilders make on barbell curls, lowering halfway down is number two. Unless you are performing 21s (described in the Advanced Training Technique section), always lower the bar to just short of your thighs. If you lower only halfway, you'll be targeting only the upper part of your biceps. You must lower the bar to your quads to stimulate the lower sections.

282. DON'T DO A WRIST CURL

Many bodybuilders make the mistake of starting their barbell curls with a slight wrist curl – bending the wrist toward their forearm before engaging the biceps. All this does is take the stress away from the biceps. Try to keep your wrist neutral at all times (ie. in line with your forearms).

TAMER EL SHAHAT

THE **BEND** ON THE **EZ-CURL** BAR WILL ALLOW YOU TO ROTATE THE PALMS SLIGHTLY INWARD, THUS PLACING **LESS STRESS** ON THE SMALL **WRIST LIGAMENTS**.

BODYBUILDING ETIQUETTE

283. Wash your gym clothes – regularly!

284. Shower after every workout

285. Under no circumstances share your razor blade

286. Do not share your comb or water bottle with anyone

287. Don't use the squat rack for barbell curls

288. Check before you strip

289. Don't stare

290. Be wary of advertisements

291. Offering advice vs being a know-it-all

292. Don't hog the equipment

293. Wipe up after yourself

294. Leave screaming for the roller coaster

295. Don't spit or leave gum in the water fountain or urinal

296. No interrupting

297. Turn off the cell phone or pager

298. Be on time for your cardio machine

299. Carry yourself with dignity

300. Stay away from the drug scene

301. Avoid growth hormone

283. WASH YOUR GYM CLOTHES – REGULARLY!

We've all heard the phrase, "It smells like a gym." The thing is, it shouldn't. Nothing is as disgusting as working out next to someone wearing month-old gym clothes. While you may be able to get by washing your gym clothes every second day, we strongly recommend doing it daily. If this is impractical, buy a second or third set of gym clothes. Having three sets of workout clothes means having to wash them only once or twice per week. Not only will your gym buddies thank you, you may even get a little bit of social life with the ladies.

284. SHOWER AFTER EVERY WORKOUT

It's not only your gym clothes that sweat and stink after a workout – you will as well! It may seem obvious, but you'd be surprised at the number of people who do their last set and go straight to school or work. All that sweat  is a great breading ground for odor-causing bacteria. Give the person next to you a break and take a shower as soon as you finish working out. If not at the gym then do it at the earliest possible time.

285. UNDER NO CIRCUMSTANCES SHARE YOUR RAZOR BLADE

This is another of those "you should know better" tips. In this day of AIDS and hepatitis, you'd think sharing a razor blade would be unheard of, but that's not the case. All it takes is one drop of blood from someone else's disease-infected body and your life may be tragically cut short. With razors costing mere pennies, save yourself a heap of potential trouble and buy your own.

286. DO NOT SHARE YOUR COMB OR WATER BOTTLE WITH ANYONE

As with sharing razors, you don't know the background of the person you are trying to help out. Head lice are still common and any number of infections can be spread by sharing a water bottle. In short, buy your own and use your own. Wash your hands after your workout and after using the restroom.

287. DON'T USE THE SQUAT RACK FOR BARBELL CURLS

This is one of those unwritten rules that you should try and follow. Nothing is as frustrating as not being able to do squats because the squat racks are all taken up by guys doing barbell curls. Barbell curls can be performed just about anywhere. If laying the bar on the floor is inconvenient, lay it on the end of a bench. Don't hinder someone's leg workout because you are too lazy to pick the bar up off the floor.

288. CHECK BEFORE YOU STRIP

Another of those unwritten rules. Don't start stripping down a bar assuming that just because there is no one close by, the bar  is not being used. As most gyms enforce the "replace your weights" rule, odds are fairly good the person using the bar stepped away for a second. This could be to use the washroom, give someone a spot, or visit the water fountain. Before taking the plates off the bar, check around to see if it is definitely free.

289. DON'T STARE

Although you are not going into a jungle, gyms do occasionally get frequented by animals! Even if some bodybuilder does have a great physique, try not to stare. As primates, most humans do not like to be stared at. Staring is a sign of aggression and provocation. It would be better to go over and compliment the person's physique and ask him how he built it, rather than staring continuously from across the gym. Another reason not to stare is that homophobia is rampant in bodybuilding gyms. That seemingly innocent stare on your part could be taken as a sign of sexual interest. You don't want some 250-pound bodybuilder getting the wrong idea! In addition, most females go to the gym to train, not to be stared at. Staring men is the reason for the proliferation of "women only" gyms. Gym clothes are often tight or provocative, but don't take that as a come-on. You don't want to be charged with stalking or harassment, and you don't want the gym to ask you not to come back.

290. BE WARY OF ADVERTISEMENTS

Anything emphasizing the human body will attract the unsavory element. Occasionally photographers or agents will bait the unsuspecting, with promises of stardom. If you develop a great physique it's possible one of these characters will approach you. Before signing any form or doing any photo shoot, check the individual's credentials. The better gyms won't allow these types through the door, but occasionally they'll find a way to slip in. Ask questions, check ID, and talk with other gym patrons. At the first sign of shadiness, drop the person. If he keeps bothering you, tell the

owner. If he starts stalking you outside the gym, contact the police immediately. If an individual tells you he works for a magazine, call the magazine's head office and check. Ask for a physical description.

291. OFFERING ADVICE VS BEING A KNOW-IT-ALL

It won't be long before you'll be seen as once of the "regulars" at your gym. Remember how you sought out more experienced bodybuilders for advice? Now you're one of those more experienced bodybuilders. With this new status comes responsibility. If someone asks for advice, then by all means offer it. Likewise if some new guy looks like he's about to hang himself from a cable machine, intervene. Don't, however, rush around the gym like some world-famous consultant after memorizing a passage from the latest issue of MuscleMag International. The regulars will think you're an idiot; the owner may or may not ask you to leave; and you run the risk of a lawsuit if someone takes your advice to heart and injuries him- or herself. There is a fine line between being helpful and being a nuisance. The truth is, many people resent being told how to exercise.

292. DON'T HOG THE EQUIPMENT

Remember how intimidating it was for you the first time you went into the gym? There are new people feeling the exact same way watching you work out. Nobody likes an equipment hog. As you rest between sets, keep an eye out for people who seem like they want to jump in but are too timid to ask. Make the offer. You are not expected to go around the gym recruiting people to work in with you; but be conscious of other members wanting to use the equipment you are using.

293. WIPE UP AFTER YOURSELF

Do you like the thought of working out in someone else's sweat? They feel the same way about your sweat. Not only is sweat a great way to pass along germs, it's downright disgusting to have to use a piece of equipment dripping with someone else's sweat. Your

gym should have towels and a disinfectant. If your gym doesn't supply workout towels (or strategically placed paper towel dispensers) bring your own. Use it to wipe up your sweat and anything left behind by someone else.

294. LEAVE SCREAMING FOR THE ROLLER COASTER

Nothing looks as stupid as some guy grunting and groaning while doing 75-pound bench presses or 100-pound squats. He may think he is impressing people but mostly he will be viewed as an idiot. Don't be that idiot. If it's the last rep on a heavy set of squats and a minor grunt or groan escapes, fine.

But there is no need to be yelling and screaming like you're doing battle with the Vikings. If being branded an idiot doesn't faze you, keep in mind that most gyms have policies on excessive grunting and groaning.

295. DON'T SPIT OR LEAVE GUM IN THE WATER FOUNTAIN OR URINAL

As disgusting as this sounds, people do it. If you have to spit out your gum, use the garbage. In fact people have choked while chewing gum during a workout, so

you may want to re-evaluate the whole gum-chewing thing. One awkward gulp on a set of heavy squats and your gum could be doing the tango with your epiglottis.

296. NO INTERRUPTING

One of the worst things you can do while working out is to interrupt someone during his or her training. All it takes is a split-second loss of concentration and you could cause the individual a grievous injury. If you need to make a comment or ask a question, wait until the person completes his or her set.

297. TURN OFF THE CELL PHONE OR PAGER

Unless you are on call for your job, turn off your cell phone or pager. Better yet, leave them in the car. Nothing is as distracting as being in the middle of a set of bench presses or squats and hearing someone's cell phone go off. Likewise you don't want your electronic device screwing up someone else's workout.

298. BE ON TIME FOR YOUR CARDIO MACHINE

Most gyms have a sign-up procedure for using the cardio equipment. Nothing is as frustrating as seeing two or three empty machines at prime time even though they are booked out on the sign-up board. If your time starts at 5:30, be ready to use it at 5:30. Don't wander over at 5:40 and then make up the 10 minutes on the back end. Why should the person booked after you have to lose 10 minutes of his or her time simply because you were late?

299. CARRY YOURSELF WITH DIGNITY

Just because you've developed a great-looking physique doesn't mean you are better than everyone else. Don't start prancing around as if you are the reincarnate of Arnold Schwarzenegger or Ronnie Coleman. Walking through the shopping mall in the dead of winter wearing a t-shirt and shorts and a weightlifting belt will only get you branded an idiot. This type of behavior does the sport of bodybuilding a great disservice. Pushing people out of the way in the gym will only get you suspended, expelled, or punched out (no matter how big you get there is always someone around the corner quite capable of dropping you). Walk with pride, not arrogance. Treat others with respect.

300. STAY AWAY FROM THE DRUG SCENE

While we probably shouldn't preach, nevertheless a few words of caution about this topic are needed. It's a fact that in their quest for ultimate size and strength, many bodybuilders turn to anabolic steroids and other performance enhancing drugs. If after many years of training you discover you have the genetics for competitive bodybuilding, then maybe (and it's a very guarded maybe) you can think about experimenting with such drugs, but this should only be done in countries where those drugs are legal. For now stay as far from the drugs and their dealers as possible. Not only is the market flooded with bogus drugs, but also many of them are illegal. The person you are buying from may be an undercover cop. Finally, even if they are a genuine drug dealer, he or she will quickly try to talk you into using other drugs like heroine and crack cocaine because of the bigger profit margins. Remember you are trying to improve your health and lifestyle, not destroy it. Illegal drugs are a certain way to an early death.

301. AVOID GROWTH HORMONE

If steroids can be classified as a drug you should probably avoid, then growth hormone is one you should definitely avoid. Unlike steroids, which stimulate muscle growth, growth hormone causes just about everything to grow. Those extra-large guts you see on some pro bodybuilders are the result of enlarged internal organs. There have been cases of healthy bodybuilders suddenly developing tumors. While results are not conclusive, the tumors' growth is believed to have been stimulated by the use of growth hormone. Our advice is to avoid growth hormone at all costs.

NUTRITION

302. Don't fall for fad diets
303. Slow and controlled
304. Experiment
305. Fat to muscle and muscle to fat
306. Low does not always mean low
307. How much protein?
308. Does my protein source matter?
309. Spaced out
310. Protein by the clock?
311. Beware of protein bars
312. Do I need fat?
313. Fat as a heart disease and cancer fighter!
314. How much saturated fat?
315. Something's fishy
316. Butter substitutes
317. Baked – when you must have your chips
318. Simple vs complex
319. The dirty dozen
320. Beware of "flavored" oatmeal
321. Sugar substitutes
322. The great pumpkin – not just for Halloween
323. Take it away!
324. Broiled or baked
325. Separate sauce
326. Limit your alcohol
327. Take your time
328. Early or late, does it matter?
329. Keep your house or apartment junk-food-free
330. Healthy on hand
331. Don't get carried away with fat-soluble vitamins
332. Vitamin C – how much is enough?
333. Fiber for regularity
334. Keep salt intake to a minimum
335. Water – the most important nutrient
336. Remove as much air as possible from airtight containers such as freezer bags
337. Limit your contact with plastic
338. Cool IMMEDIATELY
339. Nutritious but quick
340. Do not overload your freezer
341. Always wash your hands before and after handling food
342. And your cookware too!
343. Power settings
344. Beware of "good fats" for cooking
345. Eggs – still one of the best

346. Egg whites
347. Meats from bad to good
348. Complete protein for vegetarians
349. Buying vegetables
350. Steamed or raw
351. Green and sprouted
352. In the wash
353. More is not better
354. Storing meat
355. A bigger birdie?
356. Beware of bottom-feeders!
357. Can it
358. Getting fresh with fruit
359. Kiwis – the wonders from down under
360. Eat dried fruit sparingly
361. Cutting-board hygiene
362. Prioritize your meals
363. Grazing for growth
364. The blender – a bodybuilder's best friend
365. Yogurt – an alternative to milk
366. Another reason not to drink heavy
367. When artificial is better
368. Drowsy
369. The all-important bread-maker
370. Low-carb bread
371. Carbs for bodybuilders
372. Breads never best
373. Fruit vs. juice
374. Post-workout juice
375. Preworkout
376. Times may be dependent
377. What to eat?
378. Meal planning
379. Shop the outer aisles
380. Don't shop when you're hungry
381. Plate size – when illusion is reality
382. Portion size
383. Keep 'em clean
384. Breakfast – valuable planning time
385. Keep pre-workout meals small
386. Read the labels
387. Adjust your food intake
388. Have a junk meal
389. Table manners
390. Take a multivitamin
391. Buy a good cookbook!

10

302. DON'T FALL FOR FAD DIETS

Eat healthy. The human body evolved to use nutrients in balance. Don't fall for the latest fad diet, as most are unhealthy. Most diets are designed to be different from the normal way of eating. The principle aim of the diet creator is to make money, not to help you look (or feel) good.

303. SLOW AND CONTROLLED

If you have a few pounds of fat to lose don't try to lose it too quickly. Healthy weight loss is one to one and a half pounds per week. Starving yourself with an ultra-strict, low-calorie diet will destroy your metabolism, resulting in the lost weight being regained at a later date. In fact you'll probably gain back more weight than you lost.

304. EXPERIMENT

Although it will take a little extra time to experiment with what and how much you eat, the lifelong results will be well worth it. Some experts reduce eating to numbers and promote mathematics as the key to fat loss, but they don't take into account the fact that everyone is different. While the formula may say your daily caloric intake should be 3200, you won't really know until you actually consume this amount. You may lose fat on this diet, or you may pack it on. It will take you a few months of fine-tuning your caloric intake to discover how many total calories your body can handle.

305. FAT TO MUSCLE AND MUSCLE TO FAT

Since fat and muscle are two different tissues, you can't convert one to the other. Building muscle will help you lose fat because the more muscle you have the higher your metabolic rate and the more calories you will burn even at rest. But you haven't converted your fat deposits into muscle.

306. LOW DOES NOT ALWAYS MEAN LOW

Beware of food products being advertised as low-fat or low-sugar. In most cases as soon as manufacturers lower fat they increase sugar levels. Likewise many low-sugar products have high fat contents. Unless the package says "low-calories" read the label carefully.

307. HOW MUCH PROTEIN?

Protein can be considered the building material of the human body and is used to manufacture such things as red blood cells, antibodies, muscle tissue, and hormones. Hard-training athletes need more protein than sedentary (non-active) people. Try to eat .75 to 1 gram of protein per pound of bodyweight per day. If you weigh 180 pounds you should eat 135 to 180 grams of protein per day.

308. DOES MY PROTEIN SOURCE MATTER?

Protein is made up of smaller subunits called amino acids. There are around 20 amino acids; the arrangement of which determines what the protein structure is (i.e. muscle, hormone, antibody). If the body gets low in one amino acid it can usually manufacture it from other amino acids. However, there are some essential amino acids that the body cannot make. Most plant sources are missing one or more of the amino acids, while animal protein contains all the amino acids. Vegetarians need to combine specific different plant sources to get the full compliment of amino acids. (The exception is soy, which contains complete protein.) However, the simple addition of milk to the equation will assure the full allotment of amino acids are present.

309. SPACED OUT

If you follow our recommendations of eating a gram of protein per pound of bodyweight, you'll quickly realize that's a lot of protein. Don't try to consume it all in one sitting. Besides the risk of nausea, the body can really only utilize about 25 to 30 grams of protein at one time. Any excess could be stored as fat. Try eating smaller amounts of protein throughout the day. Not only is this easier on your digestive system, it will ensure that there is always building material available for tissue repair.

310. PROTEIN BY THE CLOCK?

Despite the many advantages of sleep, there is one slight disadvantage. As you hibernate your body will start drawing on its nutrient stores. It will also release catabolic hormones such as adrenalin, which can break down muscle tissue. If you are what is commonly referred to as a "hard gainer," that is, an ectomorph with a very high metabolism, you may want to experiment with consuming protein at some point through the night. Set your alarm clock to wake you three or four hours before you'd normally get up, and drink a protein shake. The body now has extra protein to use for building muscle.

311. BEWARE OF PROTEIN BARS

They are quick and convenient, but unfortunately often loaded with calories. Generally speaking, the more it tastes like a candy bar, the less healthy it is. Despite the advances made by supplement manufacturers, most of the healthier protein bars (i.e. low fat and low carb) don't taste all that great (chalk and cardboard being the most popular descriptions). Conversely, the

better-tasting bars are usually loaded with fat and/or carbohydrates. Unless you are on a strict pre-contest diet, your best bet is probably a middle-of-the-road bar (tastes OK and is not too loaded with fat and carbs). The best high-protein, low-fat, low-sugar bar is the Nitro-Tech bar.

312. DO I NEED FAT?

With all the negative press fat receives it may surprise you to learn that fat is essential to life. Not only does fat supply energy and serve as an insulator, but many vitamins and hormones are fat-soluble – in other words, you cannot metabolize them without fat. The key to fat consumption is eating the right type. Fat falls into two categories, saturated and unsaturated. Saturated and trans fats are solid at room temperature and are the big killers in our society. Those fat deposits that block arteries and cause strokes and heart attacks are primarily from saturated and trans fats. Unsaturated fats are usually liquid at room temperature and can be considered the good fats. Try to keep your intake of saturated fats as low as possible, and try to avoid trans fats altogether.

313. FAT AS A HEART DISEASE AND CANCER FIGHTER!

Include a moderate amount of fat with your uncooked or steamed vegetables. The latest research has shown that the human body needs a certain amount of fat

to absorb such cancer and heart disease-fighting compounds as alpha-carotene, beta-carotene, and lycopene. For example, if you're eating a salad, add some olive oil to keep your diet balanced.

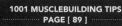
314. HOW MUCH SATURATED FAT?

As saturated fat has few redeeming qualities we suggest limiting your intake to less than 10 percent of your total daily caloric intake. Saturated fat is found almost everywhere, so you'll have to make a conscious decision to keep it as low as possible.

315. SOMETHING'S FISHY

Try to eat such fish as salmon, sardines, and herring on a regular basis. These species of fish are rich in omega-3 fatty acids. These "healthy" or "good" oils have been shown to reduce the risk of heart disease, stroke, and prostate cancer. They are also known to help your body release fat deposits as an energy source.

316. BUTTER SUBSTITUTES

If you're like most people you like to put butter on your bread or baked potato. One way to eliminate most of the calories and fat is by using a butter substitute. Real butter contains over 100 calories per tablespoon while butter substitutes average only 10 to 15. Real butter also contains about 10 to 12 grams of saturated fat, as compared to zero for most butter substitutes. However, if you are preparing for a contest or even a photo shoot, butter substitutes must be avoided.

317. BAKED – WHEN YOU MUST HAVE YOUR CHIPS

It's unfortunate that such a healthy food as the simple potato has received such a bad rap over the years. The problem of course is not so much the vegetable but what we tend to put on top of it or cook it in. Creams, butters, and cooking oils will add to the calorie content of a potato by many hundreds.

For those who like potato chips, try baked; either homemade or store-bought. We'll be honest, they don't taste quite as good as the oil-soaked variety, but with time they'll grow on you. And your waistline will thank you for it down the road.

318. SIMPLE VS COMPLEX

Besides fat and protein the other primary nutrient category is carbohydrate. Carbohydrates are either simple or complex. Simple carbohydrates (along with saturated fat the predominant nutrient in junk food) are absorbed rapidly and serve as a quick source of energy. Complex carbohydrates take longer to be absorbed (because of their larger – more complex – molecular arrangement) and supply energy over longer periods of time. Simple carbs are readily stored as fat and should be kept to a minimum.

319. THE DIRTY DOZEN

If at all possible avoid regular soft drinks. Each can contains from 8 to 12 teaspoons of sugar. At 15 calories per teaspoon that's 180 totally empty calories. You don't need to consume many soft drinks per day to add hundreds of extra calories to your diet (and waistline!). Substitute water for soft drinks.

320. BEWARE OF "FLAVORED" OATMEAL

Oatmeal is one of the most nutritious of cereals but unfortunately food manufacturers have managed to screw it up. Recognizing that most people have a sweet tooth, manufacturers have added all kinds of "flavorings" to regular oatmeal to make it more appealing. Unfortunately the word "flavored" is just another term for "loaded with sugar and calories." Avoid "flavored" oatmeal or any other similarly advertised cereal. If you want flavor, add some chopped fruit, cinnamon or berries.

321. SUGAR SUBSTITUTES

Another easy way to reduce your sugar and caloric intake is by using sugar substitutes. Even though some of them, like Aspartame, have received a lot of negative press, they are among the most tested food compounds in the world and are for the most part are

considered safe. One teaspoon of sugar contains about 15 calories while artificial contains virtually no calories. The ideal situation would be to avoid both table sugar and artificial sweeteners.

322. THE GREAT PUMPKIN – NOT JUST FOR HALLOWEEN

One of the easiest ways to fortify your diet with minerals, including zinc, is by consuming pumpkin seeds, otherwise known as pepitas. Pumpkin seeds also contain essential fatty acids that help kill parasites. For maximum nutritional benefits, seeds should be eaten raw since roasting can convert the fat into arterial-clogging plaque.

323. TAKE IT AWAY!

If you eat out and the server brings a basket of "free" bread, have her take it away. If it's not in front of you, you won't be tempted to eat it. Bread is not "free." Your waistline will "pay" for it later!

324. BROILED OR BAKED

Try to order your food broiled, steamed or baked. Broiling and baking remove fat as the cooking takes place, whereas frying and deep-frying add extra fat calories.

325. SEPARATE SAUCE

If you are ordering a meal that needs sauce, have the server bring the sauce on the side. Odds are you will add less to your meal than the kitchen staff will. Saying "no sauce" is the best route to go.

326. LIMIT YOUR ALCOHOL

Don't turn your eating out session into a drinking session. A glass of wine or a light beer may be acceptable, but excessive alcohol not only adds extra calories, it interferes with proper digestion and it impairs your judgment – making you more likely to order deep-fried foods and desserts. Besides, your workout the next day will suffer.

327. TAKE YOUR TIME

Gulping down food only results in larger pieces of food entering your stomach. This is not only bad from a digestion and absorption viewpoint, it can leave you with cramps and/or unpleasant gas problems.

328. EARLY OR LATE, DOES IT MATTER?

An enduring myth is that you must not eat carbs after 6 pm. The theory is that since you will probably be doing less exercise later in the evening there is a greater chance that any excess carbohydrate will be stored as fat. Keep in mind that the most important variable in gaining fat is your total daily caloric intake. If your intake was low earlier in the day, and provided you don't completely pig out on carbs, there is nothing wrong with having a small meal with carbs later in the evening.

329. KEEP YOUR HOUSE OR APARTMENT JUNK-FOOD-FREE

Most readers have probably heard the line: "If you build it they will come," from Kevin Costner's film, "Field of Dreams." The same holds true for junk food. "If you buy it you will eat it." If you get a craving for junk food late at night and you know it's there in the cupboard above the fridge you'll probably break down and eat it. It takes a great deal of willpower to say no to chocolate or chips late at night. On the other hand, if you have to get dressed and drive to the all-night store, chances are you'll pass.

330. HEALTHY ON HAND

To combat the late-night junk cravings try to have such healthy snacks as raisins, grapes, assorted nuts, and low-fat low-sugar cookies available. These healthy substitutes will kill your cravings without piling a load of extra empty calories into your system.

331. DON'T GET CARRIED AWAY WITH FAT-SOLUBLE VITAMINS

Vitamins are inorganic substances that are used by the body to start, maintain, or finish the various chemical reactions necessary for life. Vitamins can be divided into fat and water-soluble. Water-soluble vitamins (The B vitamins, C, and H) cannot be stored by the body and must be consumed in the diet on a regular basis. Fat-soluble vitamins (vitamins A, D, E, and K) can be stored and can reach toxic levels if amounts become too excessive.

332. VITAMIN C – HOW MUCH IS ENOUGH?

While some experts stop just short of saying it will cure cancer, most sources hold a more moderate view. Vitamin C is essential for growth and repair as well as for keeping the immune system in good health. But most current research does not support the notion that mega-dosing on vitamin C offers any benefits over traditional amounts. Keep your intake in the 500 to 2000 milligram range.

333. FIBER FOR REGULARITY

Fiber is a catchall phrase that refers to a variety of plant materials that can't be digested by the body. A diet high in fiber has been shown to reduce heart disease and cancer, prevent diabetes by controlling glucose levels, and improve digestive and excretory regularity. Try to consume a diet high in whole grains, flax seed, peas, nuts, and fruits.

334. KEEP SALT INTAKE TO A MINIMUM

Although a certain amount of salt is needed for such chemical processes as nerve impulse conduction and muscle contraction, you'll get more than you need in your diet without consciously trying. For example, two slices of bread supply more than the daily requirement. Excessive salt has been linked to heart and kidney disease. Don't add table salt to your food.

335. WATER – THE MOST IMPORTANT NUTRIENT

Water makes up over two-thirds the mass of the human body. Just about every chemical reaction in the body takes place in or involves water. Humans can live for weeks without food but only a few days without water. Try to drink a minimum of eight glasses of water a day – more if you train outdoors.

336. REMOVE AS MUCH AIR AS POSSIBLE FROM AIRTIGHT CONTAINERS SUCH AS FREEZER BAGS

The moisture in the trapped air absorbs odor from food and will form a frost. If the bag loses its airtight quality that frost will give off odors that will be picked up by other foods in the freezer.

337. LIMIT YOUR CONTACT WITH PLASTIC

One of the perils these days for males is exposure to what are called environmental estrogens. In simple terms, many of the synthetic plastics that we use for storing food are laced with chemicals that increase the level of the female hormone estrogen. Ironically much of the food we eat is stored in such containers. To reduce your exposure to such estrogen-raising compounds, try to eat only fresh food and limit your reliance on stored food. In addition, most herbicides

and pesticides mimic estrogen. Avoid using these products around your home and try to eat as much organic food as possible.

338. COOL IMMEDIATELY

If you prepare large amounts of food in advance, release as much air as possible and then put it in the fridge or freezer immediately. Do not let it cool at room temperature first.

339. NUTRITIOUS BUT QUICK

One way to guarantee healthy but quick suppers is by pre-cooking and freezing. Set aside one day a week for cooking. Prepare large amounts of stews, soups, and casseroles. Divide them into meal-sized portions and place them in airtight containers or freezer bags. You can either take them out before you go to work or school in the morning so that they are thawed out when you come home, or pop them into the microwave at dinner time. Pre-cooking nutritious food ensures that you won't succumb to grabbing something fast and junky.

340. DO NOT OVERLOAD YOUR FREEZER

Placing too much food in the freezer not only prevents proper freezing but often leads to food being left there for long periods of time. Freezing food should be for short-term, not long-term storage.

341. ALWAYS WASH YOUR HANDS BEFORE AND AFTER HANDLING FOOD

Germs are everywhere and they just love to multiply in the presence of food sources. That doorknob you just touched could harbor any number of little nasties.

342. AND YOUR COOKWARE TOO!

You probably wash the pots and pans, but how about the cutting board? Likewise, the knives and forks you use to eat with will be placed in the dishwasher but how about the large knife you used to slice the tomatoes? Any cooking utensil, no matter how large or small, needs to be thoroughly washed – and not just wiped – when you are finished with it.

343. POWER SETTINGS

For most frozen, pre-cooked foods such as soup and stew, a microwave power setting of eight for about three minutes should suffice. Even though this time will vary, at least you will know that the food was cooked beforehand and you will only have to heat the meal until it suits your needs.

344. BEWARE OF "GOOD FATS" FOR COOKING

Until recently researchers condemned all saturated fats as bad and said to cook with only polyunsaturated fats. New evidence suggests that the "good fats" are not all that good. When polyunsaturated oils are heated they undergo oxidation. This produces various new compounds that may be harmful. It has also been proven that vegetable oils can accelerate the aging process. Other studies have shown that while people who switched from saturated to polyunsaturated fats for cooking had lower levels of heart disease, mortality rates remained the same. So our advice is to only use the minimum amount of oil to cook with and drain all excess oil from food afterwards.

345. EGGS – STILL ONE OF THE BEST

Eggs have received a bad rap over the years. All the talk about the dangers of cholesterol has turned people away from eggs in droves. While eggs do contain cholesterol, they also contain choline and lecithin; two substances that keep the cholesterol in eggs emulsified and "moving" when it enters the bloodstream. Eggs are ones of the healthiest foods available and should be part of the diet of all hard-training bodybuilders.

346. EGG WHITES

If you are still worried about cholesterol, or if you just want to cut down on your fat consumption, try egg whites. Throwing away the egg yolk gets rid of all the fat and only half the protein. Many bodybuilders will make an omelet containing one egg yolk for texture and color and four or five egg whites. Vegetables can be cooked in to improve taste and nutritional value.

347. MEATS FROM BAD TO GOOD

In the hierarchy of fatty meats, pork is more fatty than beef, beef is more fatty than poultry with skin on it, poultry with skin is more fatty than skinned poultry, and skinned poultry is more fatty than fish. Within the categories of poultry, dark meat has more fat than white.

348. COMPLETE PROTEIN FOR VEGETARIANS

Vegetarians need to be very creative to ensure they are eating a balanced diet. One of the richest sources of plant protein is legumes. When combined with seeds, nuts, or grains, all the amino acids are obtained. Likewise, rice with beans or brown bread and peanut butter provide complete protein.

349. BUYING VEGETABLES

To ensure maximum nutrient content, try to buy only fresh vegetables. Don't buy unripe vegetables. Unlike fruits, most vegetables will not ripen in storage. Likewise, only buy vegetables that are in good condition. Bruised or damaged vegetables tend to be reduced in nutrient content.

350. STEAMED OR RAW

Try to eat your vegetables uncooked when ever possible. Cooking destroys much of the nutritional content. If you must eat your vegetables warm, try steaming rather than boiling. Boiling will leach out 50

to 75 percent of the nutritional content. You'll end up pouring the best part of your vegetable meal down the drain!

351. GREEN AND SPROUTED

When buying root vegetables like onions or potatoes, don't buy the ones that have sprouted. Never buy green potatoes either. The green and sprouted parts contain a poisonous chemical called solanine. If this has happened after storage cut away all green or sprouted parts before cooking.

352. IN THE WASH

As soon as you bring vegetables home from the store, wash them. This not only helps get rid of pesticides, dirt and germs, but also the nasty creepy crawlies that sometimes hang out in plants. Insects such as spiders and centipedes have been known to pop out of grapes and cabbages when least expected.

353. MORE IS NOT BETTER

Unlike meat, which should always be cooked for health reasons, vegetables and fruits should be consumed with the least amount of preparation as possible. Heating plant material not only destroys much of the nutrient content but also removes much of the taste. Carrots, for example, become tasteless after boiling.

354. STORING MEAT

For both health and taste reasons, meat shouldn't be kept for more than two to three days. For maximum freshness keep it in the coolest part of your freezer or refrigerator. As with vegetables it's a good idea to rinse the meat with water as soon as you bring it home. It's also a good idea to discard the store wrapping and rewrap the meat in foil. Under no circumstances should you put cooked meat back in the original wrapping. That's a great way to get food poisoning.

355. A BIGGER BIRDIE?

When buying poultry such as turkey or chicken, it is more economical to buy large birds, as you get a higher percentage of lean meat as opposed to fat and bone.

356. BEWARE OF BOTTOM-FEEDERS!

Despite their reputation as aphrodisiacs, oysters and other shellfish should never be eaten raw. Shellfish are examples of what are called bottom feeders. They take in surrounding water and force it back out through special filters. In this manner they capture tiny particles of food. The problem with this is that shellfish become a dumping ground for toxins and over time such compounds as mercury can rise to dangerous levels.

357. CAN IT

Although fresh is better there are times when you'll have to get your fish from a can. The two best examples of this are tuna and salmon. Tuna has been a staple of bodybuilding diets for decades. When buying canned fish, always look for fish that is packed in water alone. Avoid oils or sauces as they tend to be high in fat and salt. Once you open the tin, transfer leftovers to a sealed

container and refrigerate. Don't store it in the original tin – this not only increases the risk of food poisoning but may also give the meat a "tinny" taste. While many call light tuna "catfood grade," it carries 1/3 the amount of mercury as does albacore.

358. GETTING FRESH WITH FRUIT

Fruit are no different from vegetables and meat, the fresher the better. Unless you plan on using it for baking, give the old, on-sale fruit a pass. The nutrient content may have deteriorated by 50 percent or more.

359. KIWIS – THE WONDERS FROM DOWN UNDER

If you're tired of apples and oranges, try kiwis. Gram for gram, kiwis provide more vitamin C and minerals than oranges, apples, or pears.

360. EAT DRIED FRUIT SPARINGLY

Dried fruits have become popular in recent years and if prepared properly retain most of the nutrient content of the hydrated version. The only drawback is that the natural sugars have become concentrated (this is why raisins tend to taste sweeter than grapes). As expected, this increases the calorie content significantly. If you're trying to lose fat, keep your dried fruit intake to a minimum.

361. CUTTING-BOARD HYGIENE

It's amazing the number of people who will cut both their raw meat and bread on the same cutting board. While the meat will be cooked, rendering bacteria and germs harmless, the bread will be eaten raw. Any bacteria contained in the meat can be easily transferred to anything cut on the board afterwards. Always wash your cutting board after cutting meat products on it. Better still, have separate boards for meats, breads, and vegetables.

362. PRIORITIZE YOUR MEALS

Most people eat backwards. They have little or nothing for breakfast, a small lunch, and then a large cooked supper. In reality it makes more sense to eat the other way around. Assuming you had your last meal a couple of hours before bed, and you get six to eight hours of sleep, your body may have gone ten hours without food. The first thing you should do when you get up in the morning is get some good quality nutrients in there.

363. GRAZING FOR GROWTH

The biggest animals on the planet are constantly eating and so must you if you want to gain any significant amount of muscle mass. We don't mean literally eating every waking minute, but you should be feeding your body nutrients every couple of hours. Instead of two or three large meals, try five or six smaller meals. This not only ensures that the body is getting nutrients on a continuous basis, but smaller meals place less stress on the digestive system.

364. THE BLENDER – A BODYBUILDER'S BEST FRIEND

It's much easier to drink nutrients than eat them. In the fast world we live in, extra time is usually in short supply. Unless you take our advice and prepare meals ahead of time, you may not be able to cook five or six meals a day. One way to get round this is by blending. A blender allows you to combine a large number of nutrients into a liquid meal. It's also very fast and convenient, and when you're finished a quick rinse with hot water lets you be on your way.

365. YOGURT – AN ALTERNATIVE TO MILK

For those who are lactose intolerant, or have an allergy to milk, yogurt might be a healthy alternative. The reason many of the people who can't tolerate milk can digest yogurt is that the bacteria contained in the yogurt break down some of the problem-causing lactose. Yogurt has been linked to reduced cholesterol levels and increased longevity. If you've been avoiding protein shakes because you can't drink milk, give yogurt a try.

366. ANOTHER REASON NOT TO DRINK HEAVILY

Each gram of alcohol has seven calories. If your aim is to have a flat stomach or lose weight, either cut back your alcohol consumption or be prepared to carry a higher-than-average body-fat level.

367. WHEN ARTIFICIAL IS BETTER

One of the easiest ways to cut calories from your diet is by using artificial sweeteners. Despite the bad press some of them occasionally receive, most are apparently safe and from a nutritional point of view contain few if any calories. Try using them in your coffee, on your cereal, or even in your baking. In no time you'll have cut hundreds of calories from your daily intake.

368. DROWSY

If you start to feel drowsy after eating it usually means one of two things, either your portions are too large, or you are consuming too much simple sugar. If cutting down the portion size and/or simple sugar content doesn't alleviate the problem, consult a physician. You may be developing diabetes-related problems.

369. THE ALL-IMPORTANT BREAD-MAKER

Store-bought white bread was not created for bodybuilders. Not only have most of the good nutrients been leached out, but also it's loaded with salt. Just two slices of store-bought white bread contain the recommended daily intake of salt. Bread-makers are not that expensive and give you complete control over the ingredients. Instead of white flour you can use whole wheat, and salt and sugar can be kept to a minimum. Set it in the morning and come home to a nice fresh loaf.

370. LOW-CARB BREAD

It's not surprising with the big emphasis on low-carb diets these days that manufacturers have made low-carb breads available. As with most low-carb and low-fat alternatives, the taste is rather bland, but you are saving a heap of calories.

371. CARBS FOR BODYBUILDERS

With all this talk of carbs and calories, you'd think they were bad for bodybuilders. But it depends on your present goal. When you are bulking up you need plenty of complex carbohydrates.

372. BREADS NEVER BEST

While you need plenty of carbs, breads are never your best bet. Even whole-grain breads are a more refined product than potato, sweet potato, corn or oatmeal.

373. FRUIT VS. JUICE

Although fruit is generally made up of simple sugars, the actual fruit has loads of fiber to slow down its digestion. This is not the case for juice. Pick pieces of fruit over juice, even at breakfast.

374. POST-WORKOUT JUICE

The one time it's okay to drink fruit juice is immediately after your workout, when an insulin surge helps bring nutrients to muscles. Make sure to include some protein. Studies show that consuming carbs and protein in a 3:1 ratio postworkout brings the most muscle gains.

375. PREWORKOUT

You want to reach muscular failure during your sets, not fail because you didn't give your body enough energy. Eat anywhere from 1 hour to 2½ hours before training. Experiment with times to see which works best for you.

376. TIMES MAY BE DEPENDENT

You may find that you have to eat 2 hours before training legs but only 1 hour before training arms, because of the different stresses on your system.

377. WHAT TO EAT?

Your preworkout meal should also contain carbs and protein, but make sure the carbs are complex rather than simple. Simple carbs would be gone from your system by the time you need them.

378. MEAL PLANNING

The best results come when you plan your meals a week in advance. Then when you go shopping you know exactly what to buy and in what quanitites, making day-to-day life much easier.

379. SHOP THE OUTER AISLES

Most supermarkets keep the fresh produce, meats and dairy products in the outer aisles and the prepackaged food you should be avoiding throughout the middle of the store. Shop the outer aisles first – a cart full of healthy food will give you more willpower to avoid the cookie aisle.

380. DON'T SHOP WHEN YOU'RE HUNGRY

Going into a supermarket when you're hungry is like sending kids to a chocolate factory - you want it all. Unless you have great willpower, one of the worst nutrition mistakes you can make is buying your groceries just after leaving the gym. By then your blood sugar is low and you'll find it craving the high-calorie, sugar-loaded items. Your shopping basket will be loaded with items you'd normally avoid. And

let's face it. Once they're in your house, you will break down and eat them. If you must shop when hungry, bring a list with you and only buy what's on the list. No sweets. No junk.

381. PLATE SIZE – WHEN ILLUSION IS REALITY

Are you the type that piles your food on the largest plate in the cupboard? One of the easiest ways to reduce your calorie intake is to use a smaller plate. Even if you cover most of its surface with food, you're still eating fewer calories than the super-sized version. Many studies have confirmed this. Those who use smaller plates for their food report the same feelings of fullness as when they used larger plates, yet consumed far fewer calories.

382. PORTION SIZE

Going cold turkey on foods you've been eating for years can have disastrous results. Feelings of deprivation can set in, and then over-consumption usually occurs. Instead of going cold turkey, try reducing your portion sizes. Here's a guide: A serving of meat is about the size of a deck of cards; grilled fish should be the size of a checkbook; a pancake the size of a CD; steamed rice, enough to fill a large cup; a bagel the size of a hockey puck; pasta, enough to fill an ice-cream scoop; cooked vegetables, the size of your fist.

383. KEEP 'EM CLEAN

Although this tip has nothing to do with nutrition and calories, it does have serious implications for your long-term eating habits. The next time you are eating, try chewing your food with just your lips and gums. As comical as that sounds, this where you will be headed if you don't keep your teeth clean. Your mouth is the first stop in your digestive system, and the teeth are its machinery. All that leftover food from those four to six meals a day you are eating is a perfect breeding ground for enamel-destroying bacteria. Unless you

want to be toothless or wearing false teeth, take a few minutes after each meal and brush and floss your teeth.

384. BREAKFAST – VALUABLE PLANNING TIME

One of the best times for mapping out your daily schedule is breakfast time. As you are eating your eggs or oatmeal, decide what clothes you'll wear, what physical activities you'll engage in, and what social contacts you'll make. One of the keys to success is great planning.

385. KEEP PRE-WORKOUT MEALS SMALL

While you probably shouldn't be eating a large meal at any time of the day, this is especially true before a workout. As soon as food is ingested, the body sends extra blood to the stomach region to aid in digestion and absorption. The larger the meal the more blood. If you go to the gym immediately after a large meal, the body will start shifting some of this blood to the muscles. As expected this will interfere with proper digestion. Your workouts will suffer, as well. If you do eat a large meal, wait at least two to three hours before working out.

386. READ THE LABELS

If you intend to get serious about your eating, start learning how to read the labels on your food products. For example "light" and "low fat" are often decoys for foods loaded with sugar. Likewise some manufacturers make it seem that a food is low in calories by recommending small serving sizes.

387. ADJUST YOUR FOOD INTAKE

If you have to stop training for any reason (vacation, injury, etc), reduce your calorie intake. Regular cardio and strength training burns enormous amounts of calories. Unfortunately, your appetite may not diminish even when your energy expenditure has been greatly reduced. If you keep eating the same amount as while you were training the excess will go right around your midsection.

388. HAVE A JUNK MEAL

Unless you reach the point where you have no desire to eat junk food (yes, it happens!), pick one day a week and let loose for one meal. Have that piece of chocolate or cheesecake. Grab a candy bar or bag of potato chips. The few extra calories won't have any effect on your waistline. Notice we said junk meal, not junk day. A couple of hundred extra calories won't make any difference but a couple of thousand will!

389. TABLE MANNERS

Weight control can be summed up in the following three statements: Leave the table hungry and you will lose weight. Leave the table satisfied and you will maintain weight. Leave the table full and you will gain weight.

390. TAKE A MULTIVITAMIN

As they cost less than $10 for a three-month supply, and are perfectly safe, we strongly suggest taking a multivitamin. While they won't make any dramatic changes to your physique, they are a good way to ensure that you are receiving all the major vitamins and minerals your body needs. Take the multivitamin with your meals as vitamins and minerals have no benefits on their own. They are used by the body to catalyze biochemical reactions involving the other main nutrient groups (carbs, fats, protein, etc).

391. BUY A GOOD COOKBOOK!

It's one thing to eat someone else's great cooking, but another thing entirely to prepare your own. A good cookbook will give you creative freedom over what you eat. It will also give you hundreds of choices to spice up your eating (Muscle Meals by John Ramano and The Bodybuilder's Nutrition Book by Dr. Franco Columbu are two of the best).

SUPPLEMENTS

392. Buyer beware!

393. Knowledge is power

394. Check out the "studies"

395. Food comes first

396. Cycling for maximum benefit

397. The nutrient window

398. Whey is way better

399. Beware of soy protein

400. Use amino acid supplements with caution

401. Fruit flavor

402. Fat for fat loss

403. Creatine – bodybuilding's number one supplement

404. Insulin release for maximizing creatine absorption

405. Powder versus liquid

406. Temperature dependent

407. Creatine and caffeine – keep them separate?

408. Don't megadose on supplements

409. Glutamine – the muscle-building immunity booster

410. Meal replacement powders

411. Ephedrine for fat loss and stimulation

412. The ECA stack

413. An aspirin a day?

414. Forget the apple – try zinc!

415. Hydroxy citric acid – HCA – a safe alternative for fat loss

416. More fat loss with CLA – conjugated linoleic acid

417. Tribulus terrestris – the safe way to boost testosterone?

418. Androstenedione – not all it's cracked up to be

419. Prohormones – are they worth it?

420. Insulin mimickers – not just for diabetics

421. The java boost

422. Post-workout drink

423. Glucosamine for joint health

11

392. BUYER BEWARE!

Despite being worth billions of dollars annually, the supplement industry is poorly regulated. Just about anyone can market a product as a health food supplement. To ensure you are getting exactly what you paid for, only buy supplements from reputable companies such as Muscle Tech, Twin Lab, or EAS.

393. KNOWLEDGE IS POWER

Before taking any substance, learn everything you can about it. Even some common supplements like vitamins and minerals can be toxic in high dosages. Don't let Johnny Biceps at the local gym talk you into taking something when you don't have a clue what it is. At the very least you may be out your hard-earned cash. But you may also end up taking something that is illegal and/or dangerous to your health.

394. CHECK OUT THE "STUDIES"

Just because a supplement company claims they have studies that prove their product is effective doesn't mean everything is cut and dried and above board. Check out the studies for yourself. If the studies are legitimate they will be published in the trade scientific journals. Even then, hold a degree of skepticism. Find out who funded the study. In many cases the manufacturer is the one funding the money for the lab. The researchers often feel obligated to creatively select the data to show the product in the most positive light.

395. FOOD COMES FIRST

Never take a supplement in place of food. Food contains far more nutrients than any supplement ever could. As the name suggests, supplements should "supplement" food not replace it. For example, if you find you are not getting adequate amounts of protein through your diet, then a protein supplement makes sense. Don't, however, give a chicken breast a pass for a protein supplement.

396. CYCLING FOR MAXIMUM BENEFIT

The late Vince Gironda said the best way to maximize the benefits of supplements was to cycle the product in question. The body adapts to taking the same substances for long periods of time, resulting in reduced effects. Try taking your supplements for six to eight weeks and then taking two to three weeks off.

397. THE NUTRIENT WINDOW

One of the most popular questions received at the MuscleMag International head offices is: "When should I take my supplements?" Generally speaking the body is begging for nutrients during the hour immediately following your workout more than any other time. Have your creatine or whey protein shake already pre-mixed. This makes it very convenient to get your nutrients on the drive home or in the gym's lounge area.

398. WHEY IS WAY BETTER

There are three primary types of protein supplements, soy, milk and egg, and whey. Soy is derived from plant sources and is an incomplete protein. This means it doesn't contain the full compliment of amino acids. Milk and egg protein is complete but you'll need a blender to mix it. Whey is derived from milk and is the purist form of protein. You can mix it with a spoon

WHEY SUPERIOR!

and it doesn't cause the digestive problems that often accompany milk and egg proteins. Besides being the best source of protein for building muscle, whey protein helps boost the immunity system.

399. BEWARE OF SOY PROTEIN

Soy protein has made a comeback in recent years because of some studies that suggest it can lower the risk of certain cancers. Unfortunately soy can also elevate estrogen levels. This is not a problem for females, but for a hard-training male bodybuilder, elevated levels of a female hormone is not a desirable quality. Given that soy protein mixes poorly and has been known to cause gas, we suggest you avoid soy protein.

400. USE AMINO ACID SUPPLEMENTS WITH CAUTION

As refinement techniques improved, it wasn't long before the individual amino acids that make up protein became available. Such amino acids as arginine, lysine, glutamine, and histidine are touted to do everything from increasing growth hormone levels to speeding up protein synthesis. A few words of caution are needed. First, scientists don't know the full effects of taking high concentrations of one or more amino acids. Second, no one knows in what proportions amino acids should be consumed. Finally, amino acid supplements are much more expensive than protein supplements.

401. FRUIT FLAVOR

Despite the advances in supplement production, many people still find them rather bland in taste. One way to flavor things up is to add fruit. Place your protein powder and mixing medium (milk, juice, yogurt or water) in a blender and then throw in a banana or handful of strawberries. A few seconds later you have a great-tasting protein drink fortified with extra vitamins and minerals.

402. FAT FOR FAT LOSS

It may seem contradictory but one of the best supplements for losing body fat is medium chain triglycerides or MCTs. MCTs work by speeding up the metabolism, causing bodyfat to be consumed faster. Many biochemists say MCTs are oils that act like carbohydrates. It seems one of the byproducts of MCTs are ketones, which the body can use as an energy source. Start off by taking half a tablespoon per meal for the first week and then slowly increase the dosage to 1 to 2 tablespoons.

403. CREATINE – BODYBUILDING'S NUMBER ONE SUPPLEMENT

Creatine first broke onto the bodybuilding scene in the early '90s and has quickly leaped to the top of the supplement charts. Creatine increases muscle power by serving as a short-term energy source. When adenosine triphosphate, ATP, breaks down into adenosine diphosphate, ADP, and a single phosphate group, creatine can regenerate ATP by donating a high-energy phosphate group. The result is more energy available for contracting muscles. Start by taking 15 to 20 grams of creatine per day for 5 to 7 days, and then cut back to 3 to 5 grams per day.

404. INSULIN RELEASE FOR MAXIMIZING CREATINE ABSORPTION

Besides transporting glucose (sugar) out of the bloodstream, insulin also shuttles other substances, one of which is creatine. To maximize absorption, take your creatine supplement with a high-carbohydrate drink like grape juice. The sugar in the juice will cause the body to release insulin, which will speed the transport of creatine out of the bloodstream and into the muscles.

405. POWDER VERSUS LIQUID

As the first-generation creatine supplements came in powdered form and had to be mixed, a few enterprising supplement manufacturers jumped the gun and started marketing creatine in liquid form. There are a few problems with this. For starters creatine is not stable in liquid form. Also, despite claims to the contrary, no one is sure how effective these liquid creatine supplements are. Another factor is price. It costs more money to manufacture liquid creatine and this extra production cost gets passed on to you, the consumer. Our advice is to stick with tried-and-true powdered creatine.

406. TEMPERATURE DEPENDENT

Creatine is one of those supplements that seems to be dependent on the temperature of the mixing medium. If the liquid is too hot you may destroy some of the creatine. Conversely, cold liquid prevents proper mixing. For best dissolving results, try using lukewarm liquid. Granted warm juice is not that appealing, but you'll have the satisfaction of knowing you've maximized your creatine absorption.

407. CREATINE AND CAFFEINE – KEEP THEM SEPARATE?

A number of recent studies suggest that high doses of caffeine may interfere with creatine absorption. Taking creatine with one cup of coffee is probably no big deal but if you like to pop a couple of caffeine tablets (or a couple cups of coffee) before a workout, it probably makes sense to take your creatine a few hours later.

408. DON'T MEGADOSE ON SUPPLEMENTS

Because they are relatively cheap and promoted to cure just about every disease out there, many people take mega doses of supplements. This is not advised. Some vitamins and minerals are toxic in high doses. Likewise large amounts of creatine and protein may cause diarrhea and other digestive problems.

409. GLUTAMINE – THE MUSCLE-BUILDING IMMUNITY BOOSTER

Glutamine is an amino acid that falls into the "conditionally essential" category. This means the body can manufacture it from other amino acids, but at certain times demand exceeds the body's rate of synthesis. Glutamine is taken by bodybuilders because it keeps the body in positive nitrogen balance – the necessary environment needed to turn protein into muscle tissue. In times of stress glutamine levels may drop to the point that negative nitrogen balance occurs. The end result is a bodybuilder's worst nightmare – muscle wasting. Besides promoting muscle growth, glutamine increases production of glutathione, one of the precursors of antibodies and lymphocytes – the immune system's two primary germ-fighting cells. Although the scientific literature is lacking with regards to dosage, the anecdotal evidence suggests 5 to 10 grams per day works best.

410. MEAL REPLACEMENT POWDERS

Meal replacement powders (MRPs) are an excellent way to obtain healthy nutrients quickly and easily. While they won't replace a regular meal of food, they have the advantages of being lower in calories and easy to prepare. If you're stuck for time or trying to cut back on calories, try to make one of your meals an MRP.

411. EPHEDRINE FOR FAT LOSS AND STIMULATION

Ephedrine is one of the few over-the-counter supplements that does exactly what it claims – it promotes fat loss and increases short-term energy. Ephedrine is an example of what's called a thermogenic drug. This means it promotes fat loss by elevating body temperature. Ephedrine also provides energy because it is a sympathetic nervous system stimulant. Despite the bad press it has garnered over recent years, ephedrine is relatively safe provided you don't have a history of heart problems and you don't take megadoses. Make sure you follow the directions on the bottle. Needless to say, use it only where it is legal to do so. Never exceed recommended doses.

412. THE ECA STACK

The name ECA is derived from the first initials of the words ephedrine, caffeine, and aspirin. Bodybuilders discovered that ephedrine's stimulant and fat-burning

effects are magnified if combined with caffeine and aspirin. If you decide to experiment, the proportions are 25 mg ephedrine, 200 mg caffeine (about one cup of coffee) and one aspirin. Caffeine is also a stimulant, so those with a history of heart problems should avoid both ephedrine and high doses of caffeine. Always follow the directions on the bottle when taking supplements.

413. AN ASPIRIN A DAY?

If you have a history of heart disease in your family, check with your doctor about the possibility of taking an aspirin a day. Aspirin is commonly called a "blood thinner." It has reportedly been scientifically shown to reduce the build up of plaque on arterial walls.

414. FORGET THE APPLE – TRY ZINC!

An apple a day may keep the doctor away but zinc may cure your cold. Studies have shown that those people who take lozenges containing zinc had a significant reduction in their cold symptoms. For best results try dissolving one zinc-containing lozenge every two hours.

415. HYDROXY CITRIC ACID – HCA – A SAFE ALTERNATIVE FOR FAT LOSS

For those who don't like the stimulant properties of ephedrine, HCA may be the answer. HCA is a substance obtained from the rinds of the Garcinia fruit of Asia. HCA's primary role in athletics is to promote fat loss by decreasing fat storage. It does this by interfering with the enzyme (citrate lyase) that converts excess carbohydrate into fat. The less new fat stored, the more old stored fat will be burned during exercise.

416. MORE FAT LOSS WITH CLA – CONJUGATED LINOLEIC ACID

Like MCT oils, CLA promotes the loss of stored body fat. The exact mechanism is unknown but it is believed that CLA tricks the body into "thinking" it has more fat than it needs and so is less likely to hold onto fat stores. In addition, many biochemists believe that CLA may indirectly promote fat burning by increasing lean muscle mass. The more lean muscle mass carried by the body the higher the person's metabolism (one of the primary reasons women are encouraged to train with weights). To get the 2 to 4 grams of CLA recommended by biochemists, supplement your diet with flax and fish oils.

417. TRIBULUS TERRESTRIS – THE SAFE WAY TO BOOST TESTOSTERONE?

Sooner or later many readers will toss around the idea of taking anabolic steroids or other testosterone derivatives. We recommend against this. Not only are there health risks, but steroids are now illegal in most states. Before jumping on the pharmacological bandwagon, give tribulus terrestris a try. Tribulus is an herb that is believed to increase testosterone levels by stimulating the pituitary gland to release leutinizing hormone (LH). LH in turn stimulates the testes to produce testosterone. The recommended daily dose of tribulus is 500 to 750 mg.

418. ANDROSTENEDIONE – NOT ALL IT'S CRACKED UP TO BE

Androstenedione, or "andro," was introduced to the masses by baseball slugger Mark McGwire. When a snooping reporter spotted it in McGwire's locker, the genie was out of the bottle so to speak. Soon supplement stores couldn't keep andro in stock. This was ironic, as andro was on its way out in bodybuilding circles. Biochemically andro is a precursor to the male hormone testosterone, so in theory it should help build muscle. Unfortunately only a small amount of andro (5 to 10 percent) actually gets converted to testosterone. Another consideration is that testosterone is only one of the end products of andro. It also converts to the female hormone estrogen. Finally, most anecdotal evidence suggests andro does little to improve muscular strength or size. It may be an idea to give andro a pass.

419. PROHORMONES – ARE THEY WORTH IT?

For those of you engaged in drug-tested sports, we caution against using prohormones. As the name suggests, prohormones are compounds that serve as precursors for the manufacture of hormones. Bodybuilders and other athletes take them in the

hope they can boost their natural levels of testosterone and other muscle-building compounds. In some cases prohormones will provide a boost. However, as most anabolic compounds are banned by sports' federations, you run the risk of testing positive even though you never took the substance directly. This is especially true for the prohormones that convert to nandrolone. Before experimenting with prohormones, check to see what your sport's governing body has to say.

420. INSULIN MIMICKERS – NOT JUST FOR DIABETICS

As soon as medical science makes a discovery that has performance-boosting implications, athletes immediately update their shopping lists. Insulin mimickers are substances that either increase the sensitivity of insulin or act like the hormone. Insulin not only transports sugar through the bloodstream but also such substances as creatine and amino acids. In this respect insulin can be considered an anabolic hormone. The most popular insulin mimickers are vanadyl sulfate, chromium picolinate, alpha-lipoic acid, and Momordica charantia (also known as bitter melon). As all are fairly cheap, relatively safe, and anecdotally reported to have some merits, we suggest taking one or more with your protein or creatine supplements.

421. THE JAVA BOOST

The next time you hit the gym, take a close look at people as they come through the door. Odds are at least 25 percent of them will have a cup of coffee in hand. Coffee is one of the cheapest and most effective performance-enhancing drugs. Being a mild stimulant, coffee (actually the caffeine it contains) will give you that extra boost needed to get you through another grueling workout.

422. POST-WORKOUT DRINK

To help rebuild muscle, boost your immunity system, and recharge your energy reserves, try blending 25 to 30 grams of whey protein, 5 grams of creatine, 5 grams of glutamine, and a handful of fresh strawberries into a super post-workout drink.

423. GLUCOSAMINE FOR JOINT HEALTH

One of the few disadvantages to regular weight training is that it may play havoc on the joints over time. Veterinarians regularly prescribe glucosamine to animals to help treat and ward off arthritis and other joint problems. If you plan on lifting some serious iron for decades to come, try taking a glucosamine supplement.

CARDIO TRAINING

424. A change of heart

425. Faint or dizzy – listen to your body

426. Cardio variety

427. Target heart rate

428. Where to find your pulse

429. How to take your pulse

430. Frequency

431. The best?

432. Interval training

433. Cardio pyramid

434. Good posture – not just for weight training

435. Are two zones better than one?

436. The great outdoors

437. Sprinting

438. And for our northern readers

439. Leave the car keys at home!

440. Going up

441. External motivation – a group effort

442. Treadmills

443. Cushioned for comfort

444. Running in tandem

445. Treadmill shock

446. Blisters

447. Blister remedy

448. Blister prevention #1

449. Blister prevention #2

450. Blister prevention #3

451. Blister prevention #4

452. Start first then step on

453. Start slow!

454. Recumbent cycle

455. Cycle variety

456. Watch your step

457. Don't coast

458. The full 30 minutes

459. Stitches

460. Skipping into fitness

461. Cycling classes – putting a new spin on cardio

462. Indoor rowing – for those who don't like getting wet!

463. Cardio kickboxing

464. Stroking to cardiovascular fitness

465. Run the stairs

466. Your time is the best time

467. You are not an Olympic athlete!

468. Sip, sip, sip

469. Cleaning up – not just for strength training

470. Same days opposite days?

471. Tune in and drop out

472. Better safe than sorry

473. The talk test

12

CARDIO TRAINING

424. A CHANGE OF HEART

Although once frowned upon, it's now generally accepted that cardio training is beneficial for bodybuilders. Not only does cardio speed up fat loss, it does a better job stimulating the heart and lungs than weight training does. A cardiovascular system that's in great shape will not only contribute to your long-term health, it will give you more stamina while weight training. Finally, a healthy cardiovascular system is more efficient at removing the waste products of exercise, including lactic acid, than a slow and sluggish system.

425. FAINT OR DIZZY – LISTEN TO YOUR BODY

If at any time you feel faint or dizzy, immediately stop what you are doing and sit down. Don't try to "work through" the dizziness, hoping it will go away. Lightheadedness is one of the body's first warning signs that there is not enough blood circulation to your head and you are about to faint. As soon as you sit down, tilt your head slightly forward to increase the blood flow to the brain. If you really don't feel well, immediately notify the closest staff member.

426. CARDIO VARIETY

Although it's probably not as important with cardio as it is with weight training, it's a good idea to change around your cardio exercises every now and then. If you normally use a treadmill, try switching to a crosstrainer. Likewise if the cycle is your cardio mainstay, see what a rowing workout feels like. The body adapts fairly quickly and you'll be surprised how challenging your cardio workout will be after switching to an unfamiliar machine.

427. TARGET HEART RATE

To get the most out of your cardio workouts, strive to elevate your heart rate to what's called the "target heart rate zone." To calculate your target heart rate, subtract your age from 220. The lower end of the zone for your target heart rate will be 60 percent of this number, while 80 percent will give you your upper level. For a 20-year-old the math would be 220-20 = 200. Lower zone is .6 X 200 = 120. Upper zone is .8 X 200 = 160. For this person the target  heart rate zone would be 120 to 160 beats per minute.

428. WHERE TO FIND YOUR PULSE

Although you can find your pulse at numerous locations around the body, the best is probably the neck. The pulse in the carotid artery, located  next to the windpipe, is very pronounced. You can either hold for 60 seconds or take it for 10 seconds and then multiply by 6. For example 20 beats in 10 seconds gives a pulse of 20 X 6 or 120 beats per minute.

429. HOW TO TAKE YOUR PULSE

When taking your pulse, use one of your fingers. Don't use your thumb, as the thumb has its own pulse. This could give you an inaccurate reading, as there will be a slight difference in pulses between your thumb and areas closer to the heart. In effect you may count one beat of the heart twice.

430. FREQUENCY

Start by doing 15 to 20 minutes of cardio two to three times per week. Over a period of about four or five weeks, gradually increase it to 30 to 45 minutes, four to five times per week. You should approach cardio training like weight training – you don't start off by doing 300-pound bench presses, so don't start cardio trying to run a marathon. Start out slow and gradually increase the duration and frequency.

431. THE BEST?

In simple terms there is no "best" piece of cardio equipment. All the machines will stimulate your heart and lungs to about the same degree, and they'll all burn about the same number of calories per unit time. Having said that, you may want to experiment with different machines to see which ones feel the most comfortable. Some machines may place more stress on your joints (i.e. ankles and knees) than others.

432. INTERVAL TRAINING

To make your cardio workout more fun and exciting, try varying your intensity level. After a low-intensity warm-up of about five minutes, try alternating 30 to 60 seconds of high-intensity training with two to three minutes of moderate-intensity training.

433. CARDIO PYRAMID

Just like with weight training, you shouldn't start your cardio training at your maximum intensity level. In a typical 30-minute cardio workout, perform 5 minutes of the activity at low intensity, and then gradually increase to your maximum level for about 15 to 20 minutes. Finish off your cardio workout with 5 minutes of low-intensity training. Try not to stop cold turkey.

434. GOOD POSTURE – NOT JUST FOR WEIGHT TRAINING

Hopefully from day one you've learned that proper posture is important on all your strength-training exercises. The same holds true for cardio exercises. Never slouch or lean backwards when using any of the cardio machines, particularly the steppers, cross-trainers, and ellipticals. Doing so changes your center of gravity and places extra stress on the knees, ankles, and lower back. Always maintain an upright posture.

435. ARE TWO ZONES BETTER THAN ONE?

Even though many fitness professionals only talk of a single target heart rate zone, others divide the zone into two subzones. They call the lower, 60 to 75 percent zone, the fat-burning zone, and the 75 to 90 percent the cardio zone. In theory exercising at the lower target heart rate burns more fat calories. But keep in mind you'll burn more calories overall in the higher cardio zone. In addition, the higher zone will do a better job of stimulating your cardiovascular system. Our advice is to start out exercising in the lower zone but raise it to the higher zone as soon as your fitness level allows.

436. THE GREAT OUTDOORS

If you find your indoor treadmill workouts becoming boring, give the great outdoors a try. There's nothing like a challenging run in the fresh air on a crisp autumn morning. Running outdoors also gives you the option of running over different terrains. Even though most newer treadmills allow you to vary the incline, you are usually limited to 10 to 15 degrees. Running outdoors offers so many more different grade options. Another benefit of outdoor running is the constant changing of the scenery. Even with a cardio theater (TV and sound) or other members to observe, there is no comparison to the visual stimulation you'll experience outdoors.

437. SPRINTING

If long-distance running is not your cup of tea, try sprinting. The next time a major track-and-field event is on TV, take a close look at the leg development of the sprinters (100 and 200 meters). Many of them have legs that rival professional bodybuilders. Sprinting is an excellent way to boost the cardiovascular system as well as build and dice up the quads.

438. AND FOR OUR NORTHERN READERS

For those Canadian and northern US readers, winters brings a great option for cardiovascular training – skating. Lace on a pair of ice skates for a great way to stimulate the heart and lungs when the weather gets cold outside. And if Mother Nature doesn't cooperate, most Canadian and US cities and large towns have indoor skating rinks. Try alternating distance skating with sprints and speed skating.

439. LEAVE THE CAR KEYS AT HOME!

One of the easiest ways to burn extra calories and stimulate your cardiovascular system is to hang your car keys on the wall and walk. Any time you are going somewhere within reasonable walking distance, do so. A good, brisk powerwalk is nearly as effective as running and it's a lot easier on the joints. And let's face it, there's no comparison between the calories you'll burn walking and those you'll burn sitting behind the wheel of a car.

440. GOING UP

If you're lucky enough to work in a high-rise office building, you have another great "cardio machine" at your disposal – the stairs! Instead of huddling with the masses in an elevator, head to the stairwell and start climbing. Climbing stairs is an outstanding way to burn calories, stimulate the heart and lungs, and work the legs.

441. EXTERNAL MOTIVATION – A GROUP EFFORT

There will be days when the last thing you want to do is hop on a crosstrainer or treadmill. One way to jazz up your cardio training is to check out a group fitness class. Aerobic classes come in many formats; and guys, they are not just for women! A couple of minutes of the latest "boot camp" or "military jam" cardio class and you'll realize just where your cardio system stands. Besides the motivation you'll receive from other participants, most cardio classes include abdominal training and stretching – two things you won't get on the treadmill or crosstrainer.

442. TREADMILLS

An alternative to pounding the pavement, treadmills are by far the most popular piece of home cardio equipment. Millions are bought at Christmas time, although few are ever used. Treadmills are also one of the hardest machines to access in gyms at prime time. Running on a treadmill has numerous advantages over running outdoors. For starters the weather is a non-issue. Rain, sleet, or snow, it's always dry indoors. Another benefit is safety. Any time you have to run on the road itself, whether because the sidewalks are covered by snow or because you have to cross the road, you run the risk of being targeted by a motorist.

Many drivers take it as a violation of their civil rights if they have to slow down or stop for a runner.

443. CUSHIONED FOR COMFORT

Perhaps the biggest advantage to running on a treadmill is comfort. Most of the better treadmills have some sort of cushioning mechanism. Just like the shock absorber system on a car, cushioning places less stress on the joints than running on concrete or pavement. So if you are an avid outdoor runner who is starting to find hitting the pavement hard on the joints, give a treadmill a try.

444. RUNNING IN TANDEM

Besides safety and comfort, another benefit of using a treadmill is that two people who like to run at different speeds can work out together. Outdoors the faster runner will quickly outpace the slower. But on a treadmill the two of you will be side by side no matter what your individual speeds.

445. TREADMILL SHOCK

Try alternating running with walking at a fairly fast pace uphill, inclined between 10 and 14 (depending on fitness level). This shocks the body tremendously as you simulate walking and running up a huge hill, forcing the bigger muscles to do all the work and thus spiking your heart rate.

446. BLISTERS

Blisters are caused by rubbing and irritation of the skin. Your shoes are almost certainly the culprits – they either don't fit properly or you have run too far in them without first breaking them in adequately.

447. BLISTER REMEDY

If the blister isn't causing any pain, leave it alone. But if it's interfering with your running you should feel free to "operate" as long as you're careful to avoid infection. Sterilize a razor blade (boil it for 10 minutes), wash the area of the blister (preferably using an antiseptic like alcohol or Betadine), and make a small slit in the blister. Don't be squeamish – because the skin of the blister "bubble" is dead, you won't feel any pain. Press the fluid out. Carefully clean the area, again using an antiseptic. Let the blister dry without putting on any ointment, and cover with gauze or a Band-Aid. Problem solved.

448. BLISTER PREVENTION #1

To avoid blisters in the future, make sure that your shoes fit. They should be snug so that your foot does not rattle around inside, rubbing against the shoe and causing blisters. Make sure that

FIRST AID

you have laced your shoes tightly enough that they form to your foot. They should not, however, be too tight, and particularly not too narrow or too short.

449. BLISTER PREVENTION #2

Some manufacturers such as Thorlo, sell "blister-proof" socks. Give these socks a try. In general keep in mind that nylon socks tend to be more abrasive than cotton.

450. BLISTER PREVENTION #3

Feel free to lubricate your feet to cut down on the friction that causes blisters. Rubbing some Vaseline on your feet before runs can do the trick, but if you find that too goopy, talcum powder is a good substitute.

451. BLISTER PREVENTION #4

If you are aware of specific blister problem areas, try protecting those ahead of time. Moleskin may work, but it often doesn't stick very well to sweaty feet. Duct tape, believe it or not, is often more reliable. Put it on before your foot becomes moist, and it won't come off until you want it to.

452. START FIRST THEN STEP ON

Practically every gym instructor can tell stories of having to pick new clients up off the floor behind the treadmill. In most cases the person started the machine while standing on the belt. Even though most treadmills always start at a slow speed (usually 1 mph), if you are not used to a treadmill, this is still too fast a speed to start with. For safety purposes, place both feet to the sides of the belt, start the treadmill, and then step on once the belt is moving.

453. START SLOW!

In addition to starting the treadmill before stepping on, make sure you start at a slow speed. Don't make the mistake of bringing the belt up to 10 or 15 mph and then stepping on. You'll never get your legs up to speed fast enough to keep up. There is a good chance the staff will have to scrape you off the wall!

454. RECUMBENT CYCLE

Upright cycles force you to sit down on a chair with the legs below you, and then lean forward to grab the handlebars. This "slouched" posture is very uncomfortable for many individuals. Equipment manufacturers have addressed this by designing the recumbent cycle, which keeps the torso upright and legs out in front. This position is much less stressful on the lower back and knees. If you have avoided using the upright cycle because of lower back problems, give the recumbent cycle a try.

455. CYCLE VARIETY

Those of you who have "outgrown" standard cycling, whereby you remain seated at all times, try adding some outdoor moves. Alternate slow, medium, and high speed. Alternate seated peddling with stand-up sprints. This simulates the position you'd be in if you were climbing a hill outdoors. Not only are you stimulating your cardiovascular system to the max, but a couple of weeks of this will do your thighs wonders for your quads.

456. WATCH YOUR STEP

Although they are fast being replaced by crosstrainers and arc trainers, many gyms still have an inventory of step machines (the version by Stairmaster being the most well-known). Even though they'll give you a good cardio workout, steppers have fallen out of favor in recent years. The reason is that the relatively straight up and down motion places tremendous stress on the ankles and knees. Conversely, crosstrainers and ellipticals evenly distribute the weight across the joints. You don't suddenly have your entire bodyweight pivoting on your ankle joints. As steppers offer no cardiovascular benefits over crosstrainers and ellipticals, it is suggested you give them a pass.

457. DON'T COAST

Although there is very little difference between the various machines with regards to effectiveness – provided you maintain a brisk pace – some allow you to coast along at a less-than-productive level. The arc trainers, crosstrainers and cardio cycles are good examples. It's very difficult, however, to coast on a treadmill, as the machine is setting the pace.

458. THE FULL 30 MINUTES

Most cardio machines allow you to input various programs. This saves you the trouble of having to change the speed, resistance, or angle on the pedals or belt. The disadvantage is that most of the program modes will reset to the lowest intensity level when there is five minutes left in your program. This serves as a cool-down zone. If you want to do 30 minutes of intense cardio, either set the machine to manual mode or program it for 35 minutes.

459. STITCHES

You may find during your first few cardio sessions you develop a stitch. A stitch is caused by a spasm of the diaphragm, the muscle that controls your breathing. There are a number of possible reasons for this. If your breathing isn't controlled and disciplined, the

diaphragm may be complaining. If you are running too soon after eating, your heavy stomach may literally be tugging at the ligaments connected to the diaphragm. Or you may simply be running too fast for your body's breathing machinery to keep up. A stitch will usually go away quickly after just slowing down or stopping. If you're in a race or you just don't want to stop, however, you can often make it go away by bringing your breathing into careful control. Concentrate on belly breathing, pushing your belly out when you breathe in and relaxing it as you breathe out. Take deep breaths on the intake and exhale suddenly, even noisily. Another suggestion is to raise your hands above your head. This helps stretch out the diaphragm.

460. SKIPPING INTO FITNESS

When you were in elementary school you probably teased your female classmates for skipping rope at recess. While at one time considered a "sissy activity," skipping has gained much respect over the past couple of decades. Thanks to such celebrities as boxing great Muhammad Ali and actor Sylvester Stallone, jumping rope is now a mainstay of athletic conditioning. If you're still a holdout and think skipping rope is for sissies, give it

a try the next time you're at the gym. Start off with simple skipping exercises and progress from there. You'll quickly discover that skipping rope is not just for sissies and schoolgirls.

461. CYCLING CLASSES – PUTTING A NEW SPIN ON CARDIO

They go by different names ("Spinning" by Reebok being the most common), but essentially they are all the same. Biking classes became all the rage in the 1990s and continue to be one of the most popular forms of group cardio. A standard indoor cycling class consists of a lead bike with an instructor and 10 to 12 "followers." For the next 45 to 60 minutes the instructor will take his or her charges through a simulated bike ride. By varying the pace and tension you can come close to mimicking an outdoor bike ride. If you're looking for a means to increase you cardio intensity, give a cycling spin class a try.

462. INDOOR ROWING – FOR THOSE WHO DON'T LIKE GETTING WET!

Once indoor group cycling classes became popular it wasn't long before the rowing enthusiasts jumped on the bandwagon. As with cycling, a lead instructor takes a group of people out on a simulated rowing course. While you won't get the nice cool breeze blowing off the water, you don't have to worry about

getting wet, either. If the ergometer (rower) is one of your favorite pieces of cardio equipment, check out a rowing class.

463. CARDIO KICKBOXING

For the male readers who think aerobic classes are "just for girls," check out a cardio kickboxing class. These classes combine intense aerobic moves with various martial arts kicking and punching techniques. You'll not only be pushing your cardiovascular system to the max, your self-defense skills will be greatly improved.

464. STROKING TO CARDIOVASCULAR FITNESS

One of the most relaxing yet efficient forms of cardio exercise is swimming. Swimming will burn the same number of calories as most indoor activities, while at the same time being one of the best exercises for reducing the stress on the joints. As you can probably guess, floating in water is much less stressful on the joints than pounding on the pavement or even working on a stepper machine.

465. RUN THE STAIRS

You don't need expensive cardio equipment to give your heart and lungs a great workout. Unless your gym is on one level, there will be at least one flight of stairs available. Run up them. See how many "up and downs" you can make before you're fatigued. Try to do one extra flight per workout. It won't be long before you can run 20 or 30 flights no problem.

466. YOUR TIME IS THE BEST TIME

Don't let anyone tell you that there is a "best" time to do cardio. One of the popular beliefs these days is that doing cardio first thing in the morning is far superior to later in the day. The theory is that because your brain uses carbohydrate as a fuel source while you are asleep, you'll immediately burn stored fat if you do cardio first thing in the morning. While there is some truth to this, the difference between early morning and late evening training is not large enough to recommend one over the other. Unless you are an early riser or actually prefer doing cardio early in the morning, do your cardio workouts whenever it feels most comfortable.

467. YOU ARE NOT AN OLYMPIC ATHLETE!

Every four years doctors see a spike in exercise-related injuries. The culprit is usually over-enthusiasm brought on by couch potatoes watching the Olympics. Even if you do have the talent to be a world-class athlete, it takes years of training and dedication. Don't march into the gym with a copy of the latest gold medal winner's training program in your hand and try to follow it. Pat yourself on the back for getting off the couch, but ease into exercise at an intensity suited to your fitness level.

468. SIP, SIP, SIP

It's easy to forget the simple things when you're struggling through an intense cardio workout. Even something as seemingly unimportant as sipping water may get overlooked. You may not feel thirst so you don't bother to drink water. Unfortunately the thirst mechanism doesn't kick in until after you've become dehydrated.

1st Couch Potato

It's normal to lose four or five liters of water during an intense cardio workout. Make sure you regularly consume plenty of water during your workout. One rule is to weigh yourself before and after your workout. The difference at the end of your workout is water loss. Try to make it up by drinking water.

469. CLEANING UP – NOT JUST FOR STRENGTH TRAINING

Nothing is as revolting as getting set to hop on your favorite cardio machine and noticing a bead of someone else's sweat trickling down the console or handles. There is no need for you to join the ranks of the disgusting and inconsiderate. Always wipe down your cardio machine after your cardio workout.

470. SAME DAYS OPPOSITE DAYS?

One of the most common questions gym instructors answer on a daily basis is, "Should I do my cardio on the same day or opposite days as my weights?" There is no correct answer to this question. Performing them both on the same day will leave you a couple of days off from training each week. Of course doubling up means a longer workout. Conversely, alternating cardio means shorter workouts but more days spent in the gym. Our advice is to experiment and try both, and then decide which one feels more comfortable (or is more practical depending on your daily and weekly time schedules).

471. TUNE IN AND DROP OUT

For some, the sights and sounds of a busy gym are all it takes to get motivated. Listening to people talk or work out is all it takes to keep you pumped and committed to your training. For others, however, a workout is a time to turn inwards. If you find the normal background noise of your gym distracting as you plod through your cardio workout, try wearing a set of headphones and crank up the volume on your Walkman or iPod. Or perhaps your gym has a cardio theater so members can watch various TV channels. Either way, tune in drop out, and build muscle!

472. BETTER SAFE THAN SORRY

Most modern cardio machines are easy to use. Nevertheless there may be versions that have a tricky programming mode or operating technique. Don't risk damage to yourself or the machine by trying to figure things out on your own. If you have any doubt ask a qualified staff member.

473. THE TALK TEST

One way to determine if you're overdoing it is to use what is called the "talk test." In simple terms, you should be able to carry on a conversation with someone as you exercise. If you are gasping for breath to the point that talking is difficult, ease it back a few notches.

TAKE THE **TALK TEST!** YOU SHOULD BE ABLE TO CARRY ON A **CONVERSATION** WITH SOMEONE AS YOU EXERCISE. IF YOU ARE **GASPING** FOR BREATH TO THE POINT THAT TALKING IS DIFFICULT, **EASE IT BACK** A FEW NOTCHES.

INTERMEDIATE EXERCISES & STRATEGIES

474. Isolation exercises
475. Add weight to bodyweight exercises
476. One for thickness one for width
477. At least one upper and one lower
478. Swiss-ball crunches
479. Choosing a Swiss ball
480. At work too!
481. Roman-chair sit-ups
482. Rope crunches
483. Barbell rolls
484. Swiss-ball back extensions
485. Hack squats for that great outer-thigh sweep
486. Front squats
487. Leg extensions
488. Lying leg extensions
489. Sissy squats – don't let the name fool you!
490. Reverse hyperextensions
491. Cable pull-throughs
492. Machine abductions
493. Cable abductions
494. Adductions
495. Donkey calf raises
496. Standing one-leg calf raises
497. Hack squat calf raises
498. Seated calf raises
499. Bent-knee calf exercises
500. Standing or seated first?
501. Flat flyes
502. Incline flyes
503. Decline barbell presses
504. Neck presses
505. Cable crossovers
506. To cross over or not?
507. Flat or incline cable fly
508. Straight-arm pushdowns
509. Single-arm cable pulldowns
510. Two-arm dumbell rows
511. All three heads
512. Barbell shrugs
513. Dumbell shrugs

514. Machine shrugs
515. Shrug, not bounce
516. Shrug, not roll
517. Know when to build the traps
518. Feet on the floor
519. Upright rows
520. Dumbell or rope upright rows
521. Lateral raises
522. Lean into it
523. Bent-over lateral raises
524. It's a raise, not a row
525. Lying front raises – making like superman!
526. Arnold presses
527. Between-legs cable raises
528. Power cleans
529. Reverse pec-deck
530. Bent-over cable raises
531. Reverse-grip bench presses
532. Kickbacks
533. Rope extensions
534. One-arm cable pushdowns
535. Palms up or palms down?
536. Seated pulley concentration pushdown
537. Concentration curls
538. Arnold's way
539. Barbell concentration curls
540. One-arm preacher curls
541. When an incline bench is a preacher bench
542. Spider curls
543. Standing cable curl
544. Body-drag curls
545. Overhead cable curls
546. Lying dumbell curls
547. Wrist curls
548. Reverse wrist curls
549. Reverse curls
550. Hammer curls

13

474. ISOLATION EXERCISES

Once you reach the intermediate stage of bodybuilding (on average four to six months of regular training), you should start doing more isolation exercises. Unlike compound movements, where more than one muscle and joint are utilized, isolation exercises usually restrict the range of motion to one muscle and one joint. Don't abandon compound movements altogether, as you'll still be trying to add muscle size and strength. Instead start adding isolation exercises to develop quality in the muscle mass you have already built.

475. ADD WEIGHT TO BODYWEIGHT EXERCISES

One way to increase the intensity of your workouts without changing exercises is to add weight to some of your bodyweight exercises. You'll eventually reach the point where your bodyweight is not heavy enough on such exercises as bench dips and parallel bar dips. You may even reach a point on an exercise as difficult as chin-ups where 15 to 20 reps with just your bodyweight becomes fairly easy. If you're at this stage, try wearing a weight belt or holding a dumbell between your feet or knees when you perform parallel bar dips or chin-ups. For bench dips, have a partner place one or more flat plates across your thighs. You've now turned a warm-up or finishing exercise (which is what these exercises eventually become because of the high reps you can perform) into a basic mass movement.

476. ONE FOR THICKNESS ONE FOR WIDTH

When designing your back workouts, select at least one exercise for width (pulldowns and chin-ups) and at least one exercise for thickness (rowing movements).

477. AT LEAST ONE UPPER AND ONE LOWER

To balance out your chest development, perform at least one lower chest exercise (flat or decline presses) and at least one for the upper chest (incline presses and incline flyes).

478. SWISS-BALL CRUNCHES

They go by different names (Swiss ball, therapeutic balls, resistaballs, etc), but are all essentially the same; a large rubber ball that allows you to target the abs from a multitude of different angles. The simplest exercise is to sit on the ball so that your butt is at the front. With the legs bent, lie back until your torso is parallel with the floor. Place your hands behind your head and slowly raise your torso upward as if doing a regular floor crunch. Slowly lower back down until your torso is just below parallel with the floor. Swiss ball crunches have been scientifically proven one of the most effective abdominal exercises. And because of the balance factor, they bring in many of the smaller stabilizing muscles of the midsection.

479. CHOOSING A SWISS BALL

Unless you are using one for injury rehab and have been told otherwise by a physiotherapist, use a Swiss ball that forms a 90-degree angle between your upper and lower legs when you sit on it. This will allow for a good range of motion without putting too much stress on the lower back.

480. AT WORK TOO!

You don't need to limit your Swiss ball usage to the gym. Many physiotherapists recommend that people use them for sitting at work. Unlike a solid chair, which gives the lower back and abdominal muscles a rest, a Swiss ball forces you to use your stabilizer muscles even when sitting down. If you want to give your ab and lower back muscles an extra workout as well as improve your posture, get rid of your chair and get on the ball! Now, contrary to what you may read in some exercise magazines, do not perform heavy exercises like supine presses, curls or shoulder presses on a Swiss ball. Doing so invites injury.

481. ROMAN-CHAIR SIT-UPS

Roman chair sit-ups are one of the best exercises for isolating the lower abs. The goal, however, is to perform them like a crunch and not as the name implies, a sit-up. Position yourself on the bench with your feet locked in under the leg rollers. With your hands held to your chest or behind your head, lower backwards until your shoulders are 10 to 12 inches from the bench. Pause for a split second and then

rise back up until your torso is just short of vertical with the floor. In effect you are doing the middle third of the exercise. Going all the way down places stress on the lower back, while coming all the way up brings more of the hip flexors into play.

482. ROPE CRUNCHES

This exercise is one of the best for targeting just about all the muscles that make up the midsection. Make the midsection do the work – don't rely on the weight of your torso. Experiment with different body positions, both close to the floor and higher up. Don't rock back on your heels, as this will only create unwanted body momentum.

483. BARBELL ROLLS

Although unorthodox, barbell rolls are a great way to target virtually all the muscles that make up the midsection (abdominals, serratus, intercostals). Position a barbell on the floor with a 25- or 35-pound plate on each side. Lie down and grab the bar as if you were going to do push-ups (except that you will place most of your weight on the knees and not your toes). Instead of pushing away from the bar you roll it forward and backwards.

484. SWISS-BALL BACK EXTENSIONS

Swiss ball back extensions are the next logical step up from back extensions on the floor. The Swiss ball allows for a greater range of motion, and it forces the small stabilizer muscles of the lower torso to contribute. As you progress with both your technique and comfort, try narrowing your foot stance. This will make it more difficult to balance, providing a better overall workout.

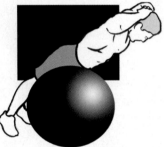

485. HACK SQUATS FOR THAT GREAT OUTER THIGH SWEEP

Many people find that after a couple of months of regular barbell squats their upper outer thighs begin to overshadow their lower outer thighs. One way to correct this is by including hack squats in your leg training. Hack squats will add a nice sweep to the outer thighs. Lie back on the hack squat machine and position your shoulders under the pads. With your legs slightly wider than shoulder width apart, feet pointed slightly outwards, lower down to a full squat (thighs parallel to the floor or slightly lower) position. Return to the starting position so that your legs are just short of being locked out.

486. FRONT SQUATS

If you find regular back squats stressful on the lower back, or if you want to target more of your lower quads and less of your glutes, try front squats. Position the bar as you would a normal set of squats but instead of resting it on your traps and back shoulders, rest it across your upper chest, arms, and front shoulders. From here the exercise is identical to back squats. Because your glute involvement is greatly reduced, you'll need to use less weight.

487. LEG EXTENSIONS

Unlike squats and leg presses, which stimulate virtually the entire leg region, leg extensions isolate the central thigh. As with

most exercises, the key is to not bounce at the bottom or lock out at the top. Also, try pointing the toes in different positions (inwards, central, outwards) to isolate different sections of the quads.

488. LYING LEG EXTENSIONS

You'll need a leg extension machine with no vertical back support attached. Sit down in the machine and lie backwards until your lower legs are hanging vertically under the leg rollers and the rest of the body is horizontal. Perform the exercise at you would seated leg extensions. By removing the bend at the hips, much of the stress is shifted from the lower to the upper thighs. This exercise is great during the pre-contest phase of training when you are trying to bring out the separation in your upper thighs.

489. SISSY SQUATS – DON'T LET THE NAME FOOL YOU!

After adapting to regular squats and leg presses, many bodybuilders are reluctant to try any leg exercise that doesn't require the use of hundreds of pounds of weight. This is too bad, since some of the most effective leg exercises require little or no weight. Despite the name, sissy squats are one of the best, and toughest, exercises for the quads. With your legs slightly wider than shoulder width apart and feet pointed slightly outwards, grab a stationary upright with one hand for support. With  your torso leaning back slightly, squat down to a full squat position. Return to the starting position so that your legs are just short of locked out. If you need extra resistance, try holding a weight plate to your chest with your free hand.

490. REVERSE HYPEREXTENSIONS

Stiff-leg deadlifts and leg curls may be the most popular hamstring exercises, but there are others. One of the best is the reverse hyperextension. As the name suggests, these are just the opposite of regular hyperextensions (more properly called back extensions). Instead of locking the legs and raising and lowering the upper body, you lock the upper body and lift your legs. The easiest way to perform this exercise is to lie face down on a high flat bench. Hold on tight with your arms and slowly lift and lower your legs.

491. CABLE PULL-THROUGHS

Cable pull-throughs are another great but seldom-seen hamstring exercise. Attach a rope to a low pulley and face away from the machine. With your legs straight, bend the torso forward and grab the rope. Slowly stand up, pulling the rope between your legs. For obvious reasons, position yourself so that the rope is still a few inches from your crotch area at the top of the exercise!

492. MACHINE ABDUCTIONS

Abductions are great for those who want to specialize on the outer-thigh-and-hip region. They are especially effective for those who play sports with a lot of lateral movement. For the machine version, adjust the leg supports so that they are in the inward position. With your knees resting against the pads, slowly push your legs out till you feel a comfortable stretch. Return to the starting position. With time you'll be able to open the legs wider.

493. CABLE ABDUCTIONS

If your gym doesn't have an abductor machine, try attaching an ankle strap to your lower leg and connect it to a low pulley. With one hand on your hips and the other holding the machine, sweep, or raise, your leg outwards and upwards to wherever your flexibility allows.

494. ADDUCTIONS

The opposite of abductions, adductions are great for working the inner thighs and small adductor muscles. When you hear of a pulled groin it's usually the adductors that we are talking about. Using the same machine, adjust the leg supports so they are in the outward position (you'll have to experiment to see how wide is comfortable). With your legs resting against the pads, slowly squeeze your legs together. Return to the outward position.

495. DONKEY CALF RAISES

Flip through copies of Joe Weider's old Muscle Builder Power magazine (the forerunner to today's Muscle and Fitness magazine) and you'll see photos of Arnold Schwarzenegger, Franco Columbu, Robby Robinson, and other great bodybuilders from the '70s performing this exercise. Despite the intimidating position involved, donkey calf raises are one of the most effective exercises for the calves. Lean across a waist-high support and, with your toes on the edge of a block of wood, have a willing training partner sit across your hips. From here perform the exercise like a regular set of standing calf raises. Be sure your partner sits across your hips and not your middle back. That would place unwanted stress on your spine.

496. STANDING ONE-LEG CALF RAISES

If your gym lacks a decent calf machine or you just want some variety in your training, try one-leg calf raises. All you need is a dumbell and a thick block of wood. Hold the dumbell in one hand and stand on the edge of the wood with the leg of the same side. With the other

leg bent behind you, flex up and down. You may need to hold on to something sturdy with your free hand for support.

497. HACK SQUAT CALF RAISES

For those who find vertical standing calf raises hard on the lower back, try the hack squat machine. Instead of facing outwards as if you were going to do squats, face inwards so that your chin is resting on the back support pad. With you toes positioned on a 2 x 4 or other block of wood, flex up and down on your toes. Make sure you maximize the stretch effect.

498. SEATED CALF RAISES

Once you develop a good foundation on your calves with standing calf raises, it's time to start specializing on the lower calves (the soleus muscle). Sit down on the machine's chair or bench and place the pads across your knees. From here, flex upwards and downwards as if doing standing calf raises. Go for the maximum stretch and both the top and bottom of the exercise. Try pointing the toes inwards and outwards to target different parts of your lower calves.

499. BENT-KNEE CALF EXERCISES

While the seated calf machine is the best exercise for working the lower calf muscles, you can modify most upper calf movements to target the lower calves. All you have to do is put a bend in your knees when you perform such exercises as standing calf raises, toe presses, and donkey calf raises. Bending the knees shifts more of the stress to the lower soleus muscle. Keep in mind that you'll need to use less weight, as your lower calves are not capable of lifting as much weight as your large upper calves.

500. STANDING OR SEATED FIRST?

When you start including both standing and seated calf raises in your workouts, the question invariably asked is what order to do them in. Physiology has one answer. The lower calf (soleus) is primarily made up of slow-twitch muscle fibers, which respond best to high reps. The upper calf (gastrocnemius) is mainly fast-twitch muscle, best stimulated by lower reps. Most experts recommend doing your upper calf training first, followed by the exercises for the lower calf.

501. FLAT FLYES

While barbell and dumbell presses are great for adding strength and size to the chest, front shoulders, and triceps, flyes are among the best exercises for isolating and shaping the chest. Flyes also make a great exercise for warming up or finishing off the chest. Grab a set of dumbells and lean back on a flat bench. With a moderate bend at the elbows and palms facing inward, lower the dumbells down and outward, until your upper arm is just slightly below parallel with the floor. Bring the dumbells back up in a hugging-type motion. Be careful you don't go too low at the bottom of the exercise. This could overstress the pec-delt tie-in (the area where your chest and front shoulders meet).

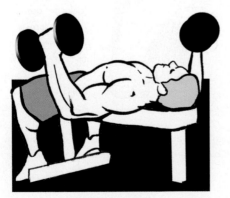

502. INCLINE FLYES

As with flat and incline dumbell presses, you can perform flat dumbell flyes on an incline bench and isolate the upper chest. Most of the tips for flat flyes apply to incline flyes: don't lower too far, keep a slight bend at the elbow, and raise them using a hugging motion.

503. DECLINE BARBELL PRESSES

If you want to target the lower and outer chest, look no further than decline barbell presses. Declines also seem to involve less front-shoulder stimulation than regular flat barbell presses. For this reason they make

 an excellent substitute for flat presses if you have shoulder problems. Instead of lowering the bar to the middle of the chest, lower it to the lower ribcage (nipple region). Experiment with different angles on the bench as well. For most people an angle of 20 to 30 degrees seems to work best.

504. NECK PRESSES

Even though the late Vince Gironda had an intense dislike of regular bench presses (he believed that wide-grip dips did more for chest development), occasionally he would let his students perform a variation of the bench press called neck presses. You may want to experiment to see how it feels. Set yourself up as if

doing regular bench presses, but instead of bringing the bar to the lower rib cage, lower the bar to where the upper chest meets the neck. Be careful not to bounce the bar off your collarbone. You may want to have a spotter standing behind you the first time you attempt this exercise, and don't try using your normal weight resistance until you get used to this variation.

505. CABLE CROSSOVERS

Cable crossovers are one of the best exercises for keeping tension on the chest muscles throughout the full range of motion. Even the famous barbell

bench press suffers from a momentary loss of tension at parts of the exercise. For stability try standing with a runner's stance (one leg forward, one leg back) between the cable pulleys. With the torso bent slightly forward, bring the handles downward so that your arms are at about 45 degrees with the torso. Slowly return to the starting position (your elbows will likely be just behind the shoulders, hands in line with the torso).

506. TO CROSS OVER OR NOT?

Even though the name cable crossover suggests "crossing over" the hands in front of the body, be careful if you do so. For an extra few degrees of movement you run the risk of gashing the knuckles of your hands. You'll get virtually the same degree of chest stimulation by bringing your hands together at the front of your body, stopping just short of having the knuckles touch.

507. FLAT OR INCLINE CABLE FLY

For a change of pace, try doing your flyes on the cable crossover machine. You can do them on a flat or incline bench. Position the bench between the two pulleys and either grab the handles yourself or have a partner pass them to you. The advantage of cable flyes over dumbell flyes is that there will be tension on

your chest throughout the full range of motion of the exercise. With dumbells you'll start losing tension as the arms approach the vertical.

508. STRAIGHT-ARM PUSHDOWNS

One of the problems with most back exercises is that the biceps end up doing much of the work. And because the biceps are much smaller than the larger back muscles, they often fail before the back muscles get the full benefit. A great way to get around this is by doing straight-arm pushdowns. Stand in front of a cable machine or lat machine that has a medium to long bar attached. Grab the bar with a shoulder-

width grip, palms facing downwards. With your arms kept locked out at all times, press down until the bar is one to two inches from your thighs. Raise the bar back up as high as possible without the weight plates touching. Because there is no flexion at the elbows the biceps are virtually eliminated from the exercise.

509. SINGLE-ARM CABLE PULLDOWNS

If you want to bring out extra detail in your back muscles, especially your lats, try this exercise. Sit down on the pulldown machine and replace the long bar with a single handle. Grab the handle with a reverse (palms facing up) grip. Pull the handle towards your torso, keeping the handle as close to your body as possible. At the bottom of the movement your elbow will be behind you and the handle will be in line with your lower ribcage.

510. TWO-ARM DUMBELL ROWS

If you find that barbell rows hit only one side of the body or are too stressful on the wrist, try dumbell rows. Most of the safety considerations of the barbell version apply to dumbell rows (i.e. slight bend at the knee, slight arch in the lower back, etc). The two primary advantages of dumbell rows is that they allow you to rotate your hands from forward to inward, as well as forcing both sides of the body to work evenly.

511. ALL THREE HEADS

Once you have a good foundation under your belt you should start specializing on the separate heads that make up the shoulder muscles. Try to include at least one exercise for the front, side, and rear deltoids in your shoulder workout. Also, if need be, include an exercise that directly works the trapezius, such as shrugs.

512. BARBELL SHRUGS

Nothing looks as impressive as a powerful set of traps (trapezius). They give the owner that strong appearance. Although most shoulder exercises indirectly stimulate the traps, the best exercise for targeting them directly is the barbell shrug. Grab a barbell with a shoulder-width grip and shrug the shoulders upwards and slightly backwards, trying to touch the ears.

513. DUMBELL SHRUGS

If you find barbell shrugs awkward, especially if they chafe your front thighs, switch over to two dumbells.

Experiment with holding the dumbells with your palms facing in or back. Perform the exercise like you would the barbell version, trying to touch your ears with your shoulders then lowering.

514. MACHINE SHRUGS

Many bodybuilders find they get a good trap workout by using a flat bench-press machine. Most serious bodybuilders use the Universal bench press more for traps than chest training! For variety try facing both away from and toward the machine. If you are tall or have long arms you may need to stand on a block of wood to get the required stretch at the bottom.

515. SHRUG, NOT BOUNCE

When doing any type of shrugging exercise, be careful not to flex at the knees and bounce the bar up with body momentum. If you can't lift it by just shrugging your shoulders, it's too heavy.

516. SHRUG, NOT ROLL

As the primary function of the traps is to elevate the shoulder girdle, it doesn't make sense to roll the shoulder blades as you are shrugging. Rolling the shoulder blades doesn't add anything extra to the movement. In fact it only increases the risk of developing a serious shoulder injury.

517. KNOW WHEN TO BUILD THE TRAPS

As with ribcage expansion, those with narrow shoulders should probably avoid building the traps. For wide-shouldered individuals, building the traps will add to the appearance of the physique, but for narrow-shouldered bodybuilders bigger traps will only make the shoulders look that much narrower. Likewise, those with short necks should probably avoid direct trap work, because heavy trap development will give you that unsightly "no neck" appearance.

518. FEET ON THE FLOOR

To ensure that you are performing your shrugs (barbell or dumbell) properly, try "forcing" the heels of your feet into the floor. This will prevent you from bouncing and flexing at the knee joint. If you find yourself using more weight on the shrug than you are squatting, re-evaluate your form! There is no way a small muscle like the trapezius can lift as much as your thighs and glutes can.

519. UPRIGHT ROWS

For those of you who want to perform extra work for both your traps and side delts all in one motion, try upright rows. Grab a barbell with a shoulder-width grip and lift it straight up the center of the body, drawing the elbows behind the shoulders at the top of the exercise. A shoulder-width grip will work more of the traps, while a narrow (6 to 8 inches) grip will bring more of the side shoulders in.

520. DUMBELL OR ROPE UPRIGHT ROWS

Those who find barbell upright rows stressful on the wrists might try performing the exercise with two dumbells. You could also use the low pulley on a cable crossover machine and attach the triceps extension rope.

521. LATERAL RAISES

With your front shoulders receiving a good workout from various chest presses and your rear shoulders coming into play on most back exercises, it's the side shoulders that need the extra work. Bodybuilders have been doing lateral raises for decades to add width to their shoulders. With your knees and elbows slightly bent, grab a set of dumbells so that

your palms face inwards. Slowly raise the dumbells out and upwards until your arms are shoulder height. Lower the dumbells until they meet in front of your quads. Resist the urge to swing the dumbells up using your torso. Concentrate on using your deltoids.

522. LEAN INTO IT
To really ensure that your side shoulders are doing most of the work on lateral raises, lean slightly forward. If you find this puts pressure on the lower back, set an adjustable incline bench at about 60 to 70 degrees and lean against it (facing the bench).

523. BENT-OVER LATERAL RAISES
Though your rear delts will probably receive adequate stimulation from your back training, a point may come when they start lagging behind your front and side delts. When this happens you'll need to target them with specific exercises. Bent-over laterals are one of the best. This exercise is very similar to the side version except you are leaning quite far forward. By holding your torso at a 30-degree angle to the horizontal, most of the stress is shifted from the side to the rear shoulders. If you find the position stressful on the lower back, try lying face down on an incline bench set at about 30 degrees.

524. IT'S A RAISE, NOT A ROW
When performing your bent-over lateral raises, make sure you keep the arms relatively straight and lift

them outwards. Many bodybuilders turn the exercise into a rowing movement by bending the elbows and pulling the arms up close to the sides. This is the body's way of cheating. It's easier to use the larger and stronger lat muscles than the smaller, weaker, rear deltoid muscles.

525. LYING FRONT RAISES – MAKING LIKE SUPERMAN!
This exercise is one of the best for targeting both the front deltoids and rotator cuff. Lie facedown on a 30-degree bench and hold a pair of dumbells down at arm's length. Slowly raise them until they are in line with your torso (think of superman flying with his arms stretched out in front of him). Slowly lower back down. For variety, try raising the dumbells in an alternating fashion.

526. ARNOLD PRESSES
Named after Arnold Schwarzenegger, Arnold presses are a variation of the standard dumbell press. Hoist the dumbells to shoulder height so your palms are facing your head. As you push upwards, rotate the palms to a forward-facing position. The advantage of Arnold presses is that they force you to do the exercise more strictly (it's harder to use body momentum to force the dumbells up) plus more of the action is directed into the side deltoids.

527. BETWEEN-LEGS CABLE RAISES
For those of you not afraid to live dangerously, try between-the-legs cable raises. Attach a shoulder-width straight bar to a low pulley and grab it so that

you are facing away from the machine with the cable running between your legs. Slowly bring the bar forward and up until your arms are parallel with the floor. Return to the starting position. Make sure you are positioned the right distance from the pulley so the cable doesn't interfere with your family planning on the way up!

528. POWER CLEANS

One of the best exercises for building upper-back and trapezius thickness is power cleans. Hold a barbell in front of the thighs with a shoulder-width grip. Now in one quick motion flick the bar away from the thighs and clean it up to your shoulders. Your palms will go from facing the thighs to facing the ceiling at the top of the exercise. Lower the weight slowly to the starting position, keeping your back flat as you do so.

529. REVERSE PEC-DECK

As the name suggests, you'll need a pec-deck machine to perform this exercise. Sit down facing the machine with your chest resting against the back

support. Grab the handles (or rest your arms on the inside of the pads) and slowly pull backwards to a comfortable stretch. Reverse pec decks are great for working the muscles of the upper back, in particular the smaller rhomboids and rear deltoids. They are also easier on the lower back than their free-weight dumbell equivalent, bent-over lateral raises.

530. BENT-OVER CABLE RAISES

To really blast the rear deltoids, position yourself in the middle of a cable-crossover machine. Bend forward and grab the right lower pulley with your left hand and vice versa. With a slight bend at the

elbows, raise the handles to shoulder height. Lower the handles back down to just short of having the plates touch.

531. REVERSE-GRIP BENCH PRESSES

An excellent way to put mass on your triceps is by doing reverse-grip bench presses. Instead of the standard palms-towards-your-feet grip, grab the bar so that your palms are facing your head. Keep your grip just slightly narrower than shoulder-width. This grip forces the elbows in closer to the body, putting more stress on the triceps and less on the pectoral muscles.

532. KICKBACKS

Dumbell kickbacks are one of the best exercises for bringing out the horseshoe shape in the triceps. Grab a dumbell, place one hand and knee on a bench for support, and lock the upper arm tight to your side and parallel to the

floor. Extend, or "kick" the forearm back until your arm is locked out. Return to the starting position so that your forearm is perpendicular to the floor (there will be a 90-degree angle between your upper and lower arm).

533. ROPE EXTENSIONS

Rope extensions are one of the best exercises for targeting the long rear head of the triceps. Attach a rope to a high pulley and turn around so you are facing away from the machine. With the elbows held close to your head, lean forward and adopt a runner's stance (one leg forward and one back). Extend your forearms away from you until your arms are locked out straight. Slowly return to the starting position. The key with this exercise is to keep the upper arms and body stationary. Only your forearms move.

534. ONE-ARM CABLE PUSHDOWNS

One-arm pushdowns can be considered the cable equivalent of dumbell kickbacks. They are great for allowing you to concentrate on one arm at a time, and are one of the best exercises for bringing out the horseshoe shape of the triceps. Attach a small handle (most people use the cable crossover handle) to a pulley

machine and position yourself so that your working arm is directly in line with the cable. Grab the handle with one hand, and with your elbow and upper arm tucked close to your sides, extend the forearm down until your arm is completely locked out at the bottom. Slowly allow it back to chest height and repeat.

535. PALMS UP OR PALMS DOWN?

When you perform one-arm cable pushdowns try experimenting with both a palms-up and palms-down grip. In theory it shouldn't make any difference but most bodybuilders find that a palms down grip shifts most of the stress to the lateral triceps while a palms up (reverse) grip seems to hit the long rear head.

536. SEATED PULLEY CONCENTRATION PUSHDOWN

This exercise can be considered the triceps equivalent of the biceps concentration curl. Sit down next to a cable machine and rest one arm on your thigh exactly as if doing a dumbell concentration curl. With your palm facing upward, extend your arm down between your legs to a locked-out position.

537. CONCENTRATION CURLS

Sit down on the front or side of a flat bench. With your elbow braced against your inner thigh, lower a dumbell to just short of lockout. Curl the dumbell up until your forearm is above parallel with the floor. Squeeze the biceps at the top of this exercise.

538. ARNOLD'S WAY

For variety try concentration curls the way Arnold Schwarzenegger performed them. Arnold would stand up, and with one elbow resting on his thighs let his other arm curl straight up and down. Arnold found that he could get a better biceps contraction by having his arm free of his body rather than braced against his thigh.

539. BARBELL CONCENTRATION CURLS

For variety try performing concentration curls with a barbell. Grab a barbell with a shoulder-width grip and bend forward until your torso is parallel with the floor. Curl the bar up and down, trying to keep your upper arm vertical with the floor.

540. ONE-ARM PREACHER CURLS

One-arm preacher curls are another of those exercises that allow you to devote full concentration to the muscle being worked. Grab a dumbell and go to the preacher bench. Place your upper arm on the pad and lower the dumbell down to a locked out position. Curl back up until your forearm is just short of vertical. As with the two-arm version, don't bounce at the bottom of the exercise. This places tremendous stress on the biceps tendon, and numerous bodybuilders have required surgery after rupturing their biceps tendon.

541. WHEN AN INCLINE BENCH IS A PREACHER BENCH

One of the nice things about one-arm preacher curls is that you don't need a preacher bench to perform the exercise. Simply stand behind an incline bench set to 45 to 60 degrees and rest your upper arm on the bench. From here perform the exercise exactly the same as the seated version.

542. SPIDER CURLS

This exercise is great for peaking the middle belly of the biceps. If the pad on your gym's preacher bench is removable, turn it around so that the vertical end is facing outwards. If not, you'll have to stand in front of the pad facing the seating bench. The exercise is performed the same as regular preacher curls but the upper arm is curling vertically rather than on an angle. Because spider curls do a better job of isolating the biceps, you'll need to use less weight.

543. STANDING CABLE CURL

One of the few disadvantages of standing barbell curls is that a point will be reached when curling the bar any higher will not produce any extra benefit. For most people this point is where the forearm is at about a 45-degree angle to the horizontal. The reason is that gravity will always be pulling straight downwards. Once the forearm starts approaching the vertical, the tension on the biceps decreases. Standing cable curls have a slight advantage since the cable will keep tension on the biceps even when your forearms are nearly vertical with the floor. So while standing barbell curls are probably the best overall biceps exercise, cable curls are a viable alternative.

544. BODY-DRAG CURLS

This exercise is great for working the biceps while minimizing forearm involvement. Instead of curling the bar upwards in an arc (starting close to the thighs, going outwards as you curl up, and coming inwards at the top), you drag the bar straight up the middle of the body. Your elbows will move behind your body as you complete the rep. Try to keep the bar no more than one to two inches from the torso at all times.

545. OVERHEAD CABLE CURLS

This exercise is great for those of you who love flexing in the mirror. Stand inside the cable crossover machine and grab the single-hand attachments. Adopt a double-biceps pose and slowly curl the handles towards the ears. For that extra contraction, hold the position for a second or two.

546. LYING DUMBELL CURLS

If you're looking for the maximum stretch in your biceps when working out, try lying dumbell curls. Lie back on a flat bench and let your arms hang

down. Slowly curl the dumbells until they are in line with the bench. You will need a higher-than-normal flat bench for his exercise.

547. WRIST CURLS

If your torso and upper arm exercises don't adequately stimulate your forearms, start including direct forearm training. The simplest is the barbell or dumbell wrist curl. Sit down on a flat bench and rest your forearms, palms up, on the end of the bench. Slowly curl the barbell toward your forearm by flexing at the wrist.

Keep your forearm flat on the bench at all times. For variety you can perform the exercise one arm at a time with a dumbell. Forearm curls primarily work the flexors of the forearm.

548. REVERSE WRIST CURLS

This exercise is great for working the extensors of the forearm. The movement is almost identical to wrist curls except that your palms are facing the floor. As the extensors are not as strong as the flexors, you'll need to use less weight.

549. REVERSE CURLS

This exercise is identical to standing barbell curls except you curl the bar upwards with your palms facing the floor. This movement is one of the best for working the brachialis (the muscle that lies underneath the biceps) and the brachioradialia (the muscle that links the upper and lower arms).

550. HAMMER CURLS

To really give the brachialis a good workout try hammer curls. Grab a pair of dumbells and, with the palms facing inward, curl them up as you would for a regular set of dumbell curls. For variety try doing the exercise on a cable pulley machine using the rope attachment. (Note: Your palms must face inward throughout the movement.)

SYMMETRY & PROPORTION

25

73

42

70

551. All about proportion

552. Uppers and lowers

553. Wide, wide, wide

554. The illusion of a small waist

555. Limit your oblique training

556. The lower calves

557. Closing the gap

14

551. ALL ABOUT PROPORTION

You may think that bodybuilding is nothing more than building the biggest set of arms, but this is simply not the case. When it comes to success in competitive bodybuilding, proportion is the name of the game. Contrary to popular belief, the biggest set of arms won't guarantee that you'll win. A great set of abs will place you as high if not higher on the winner's podium. Every couple of months, take a good look at your physique, paying close attention to proportion. Reduce the training volume on those muscles that seem to be growing fast, and increase your workload on those areas that are lagging behind.

552. UPPERS AND LOWERS

Besides the whole muscles themselves, parts of muscles may respond more quickly than other parts. For example, the upper thighs usually grow faster than the lower thighs. The upper abs tend to "come out" much more easily than the lower abs. Likewise, building the lower chest usually comes easy while filling in the upper chest takes extra work. As with overall body proportions, keep an eye on the sections of the individual muscles. Pick and choose your exercises to target both the upper and lower insertions of the muscles.

553. WIDE, WIDE, WIDE

Not everyone is born with naturally wide shoulders. In fact shoulder width has as much to do with bone structure as muscle mass. Some of the widest guys around never lifted a weight in their life. If you were not blessed with a wide shoulder structure, don't despair. Tailor your shoulder training so that your side delts receive the most work. A routine focusing heavily on side dumbell raises, cable side raises and upright rows will put inches on your shoulders and give you that yard-wide look.

554. THE ILLUSION OF A SMALL WAIST

Although most large midsections are the result of too many extra calories, there are a few unfortunates whose less-than-stellar midsections are the result of their genes. Even though these people will never have a 26-inch waist, they can create the illusion of a smaller midsection. As size is a relative term, the focus will be on trying to make the waist smaller by making the upper back wider. By adding extra size to the upper and outer lats, the waistline will start

looking smaller in comparison. If you fall into the large-midsection category, start including extra sets of wide pulldowns, chin-ups, and one-arm dumbell rows to your training.

555. LIMIT YOUR OBLIQUE TRAINING

Unless you are blessed with an ultra small waist, don't go overboard on your oblique training. Granted the

obliques don't have the same growth potential as most of the other muscles, but they are muscles just the same. Doing sides bends with heavy dumbells could cause them to grow, thus giving your waist a fat appearance. Limit your oblique training to bodyweight-only exercises, using higher-than-normal reps.

556. THE LOWER CALVES

They are called bodybuilding's diamonds and for good reason; they are just as valuable and just as elusive. They say great calves rely as much on inheritance as on hard training. There is an element of truth to this, as some of the biggest calves around belong to guys who never did a calf raise in their lives. One of the problems many people run into with calf training is that the upper calves quickly dominate the lowers. In many cases it's simply a case of not training the lower calves. But there are those who fall short in the genetic department and have what are called "high calves." This means that their calf muscles are attached high on the lower leg bones. While there is no way to lengthen the calf muscles, you can create the illusion of length by targeting the lower part of the calf (soleus). If you suffer from a high calf, or have been neglecting your lower calf training, begin your calf workouts with seated calf raises. This is the single best movement for developing the soleus.

557. CLOSING THE GAP

As most biceps exercises target the center and upper parts of the biceps, you may reach a point where there is a noticeable gap between the lower biceps and upper forearms. To fill in this gap, you need to do two things: work the lower biceps and develop the brachialis. The best exercise for targeting the lower biceps is the preacher curl, while hammer curls will do a wonderful job on the brachialis.

ROGER STEWART

INJURIES

558. Concentrate, concentrate, concentrate

559. More is not always better

560. Style vs weight

561. A warm muscle is a safe muscle

562. Avoid abs first thing in the morning

563. Stripping for injury prevention

564. Homemade is not always best

565. Check the machine

566. Change your footwear

567. You are what you eat

568. The right exercises for you

569. Modify when necessary

570. Watch the shoulder joint

571. Don't neglect the rear delts

572. Keep yourself charged

573. Listen to your body

574. RICE – more than just good eating

575. Bathroom first?

576. Acclimate to the environment

577. Bursitis – cold is best

578. Tendonitis – hot and cold

558. CONCENTRATE, CONCENTRATE, CONCENTRATE

One of the primary causes of injuries is a lack of concentration while performing your exercises. A set of squats or bench presses is not the appropriate time to be discussing or even thinking about your plans for Saturday night. One misplaced rep and you could end up in traction for six months. Always keep your mind on the task. When you bench press, for example, you develop a groove (a path the bar travels). If you get out of the groove for some reason, you risk serious injury.

559. MORE IS NOT ALWAYS BETTER

Sometimes we are our own worst enemies when it comes to training. The old philosophy of more is better may apply to many things in life, but it is not always the best approach when training. When your exercise volume exceeds your recovery abilities, a state of overtraining can occur. When this happens improvement not only ceases, but you may even lose muscle strength and size. If you suddenly start experiencing such side effects as weight loss, decreased strength, elevated resting heart rate, and a lack of motivation to train, take a week or two off and then reduce your training volume when you resume exercising.

560. STYLE VS WEIGHT

There's an old saying in bodybuilding that "strict style is king." This is especially true when it comes to injury prevention. Never sacrifice form just to place a few extra plates on the bar. If the muscle is ready for it, fine, increase the weight. But don't get caught up in a numbers game. Sloppy training style can cause long-lasting injury.

561. A WARM MUSCLE IS A SAFE MUSCLE

Few things contribute to injuries like subjecting a cold muscle to a sudden jolt of intense exercise. The human body is like a car in that it works more efficiently when it's warmed up. Before doing any heavy weight lifting, take five or ten minutes and do some light cardio to get the cardiovascular system primed. Then do a couple of light warm-up sets of each specific weight training exercise. Those ten minutes can prevent you a lifetime of suffering, and deal a severe blow to your training progress.

562. AVOID ABS FIRST THING IN THE MORNING

When you sleep, the intervertebral discs in your spine fill up with fluid. If you do any exercise that flexes the spine early in the morning, the vertebrae end up squeezing the discs, placing excess stress on them. As the day goes on the fluid drains away, allowing for greater flexibility of the spine. The bottom line is to leave your ab training until midday or evening.

563. STRIPPING FOR INJURY PREVENTION

One of easiest ways to warm up the muscles and prepare them for heavier lifting is by starting your workout wearing a heavy sweatshirt. Within the first couple of minutes of exercise you'll be sweating.

After 5 or 10 minutes, strip the sweatshirt off and finish your workout in a T-shirt or tank top.

564. HOMEMADE IS NOT ALWAYS BEST

While mom's homemade bread may put the supermarket brands to shame, the same is not always true for gym equipment. Unless the designer of the equipment is familiar with both human kinesiology and exercise technique, that homemade leg press may be a death trap. The average person has no idea of the stresses placed on machines and muscles during a typical workout. You can't just weld a few pieces of metal together and call it a leg press or Smith machine. Even if the equipment is solidly built, does it mimic the natural biomechanics of the human body? There is a good reason why equipment manufacturers spend millions of dollars designing their products. Very rarely can Johnny Bench Press duplicate this in his garage with a welding torch.

565. CHECK THE MACHINE

One of the reasons that the aviation industry is so safe is because pilots always do a walk-around before taking off. You should do the same before using any piece of gym equipment. Visually inspect the cables for fraying. Check all attachments for cracks. Make sure any adjustable seats, pads and benches lock properly.

566. CHANGE YOUR FOOTWEAR

Although the frequency may be different, you should treat your sneakers like socks – change them regularly. The lifespan for a sneaker (or cross trainer) that is used daily for weight training and cardio is about four or five months. After that they won't be giving you the support you need. Chuck them out and buy a new pair.

567. YOU ARE WHAT YOU EAT

A house or building is only as good as its foundation. The human body is in many respects similar. Despite the rantings of some so-called experts, most accept that intense exercise increases nutrient demands. All that muscle tissue you have broken down must be rebuilt. Likewise your immune system needs to be boosted to maintain your health during strenuous exercise. Nutrient intake must keep pace with your training or you'll never make gains. In addition, continuously subjecting your body to intense exercise without supplying the nutrients necessary for fuel and repair is only setting you up for an injury.

568. THE RIGHT EXERCISES FOR YOU

No matter how carefully you warm-up and how well you perform the exercises, there will be exercises that just don't feel right. For example squats, while probably being the best overall leg exercise, may place stress on the knees or lower back. If you find these areas starting to take the brunt of your squat workouts, either decrease the weight or eliminate the exercise completely. Don't keep enduring the pain just because "you are supposed to do squats." Another exercise that you may want to eliminate is barbell presses for the shoulders. In this case, the small rotator muscles of the shoulders may be damaged by repeated heavy presses. You have to weigh the benefits of a particular exercise with its potential for injury.

569. MODIFY WHEN NECESSARY

If you develop a slight injury and plan on working around it (check with your doctor first), try modifying your exercises. For example, if your rotator muscles are sore, try bending the elbows at 90 degrees when doing side raises. Likewise try doing a flye/press when training chest. Standard dumbell presses flyes can be difficult to perform when the shoulder joint is acting up. Many people find that by doing presses but with the hands rotated inwards to the flye position, the amount of stress on the shoulder joint is greatly reduced.

570. WATCH THE SHOULDER JOINT

Next to the lower back, the shoulder region is probably the most abused region of the body. This is especially true for weightlifters. All those heavy presses, both for the chest and shoulders, can play havoc with the shoulder joint. Always pay attention to  any warning signals your body may give with regards to your shoulder's health. As soon as there is any degree of inflammation, ease off the heavy pressing.

571. DON'T NEGLECT THE REAR DELTS

The rear delts are one of the most neglected muscle groups. This is because they are located behind the shoulder girdle and are not easily visible. Unfortunately, weak rear shoulders lead to a sloping forward of the shoulder. This changes the body's center of gravity, placing extra stress on the lower back. Even though the rear delts will receive indirect stimulation from most upper back exercises, you should include some direct rear shoulder exercises in your workouts – two of the best being reverse pec-deck flyes and bent-over lateral raises with dumbells.

572. KEEP YOURSELF CHARGED

Although cramping rarely leads to injuries, the possibility still exists. Most of the body's metabolic reactions are under the control of charged particles called electrolytes (biochemists call them ions). When water levels raise, and hence electrolyte levels drop, the various chemical reactions that influence muscle contraction may be impeded. One of the end results of this is cramping, but it can get much more serious. One way to combat this is to sip on a good electrolyte drink as you work out (the most popular is Gatorade).

573. LISTEN TO YOUR BODY

Very rarely will an injury pop up out of the blue. The body usually gives you warning signals. That slight lower back twinge on a set of squats is a warning not to put any more weight on the bar that day. Likewise if your shoulder is aching after you do bench presses, you may be developing bursitis. Always pay attention to any warning signals the body gives off. Failure to do so could set you back months, if not years.

574. RICE – MORE THAN JUST GOOD EATING

If you do develop a minor injury, follow the old First Aid standby of RICE. The acronym stands for Rest, Ice, Compression, and Elevation. Hopefully the words speak for themselves. First Rest the injured body part. Then apply Ice to keep swelling down. Compress the area to keep blood and fluids from accumulating. Finally, Elevate the limb to reduce pressure and fluid build-up.

575. BATHROOM FIRST?

Laugh if you may, but going to the washroom before working out could prevent injuries. Performing heavy squats or deadlifts on a full bladder will be both uncomfortable and potentially dangerous. Likewise, the less solid waste in your GI tract the less chance for cramping.

576. ACCLIMATE TO THE ENVIRONMENT

If you start training in a hotter environment, or your area experiences a sudden heat wave, modify your outdoor training accordingly. It takes the average person 10 to 14 days to acclimate (adapt to) to a hot environment. If necessary, reduce your workout volume by 25 to 50 percent.

577. BURSITIS – COLD IS BEST

A bursa is a small sack-like cavity that contains fluids to protect the joints from rubbing together. Regular exercise occasionally leads to inflammation of the bursa (called bursitis), particularly the bursa in the shoulder joint. Most experts suggest avoiding heat to treat bursitis as this could make the condition worse. Instead ice the area on a regular basis.

578. TENDONITIS – HOT AND COLD

Tendonitis is the inflammation of a tendon, which usually results from overuse of an area. One of the best treatments is to alternate ice for one minute with heat for five to seven minutes, twice a day. You should also eliminate or greatly reduce the exercises that involve that particular area.

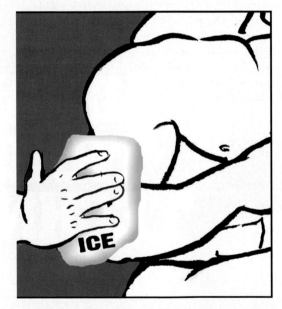

ONE OF THE BEST TREATMENTS FOR TENDONITIS IS TO ALTERNATE ICE FOR ONE MINUTE WITH HEAT FOR FIVE TO SEVEN MINUTES, TWICE A DAY.

ADVANCED
TRAINING
TECHNIQUES

579. Am I advanced?
580. Cheat reps
581. Cheat to make harder, not easier
582. When not to cheat
583. Good candidates for cheating
584. How many cheat reps?
585. Partial reps, or burns
586. Double-split routines
587. PHA Training
588. Dumbells only
589. Barbells only
590. Machines only
591. Bodyweight only
592. Freestyle
593. Ultraslow reps
594. Ultraslow – how slow?
595. Ultra-fast reps
596. Stripping
597. Down the rack
598. Race the clock
599. Triple-drop sets
600. You go, I go
601. Twenty-ones
602. Staggered sets
603. Negatives for positive results
604. Rest-pause
605. Pre-exhaust sets
606. Pre-exhaust for the shoulders
607. Pre-exhaust for the legs
608. Super growth with supersets

SUPERSETS FOR THE SAME MUSCLE
609. Thigh supersets
610. Hamstring supersets
611. Chest supersets
612. Back supersets
613. Shoulder supersets
614. Biceps supersets
615. Triceps supersets

616. Abdominal supersets
617. Calf supersets

SUPERSETS FOR OPPOSING MUSCLES
618. Quads and hamstrings
619. Chest and back
620. Biceps and triceps
621. Midsection
622. Trisets

TRISET COMBINATIONS
623. Thighs
624. Chest
625. Back
626. Shoulders
627. Biceps
628. Triceps
629. Abdominals
630. Calves
631. Giant gains with giant sets
632. Extended sets
633. Extend your chest
634. Extending your back
635. Extending the shoulders
636. Extending the biceps
637. Ten sets of ten
638. Not every set!
639. Four to six is best

16

579. AM I ADVANCED?

As much as we'd like to advise you when to proceed to the advanced level of training, realistically we can't. Everyone progresses at his or her own rate. Most people are ready for more advanced training after about a year of exercise. By this point you'll find that even by changing the exercises and splitting your workouts, your gains have slowed down. To address this situation you'll need to start applying various advanced training techniques to shock your muscles into new growth.

580. CHEAT REPS

Despite their name, cheat reps are one of the simplest ways to shock muscles into new growth. Even though most sports regard cheating as nothing but negative, controlled cheating does have a place in bodybuilding. At its simplest level cheating means using additional muscles to assist the primary muscles complete a set. For example when doing barbells, if you fail at the 8th rep but want to complete 10 reps,

you'd add just a little bit of body momentum to "swing" the weight up. However, it is important that you only start "cheating" after you have completed 7 or 8 strict reps. In so doing you will involve more cells and pave the way for bigger muscles.

581. CHEAT TO MAKE HARDER, NOT EASIER

If you perform your cheat reps in proper style, the muscle will ache more, not less. The purpose of cheating is to stimulate the muscle fibers with greater intensity, not less. If you are cheating just to lift more weight, or get the set over more rapidly, you are defeating the purpose.

582. WHEN NOT TO CHEAT

Some exercises by their very nature are not good candidates for cheating. Bouncing the barbell off the chest while doing bench presses is a great way to damage your rib cage. Barbell and T-bar rows are also

TROY TATE

poor candidates for cheating, given the vulnerability of the lower back to injury. Bouncing on preacher curls is a definite no-no. Numerous bodybuilders have ripped biceps tendons this way. As for squats, the amount of weight you'll be using makes the exercise an extremely dangerous one for cheating. Avoid bouncing out of the low squat position. Other exercises that you should avoid cheating on are stiff-leg deadlifts, seated rows, and seated barbell presses.

583. GOOD CANDIDATES FOR CHEATING

Despite the dangers of cheating on some exercises, others lend themselves perfectly to cheating. With the exception of preacher curls, virtually all biceps exercises are great candidates for cheating. All it takes is a little body momentum to get those couple of extra reps. You'll need to be a bit more creative with triceps exercises, but you can use your back muscles on most triceps exercises to do a few cheat reps. You can easily use your arms to push on your thighs when doing leg presses. Likewise you can use your thighs to help you cheat out a few extra standing calf raises. You've probably "learned" to cheat on most abdominal exercises by now. Most people cheat on ab exercises from day one by swinging the arms forward or rocking the pelvis. Try to leave such cheating for the last couple of reps.

584. HOW MANY CHEAT REPS?

This is the most frequently asked question about cheat reps. Some bodybuilders cheat from rep one, others have never done a cheat rep in their lives. Our suggestion is to pick a weight that enables you to complete 8 to 10 strict reps, and then cheat for a couple of extra reps. We should add that your cheating should be limited to a slight assistance from other muscles. When you reach the point at which you have to sway, bounce, and swing your whole body just to keep the weight moving, it's time to stop!

585. PARTIAL REPS, OR BURNS

This advanced technique was popularized by California bodybuilding guru, *Vince Gironda*. Burns are nothing more than a couple of partial reps performed at the end of a regular set. Let's say you manage to complete 10 reps on the barbell curl. While you may not be able to complete a full 11th rep, you can probably lower the bar halfway and return it to the top. The name burn comes to how the muscle will start feeling after you complete a few partial reps. Burns can be performed for just about every exercise. Be wary, however, of doing them on exercises where collapsing could place you at risk of serious injury (squats, bench presses, etc).

VINCE GIRONDA

586. DOUBLE-SPLIT ROUTINES

Once you reach a certain size and strength, you'll discover that you can place tremendous demands on your energy reserves. Ten reps with 300 pounds on the bench press will take a lot more out of you than those 100-pound sets a few years ago. By the time you get to the second muscle group in your workout it will be difficult to do it justice. One way around this is with a split routine. Train one muscle earlier in the day, and then come back later and hit a different muscle group. Instead of one long (60 to 90 minutes) workout, you perform two, shorter (30 to 45 minute) routines.

587. PHA TRAINING

PHA, or Peripheral Heart Action training was invented by 1966's Mr. America Bob Gajda. It is a great precontest advanced training technique, as it helps keep the blood circulating throughout the entire body. This burns more calories per unit of time as well as speeding up the removal of the waste byproducts of exercise. For maximum effectiveness, alternate a lower-body exercise with an upper-body movement.

588. DUMBELLS ONLY

One of the nice things about dumbells is that they force both sides of the body to do an equal amount of work. Machines (and even barbells to some extent) often let the stronger side dominate. Dumbells are also easy to get at the gym during crowded times of the day. Try the following dumbell-only exercises: dumbell rows, incline dumbell curls, seated shoulder presses, concentration curls, across-bench pullovers, triceps extensions.

589. BARBELLS ONLY

Most of the biggest and strongest guys in the world got their start working with nothing but barbells.

When it comes to building maximum strength and size, barbells are as good as it gets. Spend a couple of months doing nothing but squats, bench presses, deadlifts, curls, shoulder presses, lying triceps extensions and barbell rows, and see what happens.

590. MACHINES ONLY

We'll be the first to admit that dumbells and barbells will do more for your size and strength than other pieces of training equipment. But machines have their place. They are especially effective when you have a slight injury you need to train around. Machines are also a great way to give the joints a rest from the regular pounding of free weights.

591. BODYWEIGHT ONLY

Sometimes the simplest way to improve your size and strength is by getting back to basics – way back to basics! Before barbells and dumbells made their appearance, people got in shape by using their bodyweight. Take a look at the physiques from the old Muscle Beach days (1930s, 1940s, and 1950s). Take a couple of weeks and do nothing but chin-ups, dips, push-ups, and crunches. Not only will you be giving the joints a rest, your workouts will be quicker because there will be no waiting around for equipment.

592. FREESTYLE

As the name implies, freestyle training involves training whichever muscle you feel needs it on any given day. You may be scheduled to do legs, but perhaps the legs are still not recovered from the previous leg workout. Conversely your chest or back may be fully charged and ready to go. Keep in mind you have to be in tune with your body to train freestyle. It's easy to skip the muscles you hate training (which are usually your weaker muscles) and hit your favorite muscle groups. Don't use freestyle training to satisfy your laziness.

593. ULTRASLOW REPS

Although the time varies, most bodybuilders take four to six seconds to perform one rep. Using an ultraslow training pace, however, has a number of advantages. For starters it all but eliminates the body momentum that often accompanies faster rep paces. Another advantage is safety. Most injuries are the result of sudden stops or starts, either of which can rip ligaments or tendons. It is for this reason that slow tempos are great for training around injuries or resuming training after an injury. A slower pace also forces you to concentrate. Try lowering a light weight over 10 seconds or more. It's virtually impossible to let your mind drift.

594. ULTRASLOW – HOW SLOW?

There is no dividing line between normal-speed and ultraslow training. Most experts recommend taking at least 20 seconds to complete each rep. This works out to 10 seconds each for both raising and lowering. Experiment with different rep schemes. Also keep in mind that you won't be able to use near the weight that you can on your regular speed sets. Start with about 50 percent and don't be surprised if you have to drop it back to 25 or 30 percent.

LEE APPERSON

595. ULTRA-FAST REPS

Ultra-fast reps received their biggest boost from '60s bodybuilding superstar Leroy Colbert, the first man to develop 20-inch arms. In their simplest form ultra-fast reps are done using the heaviest weight and fastest speed possible. Now this doesn't mean bouncing the weight around in a haphazard manner. It means using good technique to perform the reps as quickly as possible. Some people call it racing the clock. Ultra-fast reps have two primary advantages: they allow you to perform more reps in a given period of time, thus completing your workout quickly, and they allow you to handle more weight than you could if using a conventional rep speed (four to six seconds per rep).

596. STRIPPING

Stripping is an advanced training technique that is both easy to learn and very effective. Let's say you are using 200 pounds on the bench press for a maximum of 10 reps. You may not be able to complete an 11th rep with the 200 pounds, but in all probability you could perform a couple of more reps with 150 or even 175 pounds. As soon as you complete your last possible rep with 200 pounds, have a training partner strip (remove) 20 or 30 pounds from the bar and then continue on for a couple of additional reps. Obviously the same weight has to be taken from either side.

597. DOWN THE RACK

Stripping is not limited to barbells. You can do the same thing with dumbells. If you are using say, 30-pound dumbells for side raises, complete the given number of reps and then place them back on the rack and grab a set of 25s. Squeeze out as many as you can manage (probably in the 3 to 5 range) and then grab the 15s or 20s. Again see how many reps you can complete. You can probably see where the name comes from. You are literally working your way "down the rack" towards the lighter dumbells.

598. RACE THE CLOCK

To really bring focus back to your workouts, try doing the same number of sets in a shorter period of time. Or try doing more sets in the same time period. Either way you will be forced to cut down on gym-chatter and other workout-wasting distractions. This is a great way of increasing intensity. Adding more weight to the bar is another form of increasing intensity.

599. TRIPLE-DROP SETS

Triple-drop sets are one of MuscleMag International publisher Robert Kennedy's favorite techniques. They are excellent for hitting the different muscle fiber types. Start with a weight that will allow you to just squeeze out 12 to 15 reps. Without stopping, grab a heavier weight that only allows you to perform 4 or 5 hard reps. Next grab a weight that allows for 8 to 10 more reps. Finally finish of with a set of 15 to 20 reps. For convenience triple-drop sets work best with machines or dumbells, but they can be employed with a barbell or if you have a couple of willing workout partners.

600. YOU GO, I GO

Nothing fancy here. One of you does a set of an exercise and then passes the bar or dumbells to the other. There is no rest in between. You go, I go works great with simple exercises like barbell curls where both of you are using the same weight. The technique is also great for friendly competitions as the both of you can try to outdo the other in the number of reps you complete.

601. TWENTY-ONES

This technique is most suited for curling movements. The name comes from the number of reps performed during the set. To do a set of 21s, select a weight about half what you would normally use for a set of barbell curls. Start by curling the bar from the thighs to about midpoint (forearms parallel to floor). Complete 7 reps. Then, without stopping, curl the bar all the way up and lower only to the midpoint. When 7 additional reps have been performed, try to force out 7 full reps. It will take a bit of experimenting to figure out a weight that will enable you to just complete 21 reps. We should add that 21 is a somewhat arbitrary number. You could do 18s (3 x 6) or 24s (3 x 8).

602. STAGGERED SETS

When you find that some of your smaller muscles (side shoulders, calves, forearms) start lagging behind, you may want to begin performing extra sets for them. One way to do this is to do the extra sets while you are resting between sets when training the bigger muscles. For example, while taking your break between bench presses, throw in a set of calf raises. Likewise, you could do a set of forearm curls between sets of squats. When performing staggered sets keep in mind that there are combinations that won't work well together. Doing forearms between sets of back or chest will interfere with your gripping strength. Staggered sets for calves may throw your leg workouts off. Make sure the muscles for which you are performing extra work don't interfere with the primary muscles being trained.

603. NEGATIVES FOR POSITIVE RESULTS

Numerous bodies of research have demonstrated that the lowering, or negative, part of the rep is just as effective as, if not more effective than, the raising (positive) part of the rep. A workout with a high percentage of negative reps will leave your muscles aching more than a workout consisting solely of positive reps will. On many exercises you will need a training partner to assist you in performing negative reps. Load the bar with slightly more weight than you can lift. Have your training partner help you lift it. Then lower it without assistance in a slow and controlled manner. You can even try stopping the bar's downward motion. Once you reach the bottom, have your training partner assist you in hoisting the bar back up. On an exercise like barbell curls you can be your own spotter. Just use body momentum to help you raise the bar back to the top position. Note: warm up well before attempting negative reps.

604. REST-PAUSE

The rest-pause technique is based on the physiological fact that a muscle will usually regain about 90 percent of its strength in 10 to 20 seconds. Select a barbell (machine, or dumbells) that will allow you to perform only one rep in positive style. After completing one rep, place the weight back on the rack. Slowly count to 10, then do another rep. Alternate these ten-second, one-rep sequences until you have completed one set of 8 to 10 reps. As with most advanced training techniques you will probably need to reduce your weight from what you would normally use for straight sets.

605. PRE-EXHAUST SETS

I invented the pre-exhaust system in the late 1960s. Pre-exhaust is one way to get around the "weak link in the chain" that brings premature failure to many exercises. For example, on bench presses the smaller triceps often give out before the larger chest muscles. To get around this, first perform an isolation exercise like dumbell flyes, which places little stress on the triceps. This will "pre-exhaust" the chest. Because the chest has already been worked, by the time you do bench presses the triceps are no longer the weaker muscle and can push the chest muscles to failure.

606. PRE-EXHAUST FOR THE SHOULDERS

The small triceps muscle gives out first on most shoulder press exercises just as with most pressing movements for the chest. Instead of starting with presses, tire the shoulders out first with an isolation exercise such as side lateral raises. Now perform a set of dumbell or barbell presses. Your still-strong triceps can push the shoulders to complete failure.

607. PRE-EXHAUST FOR THE LEGS

If you find that your lower back gives out before your legs while you do squats, try pre-exhausting the thighs with leg extensions. Leg extensions place little or no stress on the lower back, so when you get back under the bar for squats, the thighs will be the "weak link," so to speak.

608. SUPER GROWTH WITH SUPERSETS

If you're stuck for time or just want to really shock a muscle, try supersets. Supersets involve performing two exercises back to back with no rest period between sets. You can do them for the same muscle group or opposing muscles.

SUPERSETS FOR THE SAME MUSCLE

609. THIGH SUPERSETS

To really blast the thighs, try supersetting leg extensions and leg presses, or leg extensions and squats. If you are in a particularly masochistic mood, try a superset of leg presses and squats. You may have trouble walking out of the gym but you'll be quickly on your way to building two pillars of power.

610. HAMSTRING SUPERSETS

For many people, doing straight sets for the hamstrings is boring. You can easily jazz it up by supersetting lying leg curls with stiff-leg deadlifts, standing leg curls with stiff-leg deadlifts, or lying leg curls with standing leg curls.

611. CHEST SUPERSETS

With dozens of chest exercises to choose from, the number of superset combinations is almost endless. You can pre-exhaust the chest with flat flyes and then do barbell presses. You can superset exercises for the upper and lower chest; or combine free-weight (barbells and dumbells) with machine exercises. Many bodybuilders find supersetting resistance exercises with body-weight exercises very effective for the chest. Try doing a set of barbell or dumbell presses followed by a set of dips or pushups.

612. BACK SUPERSETS

Back training is similar to chest training in that you have two primary categories of exercises, those that create width and those that create thickness (for chest it would be upper and lower). You can do supersets to concentrate on width (chins followed by pulldowns) or supersets for thickness (seated rows followed by barbell or T-bar rows). Or you can perform superset combinations that target both the outer (width) and center (thickness) back.

613. SHOULDER SUPERSETS

With three separate heads to the shoulders (front, side, and rear), there is a virtual endless number of superset combinations to work the shoulders. The side raise/dumbell press superset is the most common, but front raises and side raises also work well together. You can also alternate rear delts with front or side delts. If you want to target the front delts, superset front raises and dumbell presses. A great side delt superset would be side lateral raises and narrow upright rows. Finally to target the rear delts, try reverse pec-decks with bent-over lateral raises.

614. BICEPS SUPERSETS

With biceps exercises falling into three categories (barbell, dumbell, and cable), try to alternate exercises from any two of the three categories. A basic mass superset would be barbell curls followed by dumbell curls. An excellent upper/lower superset would be preacher curls followed by incline curls (or vice versa). To really fill in the gap between the upper and lower biceps try hammer curls superset with preacher curls.

615. TRICEPS SUPERSETS

As with all muscles, try to select your triceps exercises to hit the entire muscle. Pushdowns followed by two-arm extensions are a great combo for bringing out the muscle's horseshoe look.

A basic mass and strength superset would be lying EZ-bar extensions followed by bench dips.

616. ABDOMINAL SUPERSETS

Ab training is similar to chest training in that you can target both the upper and lower sections of the muscle. Probably the most effective abdominal superset would be crunches followed by reverse crunches. You can substitute leg raises for the reverse crunches if you wish. A great upper ab superset would be crunches followed by Swiss ball crunches. To blast the lower abs try reverse crunches followed by hanging leg raises or leg raises from the floor.

617. CALF SUPERSETS

The four primary calf exercises are standing calf raises, toe presses on the leg press, donkey calf raises, and seated calf raises. To target the upper calves, select any two of the first three. If you want to bring in the lower calves do the seated calf raise and one of the first three.

SUPERSETS FOR OPPOSING MUSCLES

618. QUADS AND HAMSTRINGS

If you want to reduce your legs to quivering masses of jelly try supersetting lying leg curls with squats or stiff-leg deadlifts with leg presses. For speed, as most gyms have the two machines next to one another, try supersetting lying leg curls with leg extensions.

619. CHEST AND BACK

Two of bodybuilding's all-time greats, Arnold Schwarzenegger and Sergio Oliva, often supersetted chest with back. The combination king in this case would be chin-ups followed by flat barbell presses (or vice versa). Other popular chest/back supersets are flat dumbell presses and front pulldowns, incline flyes and rows, and chin-ups and dips (many gyms have the dip/chin-up bar combo machine).

620. BICEPS AND TRICEPS

Nothing feels as good as having both the triceps and biceps pumped full of blood at the same time, and the best way to do this would be to perform supersets for both muscles. Try alternating standing barbell curls with lying barbell extensions (skull crushers), incline curls with two-arm dumbell extensions, or pushdowns with cable curls.

621. MIDSECTION

Since the abdominals and spinal erectors (lower back) work opposite to one another, they make a great superset combination. Crunches alternated with back extensions will do wonders for the midsection core. Reverse crunches superset with stiff-leg deadlifts are

another great combination. You can even superset Roman chair sit-ups with lying leg raises on the same chair (just flip over and lie back on the decline pad).

622. TRISETS

Trisets are an extension of supersets. As the name suggests, you group three exercises together and perform them in a row. Trisets are a great way to shock a muscle that has plateaued and needs a good wake-up call. If trisets have a disadvantage it's that they may be difficult to perform in crowded gyms. As soon as you leave a machine someone else jumps on it. For this reason try to limit your triset training to barbells and dumbells, or come in when the gym is less crowded (mornings, midday, and late evenings).

TRISET COMBINATIONS

623. THIGHS

The most effective triset combination for the legs is squats, leg presses, and leg extensions. A great free-weight triset for the thighs would be squats, lunges, and split squats. If you like machines try leg presses, leg extensions, and hack squats.

624. CHEST

Popular trisets for the chest include flat dumbell presses, incline dumbell presses, and flat dumbell flyes; incline barbell presses, incline dumbell presses, and incline dumbell flyes; flat barbell presses, dips, and push-ups.

625. BACK

Trisets for the back can include all width or all thickness exercises, or combinations of both. For beefing up the back's thickness try barbell rows, seated rows, and T-bar rows. To bring out the back's V-shape try chin-ups, wide pulldowns, and reverse pulldowns. To work on both sections of the back during the same workout try chin-ups, reverse pulldowns, and T-bar rows.

626. SHOULDERS

To bring out all three heads of the shoulders try a triset consisting of front, side, and rear raises. To bring in the traps perform a triset of side raises, upright rows, and dumbell presses.

627. BICEPS

Because the biceps are small (and they get a good workout when you train back) you can easily overtrain them with too many intense sets of trisets. Do no more than one or two trisets per workout for the biceps. Popular trisets include barbell curls, dumbell curls, and cable curls; preacher curls, narrow-grip chin-ups, and hammer curls.

628. TRICEPS

Like the biceps the triceps are small and get a good workout when you train chest and shoulders, so limit your trisets to one or two sets. A great all-around triset is lying EZ-bar extensions, pushdowns, and bench dips. Another great triset is two-arm dumbell extensions, lying dumbell extensions, and narrow-grip push-ups.

629. ABDOMINALS

To jazz up your abdominal training try a triset of crunches, reverse crunches, and leg raises. If you want to bring out the lower abs try hanging leg raises, Roman chair sit-ups, and lying leg raises. If it's the upper abs you want to target try crunches, Rope crunches, and Swiss ball crunches.

630. CALVES

As with supersets you really only have standing calf raises, toe presses, donkey calf raises, and seated calf raises, to pick from for trisets. Remember if you want to directly target the lower calves, one of your three exercises should be the seated calf raise.

631. GIANT GAINS WITH GIANT SETS

If you are wondering whether you can perform more than three exercises for the same muscle in the superset fashion, the answer is yes. They are called giant sets and you'll need to do only one or two giant sets to shock the muscle into new growth. For smaller muscles like the biceps and triceps, one giant set is more than enough. Even though your goal is to keep the rest interval

between exercises to a minimum, you'll probably need to take a minute or so between the third and fourth exercises.

632. EXTENDED SETS

Extended sets are one of the best ways to push a muscle past the point of normal failure. As an example let's look at the triceps. After going to failure on a set of lying EZ-bar extensions (skullcrushers), bring the bar to the midpoint of the chest and start performing narrow presses. Even though you can't do additional reps in the lying extension, your still-fresh front shoulders and chest will allow you to "extend" the set with narrow presses. The key to extended sets is to first perform an isolation exercise and then follow it up with a compound movement.

633. EXTEND YOUR CHEST

One of the best extended-set combinations for chest is flat flyes and presses. Start off with an isolation exercise such as flat or incline flyes. When you tire, switch over to incline presses. You will be stronger in the pressing movement because you are using more of your front shoulders and triceps.

634. EXTENDING YOUR BACK

Two of the best back exercises for extended sets are wide and reverse pulldowns. After going to failure on the wide pulldowns, grab the bar with a reverse (shoulder width, palms facing upwards) grip and start doing narrow pulldowns. You'll still be working your back, but the narrow reverse grip will bring more of your biceps into play, allowing you to continue the set.

BINAIS BEGOVIC

635. EXTENDING THE SHOULDERS

To really give the shoulders a great workout, try a combination of side raises and dumbell presses. The isolation side raise exercise will fatigue your front shoulders, while the dumbell press will allow you to bring in your front shoulders and triceps, thus allowing you to extend the set. When you extend a set you bring more muscle cells into play and thus increase strength and muscle mass.

636. EXTENDING THE BICEPS

Although not as convenient a muscle as some others for doing extended sets, it can be done with a bit of creativity. Start with drag curls and then switch over to regular barbell curls. While not a pure isolation exercise, drag curls do have less front shoulder and forearm involvement than regular barbell curls. After going to failure on drag curls, you can extend the set with regular barbell curls for extra reps. Tom Platz extends his incline biceps curls by performing partial curls when he can no longer perform a complete curl.

637. TEN SETS OF TEN

This advanced technique was first popularized back in the 1940s and 1950s by bodybuilding legends Reg Park and Vince Gironda. It has made a comeback in recent years under the name "German volume training." Regardless of who invented it, the technique is one of the simplest yet effective ways to gain muscular size and strength. As the name suggests, you perform just one exercise for each muscle, trying to complete 10 sets of 10 reps. This technique has a number of advantages. For starters you need only one piece of equipment. No need to be waiting around for additional items in the gym. Second, because you are doing continuous sets of one exercise, you don't have to worry about cooling down between separate exercises. Finally, the technique is one of the best for

thoroughly fatiguing a muscle. When you do multiple exercises for one muscle you must warm up on each exercise. While these warm-ups are valuable, they do take time and effort away from your ultimate purpose of building muscle.

638. NOT EVERY SET!

Because of the nature of advanced training we strongly urge you to avoid doing advanced techniques on every set (the obvious exception being 10 sets of 10). Start by making your last set of the day an advanced set. Over time add one or two sets per workout.

639. FOUR TO SIX IS BEST

Besides limiting the number of advanced sets per workout, you should also limit the number of weeks that you are training at a high intensity level. The human body is like a car battery in that it needs to periodically recharge. Training all out, month after month, will probably leave you in a severe state of overtraining. Limit your advanced techniques to four to six weeks' duration.

OVERCOMING STICKING POINTS

640. Re-evaluate your diet
641. Protein – the true bodybuilder
642. Cycling for success
643. Change the order
644. If it doesn't work – don't do it!
645. Get rid of them!
646. Prioritize
647. Asymmetric training
648. One side fits all
649. When one side doesn't fit all
650. One more rep or one extra plate
651. Specific sticking
652. Unsticking the calves
653. Calf priority
654. Hamstring priority
655. Thicker bars for thicker forearms
656. The overworked biceps and triceps
657. Change it up
658. Try a different angle
659. The big three
660. Try a different gym!
661. Hit the woods!
662. Vary the reps
663. Change the tempo
664. Hi-Lo training
665. One muscle per workout
666. One rep per set
667. Staggered workouts
668. Every-other day training
669. Making new progress by not training
670. Avoid negative thoughts
671. A change of clothes
672. Read everything
673. Instinctive training – the most advanced technique

17

640. RE-EVALUATE YOUR DIET

Many times the reason for your lack of progress doesn't lie with your training. The late Vince Gironda said bodybuilding is at least 80 percent diet. While some may argue with Vince's number, most accept that lousy eating habits will derail your progress just as fast as haphazard training. If you're following the typical North American diet of burgers, fries, and cheesecake, you might as well give up training right now. Before you make any adjustments to your training, get your nutrition house in order. Odds are you'll start seeing progress within a very short period of time.

641. PROTEIN – THE TRUE BODYBUILDER

It stands to reason that since muscles are primarily composed of protein, any activity that stimulates muscle growth will place increased protein demands on the body. If you are not consuming adequate amounts of protein your training progress will come to a halt. Although there is much debate over exact figures, the consensus seems to be that athletes engaged in strength sports (bodybuilding, weightlifting, football) need between .75 and 1 gram of protein per pound of bodyweight. Do a quick check of your daily protein intake and see where you stand. Overcoming that sticking point may be just a few grams of protein away.

642. CYCLING FOR SUCCESS

The human body has remarkable powers of adaptability. The soreness you experience following a new exercise quickly disappears after a few workouts. To keep progressing with your workouts you need to keep the body guessing. One of the best ways to do this is by cycling your workouts. Try alternating six to eight weeks of high-intensity training with an equal period of medium-intensity training. Every two months or so, throw in a couple of weeks of low-intensity training. You'll keep making progress by cycling your training intensities in this manner.

643. CHANGE THE ORDER

Another simple way to shock the muscles is by switching around the exercises in your training program. You can switch the muscle group order, exercise order, or a combination of both. The beauty of this shocking technique is that it's simple and doesn't require you to learn any new exercise. Surprise the muscles in any way and they will keep growing.

644. IF IT DOESN'T WORK – DON'T DO IT!

Someone once said that it makes no sense performing the same action and expecting a different outcome. The same holds true for training. It doesn't make sense to keep doing the same workout with the same weights, month after month (in many cases year after year), and hoping that someday it will pay off though you get no results. If after a couple of months your size and strength levels haven't improved, scrap the routine and try something different.

645. GET RID OF THEM!

If changing your entire training routine sounds too drastic, at least get rid of some of your exercises. You can combine muscles in the same way and perform a similar number of sets and reps, but get rid of the exercises you've been doing for the past few months (or years!) and select a whole new bunch.

646. PRIORITIZE

While the odds of all your muscles stalling at once are slim, chances are you'll notice a couple of stragglers. When this happens the first order of business is to rearrange your training schedule. Odds are the muscles lagging behind are the ones you train later in your workouts. To bring them up to scratch you have to prioritize. To do this, start your workouts with your weaker muscles. This way you'll be able to use your full energy to train them properly rather than going through the motions later in the workout.

647. ASYMMETRIC TRAINING

In this fast-paced world of ours it seems the goal with every venture is to rush through it as quickly as possible. In the gym setting this often translates into training both sides of the body at the same time. There is nothing wrong with this, as many of the best exercises (squats, bench presses, chin-ups) are performed this way. Still, training one side at a time (called asymmetric or unilateral training) does have a role to play. First of all, you can hit both sides with equal intensity. With barbell and machine exercises, the stronger side tends to do a little more of the work. Another benefit is that you can concentrate better when you train each side separately. You don't have to split your focus between two sides. Finally, neurophysiologists tell us that the brain has to "split" the nerve impulse when you train both sides at the same time.

648. ONE SIDE FITS ALL

Although there are too many exercises to list, here are some suggestions for asymmetric training to help you overcome sticking points:

Biceps:	One-arm cable curls
	One-arm dumbell curls
	Concentration curls
Triceps:	Dumbell kickbacks
	One-arm extensions
	One-arm pushdowns
Shoulders:	Front dumbell raises
	Side dumbell raises
	Cable raises (front or side)
Calves:	Dumbell calf raises
	One-leg standing calf raises on machine
	One-leg seated calf raises
	One-leg toe presses
Hamstrings:	One-leg lying leg curls
	One-leg standing leg curls
Back:	Dumbell rows
	One-arm pulldowns
Quads:	One-leg extension
	One-leg leg press
Chest:	One-arm pec deck
	One-arm cable crossover

649. WHEN ONE SIDE DOESN'T FIT ALL

Even though just about every exercise you can think of can be performed asymmetrically, there are a few you should probably avoid. For obvious reasons don't try one-legged squats. The torque placed on the knees and lower back is just too great – not to mention that you may have a hard time balancing. The same goes for deadlifts, especially stiff-leg deadlifts. Most chest exercises are difficult to perform asymmetrically because of stability issues.

650. ONE MORE REP OR ONE EXTRA PLATE

A simple way to shock the muscles is simply to push yourself a little harder each workout. Try to do one extra rep with the same weight you used in the previous workout, or try to get the same number of reps with a slight increase in weight. Either technique will increase the intensity level of your training. Unless you have a phenomenal memory, make sure to record everything in a journal. *(To order the No Pain - No Gain Training Journal call toll free: 1-888-254-0767)*

651. SPECIFIC STICKING

At some point you may find that your overall progress is going fine, but in one or two exercises you don't have the same degree of strength throughout the full range of motion. A classical example is the bench press. Many people find that they have what's called a "sticking point" at some point in the exercise – usually just short of locking out. One way to correct this is by using the power cage. Set the cross bars an inch or two below your sticking point. You now perform reps that specifically work the point that is giving you difficulty. You'll also be able to use heavier weight, as you are not performing a full range of motion.

652. UNSTICKING THE CALVES

Unless you are one of the few lucky individuals blessed with great calf-building genes, you'll have to be very creative to keep your calves growing. One way to do this is by varying your foot stance. Keeping your feet slightly less than shoulder width apart forces you to rise up on the outside of your feet, thus targeting more of the outer head of the calves. Conversely, a wide stance forces you to rise up on the big toe, shifting more of the stress to the inner calves. Try alternating both stances in the same workout.

653. CALF PRIORITY

If you are like most bodybuilders you probably leave your calves till last in your workout. A few half-hearted sets and you're out the door. Is it any wonder your calves are slow to respond? If you want to bring your calves up to the level of the rest of your body, train them first in your workout. Calf training doesn't require much energy and won't interfere with training your other muscle groups.

654. HAMSTRING PRIORITY

As the calves play a role in leg curl exercises for the hamstrings, you want to minimize them as much as possible. The way to do this is by pointing your toes. When your toes are pointed toward the shin the calves play a major role. But point the foot away from the lower leg and it's almost all hamstrings.

655. THICKER BARS FOR THICKER FOREARMS

The forearms can be considered the calves of the upper arms. Not only are they painful to train, they can be stubborn. Some bodybuilders find that their forearms grow just by training the other muscle groups. Others find that they need to attack the forearms head on with direct exercises. An easy way to indirectly train the forearms is to use a thicker bar when you train the other muscle groups. Olympic bars come in varying sizes, and using a thicker bar forces the forearms to contract harder to hold on to. Two of the best exercises for using a thicker bar are barbell curls and deadlifts.

656. THE OVERWORKED BICEPS AND TRICEPS

Probably the two most overtrained muscle groups in the body are the biceps and the triceps. Chest and shoulder training brings in the triceps while the biceps are heavily involved in most back exercises. If you find that one or both of these muscle groups are not responding, try working them on separate days from the other muscles. Also, you don't want to work biceps the day before or after back, or triceps the day before or after chest.

657. CHANGE IT UP

One of the most effective ways to wake up stubborn muscles is by changing your grip, or attachment on the machine. For example, while most people regularly perform wide-grip pulldowns, few experiment with other attachments. You can use the double-D normally used on the seated row. Or you can use a shorter bar with the hand grips facing inwards. You can even use the single handle normally found on the cable crossover machine. The same approach can be used on the seated row. Instead of using the v-bar attachment, try one of the longer bars and pull it to the mid-chest rather than the lower ribcage.

658. TRY A DIFFERENT ANGLE

Sometimes shocking a muscle into new growth can be measured in degrees. Instead of performing your barbell or dumbell presses on a flat bench (180 degrees), try inclining it just 5 or 10 degrees. Likewise, if you normally use a 30-degree angle for inclines, drop it to 20 or 25 or increase it to 35 or 40. To really spice things up, try changing the angle on every set. Start completely flat and work your way up to 45-degrees in 5 degree-increments.

659. THE BIG THREE

Sometimes the key to breaking out of a training rut is simplicity. Take a month or two and do nothing but squats, deadlifts, and bench presses. These three basic, compound movements will work the entire body as well as allow you to let your ego run wild. You can either perform all three on the same day for an average of 6 to 8 sets each, or take three days a week and do them separately. Concentrate on using as much weight as possible on each lift. We can almost bet that your training rut will quickly be a thing of the past.

660. TRY A DIFFERENT GYM!

Even though it's one of the more expensive options for breaking out of a training rut, the results are worth it. Switching gyms will give you access to new equipment and a new atmosphere. A month's membership at most gyms costs about $50, but it may be the best $50 you ever invested.

661. HIT THE WOODS!

Those of you who read Arnold Schwarzenegger's "Education of a Bodybuilder" will recall how he and a few of his buddies would load up the car with weights and go into the woods and train. The combination of fresh air and "back to nature" feel can do wonders for muscles that are used to the staleness of a gym environment. Don't have access to woods? Set up a bench in your back yard.

662. VARY THE REPS

Another easy way to shock a muscle into new growth is by changing your rep scheme. No doubt you've probably been following one of the classic 6-to-8 or 10-to-12 rep schemes. Try doing high reps (15 to 20) with light weight, or low reps (4 to 6) with heavy weight. Presto! Your sticking point is history.

663. CHANGE THE TEMPO

If you're like most bodybuilders you're probably following a 2-0-2 tempo (two seconds to raise, no pause, two seconds to lower). Like most training techniques, the muscles quickly adapt to rep tempo. Try changing your tempo. Instead of a 2-0-2, try a 3-1-3 tempo. Not only are you adding a pause to the set, you are raising and lowering in a slower manner, which will stress your muscles differently. There are an almost infinite number of tempos. Experiment to see which one shocks your muscles into new growth.

664. HI-LO TRAINING

To both shock the muscles and to lessen the stress on your recovery system and joints, try alternating a high-rep/low-weight day with a low-rep/heavy-weight day. This type of training also ensures that both major muscle fiber types are hit. The heavy weight/low reps will stimulate the fast-twitch muscle fibers, while the light weight/high reps will target the slow-twitch muscle.

665. ONE MUSCLE PER WORKOUT

Shock a stubborn muscle by giving it your undivided attention. Instead of hitting a couple of muscle groups during the same work out, devote your entire workout to just one muscle. Not only do you not have to split your focus, but you'll have the time and energy to hit the muscle from every conceivable angle. Another advantage is that the blood (pump) will stay in your targeted area. It won't be stolen away when you go to work another muscle group.

666. ONE REP PER SET

Although we don't really advocate one-rep-per-set training, sometimes it can be just what the weight doctor ordered. Shocking a muscle out of a rut can require drastic measures. If you decide to go the one-rep-per-set route, make sure your technique is impeccable. Your muscles are not used to the heavy weight and the slightest deviation from proper form could cause an injury. Stay in the groove. In addition, be sure to warm up your muscle thoroughly before attempting a 1RM weight.

667. STAGGERED WORKOUTS

A few individuals may have to take drastic steps to shock their systems out of a training rut. For some inexplicable reason their bodies adapt to workouts on an almost daily basis. One way to combat this is by staggering workouts. You literally perform a completely different set of exercises during every workout. No two workouts are the same. The muscles are always kept guessing as to what you're going to hit them with next. Television's Incredible Hulk, Lou Ferrigno, frequently made use of this training principle.

668. EVERY-OTHER DAY TRAINING

This technique was made famous by the late Mike Mentzer. Even though you may be training different muscle groups on consecutive days, you are still stressing the recovery system. One way to get around this is by taking a day off after every workout. This way the body is fully recharged before you subject it to another grueling workout.

669. MAKING NEW PROGRESS BY NOT TRAINING

Contrary to popular belief your muscles don't grow in the gym when you train, they grow after you leave. Even those with remarkable powers of recovery will find training year-in, year-out to be draining. One of the primary reasons for a cessation of progress is overtraining – never allowing the body to fully recover. This is especially true for advanced bodybuilders, as their strength levels allow them to place incredible demands on their recovery systems. Even though it probably goes against your training philosophy, take a couple of weeks off each year and do absolutely nothing. You'll find your enthusiasm level will go through the roof, all those nagging little aches and pains will disappear, and most of all, you'll make some of the best progress of your life when you get back to training. You may find yourself stronger by your first workout back, but if not, it'll come soon after.

670. AVOID NEGATIVE THOUGHTS

Sometimes the easiest way to overcome sticking points is to simply believe that you can. Try to avoid negative thoughts. Don't get into the mindset where you always look at things as being hopeless. Remember, you decide whether you can or can't do something. Change your attitude and surprise the world with your new advancement.

671. A CHANGE OF CLOTHES

In many respects wearing new clothes symbolizes a new beginning. As physical stagnation is often related to following the exact same daily routine, try a simple change of workout clothes. If you're like most people, you've been cycling the same couple of pairs of workout duds week after week. A new set of workout clothes will not only make you feel better, but other gym members will notice and compliment you. That can only make your workouts better.

672. READ EVERYTHING

Buying this book was a start, but there are others. The most successful bodybuilders are generally the ones who read the most about training and nutrition. Try to buy at least one bodybuilding magazine a month to keep up on the most recent training tips, supplements, and eating plans. There is a wealth of information out there just waiting to be tapped. Take advantage of it.

673. INSTINCTIVE TRAINING – THE MOST ADVANCED TECHNIQUE

When you start bodybuilding it's important to follow an organized program. Read books and magazines, and never be afraid to ask someone for advice. Eventually, however, you'll reach a point where you are more in tune with your body. You'll know its strengths and weaknesses. You'll have discovered what works and what doesn't. In short, you will have developed an instinct for training. Instinctive training allows you much more room for creativity. You can modify your routine as the situation, and the feeling of your body, dictates. Don't use instinctive training until you are quite advanced as a bodybuilder, and don't use it as an excuse for being lazy. You will only hurt yourself.

COMING BACK
AFTER A LAYOFF

674. The first one

675. What to wear

676. Comeback sets, reps, and duration

18

674. THE FIRST ONE

Perhaps no workout is as important as the first one following a layoff. The problems usually arise when you rush back into the gym and try to pick up where you left off. At the very least you'll be too sore to move the next day. Often, however the end result is a serious injury. If it took years to condition the body to rep with hundreds of pounds, what makes you think you can do it all the first workout back? Start out with a simple, one-exercise-per-muscle-group program, using a moderate weight – say about 50 percent of where you left off. Your goal at this stage is to ease safely back into training, not set records.

676. COMEBACK SETS, REPS, AND DURATION

You may have been doing 10+ sets per bodypart at one time, but trust us, your system won't be able to handle such a training volume the first couple of workouts back. Start out by doing 1 or 2 sets per muscle group, for about 12 to 15 reps per set. Even if your strength levels haven't dropped that much, resist the urge to pile the plates on the bar. Keep the weight light to moderate. Stick with this simple routine for about two weeks. By the third week add an extra set. Only after you have about a month of regular training under your belt should you consider split routines and multiple exercises per bodypart.

TITO RAYMOND

675. WHAT TO WEAR

If you normally trained in a T-shirt and shorts, try switching to a sweatshirt and track pants. The extra clothing will keep the muscles warm and also keep you from getting depressed about your appearance. Odds are you haven't physically lost any muscularity, but most people assume they have, and so hate to look in the mirror. After a few weeks of regular training you can switch back to your regular training outfit.

RELAXATION & RECOVERY

677. Rest

678. The all important 48 to 72

679. Recognition - the first step in stress management

680. Lunchtime

681. Massage

682. Stroking to perfecting

683. Kneading you

684. Friction

685. Chopping

686. Vibration

687. For lactic acid removal

688. Massage – the don'ts

689. Exercise - the endorphin boosters

690. A cure for insomnia?

677. REST

The Greeks are believed to have been the first to discover that if a sick person were allowed to rest, he or she would recover faster. Bodybuilders often forget that a good night's rest is just as important as regularly doing squats or bench presses. Subjecting your body to an intense one or two-hour workout and then staying out all night drinking and partying won't do your muscle-building strategy any favors. We are not suggesting that you abandon your social life, but you must give your body time to recover. Why do babies spend so much time sleeping and resting? It's because their bodies are in a rapid stage of growth. If you plan on growing, try to obtain at least seven hours of rest on most nights of the week, and more if you can. The occasional late night/early morning is fine, but don't make it a habit.

> BODYBUILDERS OFTEN FORGET THAT A GOOD **NIGHT'S REST** IS JUST AS **IMPORTANT** AS REGULARLY DOING **SQUATS OR BENCH PRESSES.**

KEVIN ASHER

678. THE ALL IMPORTANT 48 TO 72

The same applies to bodybuilding. You need to give the muscles at least 48 to 72 hours of rest between workouts for adequate recovery. In fact as you get stronger you'll find that 72 hours will probably be the bare minimum that you'll need between workouts. For a large muscle group like legs, chest, or back, you may need a full four to five days between workouts.

679. RECOGNITION – THE FIRST STEP IN STRESS MANAGEMENT

The rigors of modern daily life have added a new term to 21st-century vocabulary – stress! Stress can take many physical and psychological forms; and left untreated can lead to severe health problems. The first step in combating stress is to determine the source of the stress. Is it school, work, money problems, or your home environment? The next step is to face the problem head on and find solutions. If no solutions exist (or are impractical at the moment), you must learn coping strategies.

680. LUNCHTIME

If you're like most people, your job is a source of stress. One of the easiest ways to reduce work-related stress is to fit in a 20-minute workout over lunchtime. This helps you forget the rigors of the morning and puts you in a better mindset for the afternoon. The fact that it will burn off a few extra calories is an added bonus! Exercise is the best stress reliever.

681. MASSAGE

The Chinese were the first to use massage as a serious form of relaxation. Unfortunately in Western society massage has been tied to the sex industry. This is too bad, as massage is one of the best techniques for relaxing the mind and as an athletic recovery aid.

Check out the yellow pages of your phone book, or ask around for the nearest legitimate massage clinic. Look for a RMT, or registered massage therapist, as opposed to a "relaxing massage." One of the keys to your bodybuilding success could be just a rub away!

682. STROKING TO PERFECTING

Stroking is one of the easiest massage techniques to learn. It is performed with the fingers or thumbs on small areas and with the full hand on large areas. It is applied superficially while stroking toward the heart. This action assists venous blood flow and lymph circulation. Stroking is the primary technique used to get the patient accustomed to the physical contact of the massage therapist. It is composed of light gliding movements over the skin with little attempt to manipulate the deeper tissues. Stroking is commonly used at the beginning of a massage session.

683. KNEADING YOU

Kneading is a form of massage whereby the therapist massages the muscles in a deep, firm, clockwise circular motion, or in a straight back-and-forth movement across the muscle. Connective tissues and muscles are gently squeezed and rolled by the fingers in a milking action. This technique is more forceful and deeper than stroking. One form of kneading involves rolling a cylinder across the muscles.

684. FRICTION

In this massage technique the edge of the hand, fingers, thumbs, or palms is used in a back-and-forth motion over the top of the skin. This is deep-penetrating technique used to relieve trigger points, which are localized areas of tenderness within the muscle.

685. CHOPPING

As the name suggests, this massage technique involves an alternate chopping-type movement. Chopping is used in situations where relaxation is not the desired effect, such as before an athletic event or training session. We should note that the fulcrum of the movement is at the wrist rather than the elbow or shoulder, because striking the patient too hard could be painful and cause injury.

686. VIBRATION

Vibration involves making the hands or fingers tremble to create a firm rapid shaking of deep tissue. This technique is one of the most difficult to master. A variation of this technique is to rest the part of the body that is being massaged in a bath of water that is being vigorously circulated. The best examples of this include whirlpool baths, hot tubs, Jacuzzis, and small portable foot baths.

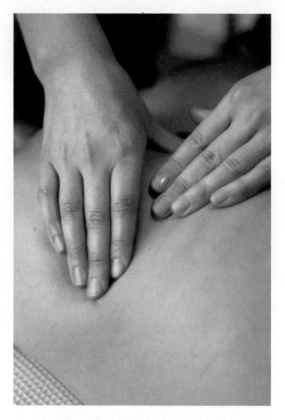

687. FOR LACTIC ACID REMOVAL

For effective removal of lactic acid following a workout, two sessions of massage are recommended. The first session removes the lactic acid from the muscles. The second session helps remove the lactic acid from the body (after it diffuses from the muscles into the bloodstream). The product GAKIC is designed to reduce lactic acid and other metabolic byproducts so that rep-failure is delayed to a proven 10.5 percent.

NEVER PERFORM **MASSAGE** ON SOMEONE WITH A **SEVERE INJURY.** INJURIES REQUIRE THE ATTENTION OF **SPECIALISTS.**

688. MASSAGE – THE DON'TS

Like all beneficial techniques, massage can be detrimental if used in the wrong situations. Never perform massage on yourself or someone else if either one of you is battling a severe flu. A good massage is like vigorous workout and when ill the body needs rest. Never perform massage after donating blood. The body needs time to bring its fluid levels back up to normal. Finally, never perform massage on someone with a severe injury. Injuries require the attention of specialists. Unless you are a licensed massage practitioner, leave the injured alone!

689. EXERCISE - THE ENDORPHIN BOOSTER

They are called natural opiates, and are believed to be one of the primary reasons that some people get addicted to exercise. Endorphins are biochemicals that block pain receptors and produce feelings of relaxation and euphoria. Numerous studies have shown that those people who engage in regular exercise are much less prone to anxiety attacks and depression. So if you are regularly stressed out from work or life, try a quick 15-to-20 minute bout of exercise to pump up your endorphin levels!

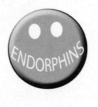

690. A CURE FOR INSOMNIA?

One of the natural therapies being experimented with for curing insomnia is exercise. Exercise helps to relax the sympathetic nervous system, and the endorphin rush helps reduce anxiety and induce sleep. If you regularly suffer from insomnia or even the occasional bout of sleeplessness, try performing your workouts in the evening. In studies, the best results are achieved when the exercise session is performed about two to three hours before bed.

RICKY MARCONI

BODYBUILDING
ON THE ROAD

691. Creativity on the road
692. Hotel gyms – a sign of the times
693. The traveling road kit
694. Sissy squats
695. Chair lunges
696. Limbo squats
697. The uppers with one-leg calf raise
698. The lowers with squat-down calf raises
699. Pushups – that old chest standby
700. Dips between chairs
701. Dips between chairs with feet elevated
702. Pushups with the legs elevated
703. Chins between chairs
704. Chest expander rows
705. Side raises to the front, side, and rear
706. Chest expander laterals
707. Chest-expander upright rows
708. Chest-expander curls
709. Crunches
710. Lying leg raises
711. Reverse crunches

691. CREATIVITY ON THE ROAD

It's a fact that people travel around more now than at any time in history. Modern transportation methods mean vast distances can be covered in short periods of time. For the average Joe or Jill, this causes no major inconveniences, but for the aspiring bodybuilder, frequent travel can cause havoc. Don't despair, however, as most cities have gyms that will allow you to work out for $5 to $10. If all else fails you can bring a few simple weight-training items with you, at least a couple of dumbells, and perform a couple of bodyweight exercises. There is no need to abandon your training simply because you are away from your regular workout place.

692. HOTEL GYMS – A SIGN OF THE TIMES

In the competitive world of travel and lodging, it's not surprising that many hotels cater to fitness enthusiasts these days by offering workout facilities. Even some of the smaller hotels and motels will have a few weights and a couple of pieces of cardio equipment. Go online to check out the hotels in the city you're traveling to, or pick up a travel or tourism guide before you go. All the hotels will be listed as well as the facilities offered by each. If you are dedicated to your workouts, it's worth the few extra dollars to book with a hotel that has a gym.

693. THE TRAVELING ROAD KIT

If your job requires extensive traveling you may want to invest in a few items that will enable you to work out on the road. No need to spend big bucks, either. A chest-expander set (strands) can be bought for as little as $15 to $20. A piece of one- or two-inch dowel will cost about $5. There are even telescopic bars available for a few dollars more. If you do most of your traveling by car you can add a set of adjustable dumbells and a small flat bench to your workout kit.

694. SISSY SQUATS

Although the average hotel room doesn't have a squat rack, there is no reason to miss leg day. Grab a doorway or door handle with one outstretched arm, and, with your torso leaning slightly backwards, squat down until your thighs are parallel with the floor. Slowly return to the starting position. If your legs are used to squatting hundreds of pounds on regular squats, then sissy squats with your bodyweight may seem light. But try 3 or 4 sets of 20 to 30 reps and see how your thighs feel.

695. CHAIR LUNGES

Most hotel rooms have a chair. Place one foot on the chair, and with the other leg kept straight, lunge forward until you feel a comfortable stretch. Perform 15 to 20 reps and then switch legs. Try to make sure the knee of the working leg doesn't go out over your toes.

696. LIMBO SQUATS

Open the bathroom door and grab both sides of the doorframe with your hands. Lean as far back as possible, and squat down until your thighs are parallel with the floor. This exercise is very similar to sissy squats, but by holding on with two hands you can isolate the thighs better. If you perform 3 to 4 sets of this exercise, not only will your thighs be howling, but it will do wonders for your limbo dancing later that night!

697. THE UPPERS WITH ONE-LEG CALF RAISE

All you need for this is a two to three-inch object to stand on. If you're in a city the phone book will do. If not you may want to bring along a short piece of two-by-four. Place the book or wood in the middle of a doorway. With one hand holding the door or doorway for support, stand on the object with one foot. Bend the nonworking leg up to your butt and hold your foot with your free hand. From here perform 15 to 20 reps (or more) of standing calf raises. Switch legs.

698. THE LOWERS WITH SQUAT-DOWN CALF RAISES

As the previous tip primarily works the upper calves, you need to also do something for the lower calves. Using your trusty phone book or block of wood, stand on the edge with both feet, heels hanging out over the edge. Squat down until your thighs are parallel with the floor. From here start doing calf raises as if you were using the seated calf raise machine. When you reach the point that you can do 30 reps nonstop, try performing the exercise one leg at a time.

699. PUSHUPS – THAT OLD CHEST STANDBY

Pushups have probably been done for thousands of years. To this day they are a core exercise of military and athletic conditioning. You can think of them as reverse bench presses. Instead of the bar moving away from your stationary body, your body moves away from the stationary floor. To isolate the chest more, keep the hands wider than shoulder width apart. To bring more of the triceps into play, position the hands about 10 to 12 inches apart. For a great all-around chest, triceps, and shoulder workout, place the hands shoulder-width apart. Perform 3 to 4 sets to failure.

700. DIPS BETWEEN CHAIRS

Place two chairs about shoulder width apart. With your body face down, your feet on the ground and hands placed firmly on the chair seats, slowly lower your body between them. Because of the angle that your arms are in relation to your torso, dips between chairs primarily work the lower, outer chest. To make this movement harder you can elevate your feet on a third chair.

701. DIPS BETWEEN CHAIRS WITH FEET ELEVATED

If you want to target the triceps, place the heels of your feet on the side or end of the bed (or a third chair) and your hands on the other two chairs (Your body is face up).Please make sure the chairs are stable! Slowly lower your body down between the chairs to a comfortable stretch. This exercise is a pure triceps exercise.

702. PUSHUPS WITH THE LEGS ELEVATED

Position your body so that the feet are on a chair (the edge of the bed will do). With the hands resting on the floor, perform the exercise like a standard pushup. Because of the angle of the arms with respect to the torso (about 120 degrees) most of the stress is placed on the upper chest. In effect you are doing an incline bench press. In addition, because of gravity forcing the weight of your body downward, you are actually working against greater resistance.

703. CHINS BETWEEN CHAIRS

The lats are probably the hardest muscles to work without specialized equipment. If you have a sturdy broomstick, doweling or metal pipe you can do a variation of the chin-up. Position two chairs about four feet apart and place the stick across the seats. Obviously this will not work if the broomstick slides around – be sure it's very secure, stable, and strong. Lie face up on the floor between the two chairs and grab the stick as close to the chair seats as possible (not only is this the most effective width for working the lats, there is less chance the stick will break.). Pull yourself upward until your chin is about an inch from the bar. Slowly lower back down to just short of the floor. Although we are calling this exercise a chin-up,

it's really more of a rowing movement because your arms are being pulled towards the body at about 90 degrees rather than the 180 degrees of a standard chin-up.

704. CHEST-EXPANDER ROWS

You'll need one of those portable chest expander spring sets (strands) to do this one (the most popular consist of four or five 2-foot springs attached to handles on both ends). Anchor one end of the springs at the floor. Try lifting up one leg of the bed and slipping it through the handle. Stand at arm's length from the attached handle, and grab the other handle with both hands. Slowly pull to your mid-chest. Make sure you keep your legs slightly bent. You can also do this exercise with one hand, similar to a one-arm dumbell row.

705. SIDE RAISES TO THE FRONT, SIDE, AND REAR

Grab two large books or small suitcases and slowly raise them to the front, side, or rear (lean forward for this one). If you have access to only one book or suitcase, perform the exercise one side at a time. Grab a door or some other stationary upright for support.

706. CHEST-EXPANDER LATERALS

Once again you'll need your trusty chest expander. (Ironically the most awkward muscle group to work with this apparatus is the chest) Secure one handle to the floor (under the leg of the bed or under your foot) and raise the other handle to the front or side. You'll probably need to use only one or two springs for this exercise.

707. CHEST-EXPANDER UPRIGHT ROWS

If you want to bring your traps into your on-the-road shoulder training, try upright rows. Anchor one end of the springs to the floor (hold under your foot or a bed leg) and pull the other handle up the center of the body with both hands. As you are pulling upwards, let the elbows flare out to the sides and then pull them behind your shoulders.

708. CHEST-EXPANDER CURLS

With one handle anchored, curl the other one upwards in a curl motion. For variety you can perform the exercise either with both the anchored handle and working arm on the same side or on opposite sides.

709. CRUNCHES

You don't need fancy equipment to do crunches in the gym, and the hotel room is no different. Lie down on the floor with your knees bent and feet flat on the ground. Perform the exercise as if you were back in the gym. To make the exercise more difficult, try elevating your feet (resting them on a bench or chair) For variety twist to the sides as you lift upwards (this brings the obliques into play).

710. LYING LEG RAISES

Again nothing fancy here. Lie on your back, and with a slight bend at the knees, slowly lift your legs upwards until they form about a 45-degree angle with the floor. Slowly lower until your feet are a few inches from the floor.

711. REVERSE CRUNCHES

Adopt the same position as with a leg raise, but instead of lifting the legs upwards, draw your knees back towards your chest. Try to keep your lower legs parallel with the floor as you move your legs back and forth. This is an excellent lower ab exercise.

CIRCUIT
TRAINING

712. Strength and cardio in one

713. When lighter is better

714. Don't get caught up in the numbers

715. Compound your circuit

716. Rotate your circuit

717. Up, down, all around

718. When not to circuit train

21

712. STRENGTH AND CARDIO IN ONE

Although other types of training are better for pure strength and size, circuit training does have one big selling point – it's a great way to stimulate both your muscular and cardiovascular systems all in one workout. Instead of doing multiple sets for one muscle and then moving on, you perform one set per body part in a circuit. If you keep your pace up you'll also raise your heart rate to the target heart rate zone. A 30-minute circuit will provide nearly the same cardiovascular benefits as 30 minutes on a cardio machine, and the body will continue to burn calories even at rest.

713. WHEN LIGHTER IS BETTER

You may be capable of hoisting some pretty mean weight on your regular exercises, but you'll have to scale it back when circuit training. Doing a set of exercises in a circuit will tax you more than doing straight sets with a minute or two in between each set. Start out with about 50 percent of the weight you'd normally use and go from there. In fact, you may have to lower the poundages down to 25 or 30 percent of what you'd normally use.

714. DON'T GET CAUGHT UP IN THE NUMBERS

When you first start out circuit training, only perform one exercise per bodypart. If you split the legs into three muscles (thighs, hamstrings, calves), the torso into three muscles (chest, back, shoulders), the arms into two (biceps and triceps), and the abs into upper and lower, that means a total of 10 exercises. Start out by doing two circuits, and over a few weeks bring it up to three or four circuits.

715. COMPOUND YOUR CIRCUIT

When selecting your exercises, choose compound rather than isolation movements. For example, squats, deadlifts, and bench presses will make you breathe much harder than such isolation exercises as kickbacks, leg extensions, and concentration curls. Compound movements will also stimulate more of your body musculature than isolation exercises.

716. ROTATE YOUR CIRCUIT

Circuit training is no different than regular training in that the body will adapt to the movements. Every three or four weeks rotate the exercises to keep shocking the body. The variety will keep your muscles growing.

717. UP, DOWN, ALL AROUND

Although you may develop your own order of preference, it's best to alternate an upper body exercise with a lower body movement. This not only stimulates the cardiovascular system to the maximum, but also contributes to venous blood return to the heart.

718. WHEN NOT TO CIRCUIT TRAIN

For obvious reasons, circuit training is difficult to do in a crowded gym. The odds that you'll be able to do 10 or more exercises in a row without interruption are slim to nonexistent. As most gyms are crowded between 4:30 and 8:30 pm, we suggest coming in much earlier or later in the day. You may even have to leave your circuit training until the weekend.

COMPOUND MOVEMENTS WILL ALSO **STIMULATE** MORE OF **YOUR BODY** MUSCULATURE THAN ISOLATION EXERCISES.

STEPHEN D'ANGELO

COMPETITIVE BODYBUILDING

719. You're still a winner in our eyes
720. Don't procrastinate!
721. Don't compare yourself to Ronnie, Jay or Arnold

WHY COMPETE

722. Improved progress
723. Competition builds knowledge
724. Bringing out the best
725. It's safe

YOUR FIRST CONTEST

726. Watch the first one
727. What to look for
728. Which contest?
729. Open or closed?
730. And for teens
731. Which federation?
732. Which weight class?
733. How will I be scored?
734. Is the scoring fair?

719. YOU'RE STILL A WINNER IN OUR EYES

Even if you never decide to compete in a bodybuilding contest you're a winner. Most people don't even go for a daily walk, much less commit to a regular cardio and weight training program. You've probably done more for your physical health in the last year than the next 100 people will in their entire lives. So pat yourself on the back. We sure will!

720. DON'T PROCRASTINATE!

If you've been working out for a few years and have developed a physique that garners rave reviews, then give competitive bodybuilding a try. Don't be one of those guys you see in the gym who sports as much muscle as some of the pro bodybuilders but constantly says, "No, I'll wait till next year." Guess what? Next year becomes the next five or ten years, and before they know it their best competitive years are behind them. Don't procrastinate! It's a shame when you see guys in the audience sporting physiques that could have won the show they were watching.

721. DON'T COMPARE YOURSELF TO RONNIE, JAY OR ARNOLD

If you wait until you look like Mr. Olympia you'll never compete. These guys are one in a million. Take the great physique you have right now and compare it to the other guys in your gym. If you think you are as good, if not better, chances are you're ready for your first contest. Have photos taken so you can really analyze your physique.

WHY COMPETE

722. IMPROVED PROGRESS

One of the biggest reasons for competing is that it will help you make better progress. Competitive bodybuilding forces you to improve your eating, get stricter on your technique, and modify your exercise program, all of which are great for breaking people out of a training rut.

723. COMPETITION BUILDS KNOWLEDGE

Pre-contest bodybuilding is quite different from off-season training. When you decide to engage in a bodybuilding contest you'll have to increase your knowledge base tremendously. It's a fact that those who compete regularly are more knowledgeable about training and nutrition than those who just dabble in non-competitive bodybuilding.

724. BRINGING OUT THE BEST

There is nothing like preparing for a bodybuilding contest to bring out the best in someone. A fifth-place finish this year will motivate you to train harder and place first next year. Take it on and force your progress into the fast lane.

725. IT'S SAFE

Despite the occasional report of a bodybuilder collapsing because of dehydration (usually brought on by diuretic abuse), bodybuilding is virtually 100 percent safe. Unlike such sports as wrestling, judo, and boxing, where inadequate preparation can put you in hospital, the only thing that may get bruised in a bodybuilding contest is your ego!

YOUR FIRST CONTEST

726. WATCH THE FIRST ONE

Although many people go into their first contest cold turkey, we advise you to make your first contest a spectator event. Pick a local show and attend both the pre-judging and evening show. It's much more relaxing sitting in the audience than standing onstage. Once you have a general idea what's involved, start preparing for next year!

727. WHAT TO LOOK FOR

While sitting in the audience at your first show, sit back and observe "the big picture." Watch the judges. Which competitors do they call out the most? What seems to impress them the most? What music seems to get the judges' and audience's attention? Make mental notes of everything you observe at both the pre-judging and evening show.

728. WHICH CONTEST?

Bodybuilding contests are organized like most major sporting events these days. You start at the provincial or state level (big cities also have city championships) and then work your way up to the regionals, nationals, and finally the world championships. If you win your weight class at the world championships you receive your pro card. This means you can enter pro bodybuilding shows. In other words, you don't start at the national level. You must win or place high in a lower level show.

729. OPEN OR CLOSED?

Once you decide on which contest to enter, check to see if it is open or closed. A closed show means you

BERRY DEMEY

COMPETITIVE BODYBUILDING

must live in a certain geographic area to enter. Open shows are open to anyone, regardless of residency.

730. AND FOR TEENS

Most shows offer a teenage division. To compete in such shows you must be 19 or younger.

731. WHICH FEDERATION?

Throughout the history of competitive bodybuilding, a number of different federations have emerged to govern the sport. The largest is the International Federation of Bodybuilders (IFBB), but there are others. You have to decide early in your career which federation you want to become associated with, as competing in one federation usually gets you banned from the others.

732. WHICH WEIGHT CLASS?

Most contests are broken down into weight divisions. Such an arrangement makes the contest more equitable for shorter and smaller bodybuilders. The strategy employed by most bodybuilders is to compete at the top of the weight class. Keep in mind that you'll make a bigger impact on the judges as a ripped middleweight than smooth light heavyweight.

The five primary weight classes are:
Lightweight – under 154 pounds
Middleweight – 155 to 176 pounds
Light-heavyweight – 177 to 198 pound
Heavyweight – 199 to 219 pounds
Super-heavyweight – over 220 pounds

733. HOW WILL I BE SCORED?

Ask the average person on the street and he'll tell you the guy with the biggest muscles will win. But that's not how it works. Muscle size is but one aspect that the judges will award you points for. They'll also scrutinize you on symmetry (how your right and left sides compare to one another), muscle proportion, shape, definition (how lean you appear), and posing. While you don't have to be the best in every characteristic, you'll definitely need to score high in all of them to win.

734. IS THE SCORING FAIR?

The judges at most contests are like the bodybuilders themselves; they are working their way up the competitive hierarchy. By the time they reach the national level, the judges have years of experience under their belts. Many are former bodybuilders themselves, so they know what the contestants are going through and do their utmost to be fair. To guard against bias, the highest and lowest score are usually eliminated at the end of each round.

THE FOUR
ROUNDS

735. Round 1 is number 1

736. When relaxed is not relaxed

737. From the front, side & rear

738. Can I pick my best side?

739. The seven wonders of Round 2

740. Front double biceps

741. Back double biceps

742. Side chest

743. Side triceps

744. Front lat spread

745. Rear lat spread

746. Abdominal and thigh

747. Not too hard

748. Smile!

749. Do the twist

750. Lean into it

751. Reading the judges

752. Round 3 – room to be free

753. Posing – how long?

23

THE FOUR ROUNDS

735. ROUND 1 IS NUMBER 1

Although it's the most basic round, it is where you make the first impression on the judges. You can win or lose the contest in the first couple of minutes if you let your mind wander. This is especially true if the contestants are equally balanced. From the moment you step onstage until you exit, try to keep focused, and keep your body tight. At any given instant one of the judges may be looking at you.

736. WHEN RELAXED IS NOT RELAXED

Although it's called the relaxed round, you are never actually relaxed. Always keep your muscles contracted and your stomach tight. Practice doing this. Depending on the number of competitors you may be out onstage for 15 to 20 minutes … or more.

737. FROM THE FRONT, SIDE & REAR

The four "poses" that make up Round 1 are the front, left side, rear, and right side, relaxed poses. As soon as you take your position onstage, tense your abs and lats to highlight your waist-back differential. To bring the calves out, try pushing on the floor with your heels and the balls of your feet. When you turn to the side, make sure your triceps, chest, quads and hamstrings are flexed.

738. CAN I PICK MY BEST SIDE?

No! During Round 1 you'll be asked to display both your left and right sides to the judges. This may seem redundant, but few bodybuilders are perfectly symmetrical. Odds are that one bodypart will be less developed on one side. In the vast majority of cases the difference is negligible, but in a few cases it stands out. The judges want to see if this is the case.

739. THE SEVEN WONDERS OF ROUND 2

Round 2 is where you get to show the judges how you stack up against your opponents. It's cold and clinical, but it's probably the round that does the most to rank the competitors. There are seven mandatory poses that have been adopted over the years because they show the judges the entire body. Any weaknesses will quickly be highlighted. Make sure you have these seven mastered before you step onstage.

740. FRONT DOUBLE BICEPS

The front double biceps is the most familiar pose to bodybuilders and non-bodybuilders alike. Besides showing the biceps, it highlights the legs, lats, and triceps. In fact, other than the central back and hamstrings, every major muscle group in the body is exposed. If you are one of the biggest competitors in the contest (you'll quickly discover where you stack up at the pre-judging), hit this pose straight on. By this we mean everything is square. This will show the judges your size advantage over the other competitors. If you can't match the mass of some of the larger contestants, bend one knee slightly and add a slight twist to your torso. This will emphasize your proportion.

741. BACK DOUBLE BICEPS

As with the front version of this pose, the back double biceps displays just about every muscle in the body. Besides your arms, make sure your lats, legs, and shoulders are fully flexed. As with the front version, hit the pose square or with a slight twist, depending on your size and proportion.

742. SIDE CHEST

Arnold Schwarzenegger used to dwarf most other competitors with this pose. Nowadays guys like Ronnie Coleman and Jay Cutler reign supreme. Besides the chest, this pose highlights the arms and legs. To bring out the striations and muscularity in the arms, clasp your hands and push them together. Likewise, bend the knee of the leg closest to the judges and rise up on the toes to flex the calf. Doing this also shows the development of your hamstrings and quads. If you have one of the largest chests in your weight class, keep your entire body straight up and down. If you are giving size away to other competitors, tilt your torso slightly towards the judges and keep your hands further away from the body. This will put the emphasis on your muscularity (hopefully!) and proportion.

743. SIDE TRICEPS

This pose is similar to the side chest in that you set the legs in the same position. Lock the arm closest to the judges in the down position. Reach behind your back with the other hand and grab your hand or wrist. Keep your abs tight and slowly twist your torso back and forth to give all the judges the same angle of view.

744. FRONT LAT SPREAD

Set your feet shoulder width apart and pointing slightly outwards (so you have a V-stance). With your thumbs on the side of your lower ribcage, slowly push your elbows and shoulders forward. Pull your waist in and keep your abs tight.

745. REAR LAT SPREAD

Set your feet shoulder width apart and pointing slightly outwards. Start the pose by squeezing the shoulder blades together, then slowly spread them outwards. If you want to see perhaps the greatest rear lat spread of all time, rent the documentary Pumping Iron and watch Franco Columbu.

746. ABDOMINAL AND THIGH

Although some of the other poses get more attention, it's the thigh and abdominal pose that really displays your shape and proportion. You may be ripped over the rest of your physique, but it's the abdominal region that will show how lean you really are. Display a solid set of six-pack abs to the judges and you're on your way up in your placing. Likewise, show great leg development and people will realize you pay attention to both your upper and lower body. Place both hands behind the head. With one leg extended forward, exhale all the air from your lungs and flex your abs. Make sure you are flexing your thighs just as hard as your abs.

747. NOT TOO HARD

The key to successful posing is to flex hard enough to bring out all the striations and ridges without cramping up. This is why you must practice holding poses weeks, if not months, in advance. Another reason not to overdo it on flexing is that the muscles (and you!) will start shaking. You don't want to step onstage and start looking like an overgrown jackhammer!

748. SMILE!

Despite the agony that you'll go through while posing, try to maintain a smile at all times. Posing is just as grueling as an intense workout, but you have to make it appear effortless. All things being equal (size, shape, definition), a smiling competitor will garner more points than a grimacing one.

749. DO THE TWIST

Because the judges will be sitting in a line, they'll all have a slightly different angle of view. Slowly twist (or pan) your body and look each judge in the eye as you do so. It would be a shame to lose a contest simply because of a bad view!

750. LEAN INTO IT

Because the judges are sitting below you, their angle of view is compromised to begin with. Don't make the mistake of many bodybuilders and lean backwards. This will only give the judges great view of your nostrils and armpits. It makes more sense to lean slightly forward to highlight your physique to its greatest advantage. You'll need to practice this. Posing while leaning slightly forward is not as easy as you may think.

CHRIS CORMIER

751. READING THE JUDGES

In most weight classes the top three will quickly stand out from the rest; and of the top three, odds are the winner will be easily determined. The judges usually call forward the top three bodybuilders for the first comparison. They then work their way down the line until virtually all the competitors in the class have been compared. If you find yourself called out early and frequently, there is a good chance you are near or at the top. If you don't get called out at all, you are not going to place.

752. ROUND 3 – ROOM TO BE FREE

It's called the free-posing round, and for good reason. This is the stage in the contest where you get to let your physique and personality shine. You may have been a "bump" on the log during the first two rounds, but now you get to stand on your own. Your goal in Round 3 is to highlight your best features and minimize your weak points. Make sure to use music to your advantage in this round.

753. POSING – HOW LONG?

Most bodybuilding federations limit posing routines to 90 to 120 seconds. This means you have less than two minutes to prove to the judges that you have the best physique on the stage that day. If your body is lean and your posing crisp, you will impress the judges.

DESIGNING YOUR POSING ROUTINE

754. Music selection

755. You can't go wrong with upbeat

756. Don't let your music overshadow your physique

757. Turn on the radio

758. A splice of life

759. Splice with care

760. Two is good, three is better

761. How others do it

762. Photos don't lie

763. True friends don't lie, either!

764. Poetry in motion

765. Which poses?

766. Double up

767. Mirror mirror on the wall

768. Practice ALL the poses

769. Should I include the compulsories?

770. To dance!

771. More than one?

772. Round 4 – bodybuilding's free for all

773. Confrontation within reason

774. Pre-contest exercise

754. MUSIC SELECTION

The first step in putting together your posing routine is choosing your music. Pick your music so that it suits your physique. Large bodybuilders can get away with classical because they have overpowering physiques. Mind you, we're talking "Battle of the Valkyries" here, not Mozart. Most bodybuilders, however, will need to choose their music with caution. This is not the time to pose to an unknown piece of music.

755. YOU CAN'T GO WRONG WITH UPBEAT

All things being equal, the best music selection is something current (most audience members fall into the 20- to 40-year-old age group) and upbeat. Not only is upbeat dance music the best for hitting poses to, it has the added benefit of getting the audience involved. It won't take long before someone starts clapping and before you know it the whole audience is rooting for you. In a close contest such audience favoritism can sway the judges to your side (they are human after all).

756. DON'T LET YOUR MUSIC OVERSHADOW YOUR PHYSIQUE

One of the key points in choosing your music is that it should compliment your physique, not obscure it. Powerful music selections like the themes from Star Wars, 2001 A Space Odyssey, and even Rocky, can sometimes leave the audience and judges concentrating more on the music than your physique. Such things as laser blasts and computer-generated voices tend to be distracting.

757. TURN ON THE RADIO

If you have trouble choosing your posing music, try doing this as you're driving around in your car: picture yourself posing to the various songs on the radio. As the music goes up in tempo, visualize hitting a double-biceps pose. When the music goes down, crunch a most muscular pose. Before you know it, you'll have narrowed your song choices down.

758. A SPLICE OF LIFE

As you're deciding on your posing music, you'll discover that parts of some songs work, while other parts are awkward. In recent years many bodybuilders have taken advantage of this by splicing parts of different songs together. For example you could start with a slow piece, and then launch into an upbeat dance tempo. Match your poses to the music style. Start with graceful poses accompanied by the slow or classical music, and then combine your best muscular poses with the upbeat dance or rock music. Same bodybuilders alternate between graceful elegant poses and all out mass-muscle poses.

759. SPLICE WITH CARE

Nothing sounds as ridiculous as two or three songs spliced together in an amateurish fashion. If you decide to go this route, make sure the pieces flow together without the cuts being obvious. If you have the money, get a professional sound engineer to do the job for you. At least get a friend with a CD burner to help you out.

760. TWO IS GOOD, THREE IS BETTER

Once your CD is complete, make at least one, if not two, extra copies. CDs are easily lost. This is especially true backstage, as competitors have been known to "hide" the music of their competition. You also have the tape or CD players to think about. Play it safe. Bring two copies with you and have a spare in the car.

761. HOW OTHERS DO IT

One of the best ways to create a posing routine is by watching others. Unless you live in or near a large city, you'll probably get to see only one live bodybuilding contest a year. The next best thing is TV and videos or DVDs. In fact we encourage you to start a collection of bodybuilding contests. At least once a day watch one with paper and pen in hand. Pay close attention to the individual poses, and also to how the competitors move from one pose to another (called transition).

FRANK ZANE

762. PHOTOS DON'T LIE

A couple of months out from the contest, have a series of photos taken. Don't just shoot the compulsories, either. Photograph as many poses as possible, including the variations. Sort the poses into good (will use in the contest), fair (may use in the contest), and poor (not a chance you'll use). Remember, you have about 90 seconds to show your physique to the best of your ability. Use your time wisely.

763. TRUE FRIENDS DON'T LIE, EITHER!

Most bodybuilders see only their good points, and choose to ignore (or honestly don't see) their less-than-stellar bodyparts. This is where a couple of trusted friends come in. They can be brutally honest with you and tell you which poses to use and which to discard.

764. POETRY IN MOTION

While photos are great for evaluating individual poses, they don't show what you'll look like moving from one pose to another. If you have access to a video camera, tape your posing routine for evaluation. Besides the individual poses, pay close attention to how you move between poses. Do you appear awkward or graceful? Does it look stop/start, or can it be described as poetry in motion? The best bodybuilders flow almost effortlessly between poses.

765. WHICH POSES?

When selecting your poses remember you only have about 90 seconds to perform them. As it takes a few seconds to hold each pose and another few of seconds to move between them. You'll only have time for about 10 to 15 poses. Start with your second-best pose first to make a good impression. Likewise, conclude with your best pose to leave a lasting impression. Choose the middle poses to highlight your best points and minimize your weak points.

766. DOUBLE UP

If you are new to bodybuilding and your physique lacks the development to master 15 or 20 poses, double up on your best ones. Eight to ten good poses performed twice (in different sequences and from a slightly different angle if possible) will get you more points than adding poses that make your physique look mediocre.

767. MIRROR MIRROR ON THE WALL

As soon as you start putting your posing routine together, arrange a couple of mirrors (the more the better) around your practice area. You want to be able to see all your muscles as you flex them. One of the reasons many bodybuilders have poor control over their back muscles is that they can't see them. They spend hours hitting chest and arm shots and then throw in a couple of back poses as an afterthought.

768. PRACTICE ALL THE POSES

We are sure by now there are poses that you have been hitting since your first day in the gym (the double biceps being the most common) and others you have never even heard of. Practice all the poses with equal determination. In fact you should practice the unfamiliar ones more, as they'll be the ones that need the most work.

769. SHOULD I INCLUDE THE COMPULSORIES?

There are two schools of thought on including the compulsories in your free posing. On one hand you've already done them in Round 2, so is there a need to do them again in Round 3? The other view is that since the compulsories are the best ones for showing your physique, you should include them in your free-posing routine. Our advice is to go by development. If the compulsories are in fact the ones you look best in, then use them frequently in your posing routine. On the other hand if these poses are less than flattering, try to limit them. Keep in mind, if you don't include any of them the judges will suspect you are trying to hide something!

770. TO DANCE!

If you saw the moving Pumping Iron, you'll remember Arnold and Franco Columbu posing under the scrutiny of a dance instructor. One of the things that separated Arnold from most other competitors was his attention to detail, even onstage. Unlike some of the other big bodybuilders of the 1970s (Sergio Oliva being probably the best example), Arnold moved gracefully from one pose to the next. If you have a friend who is into dance or ballet, recruit him or her to help you with your posing routine. Your friend probably doesn't know a double biceps from a lat spread, but he or she can certainly help you with the transition between poses. The most famous Mr. America, John Grimek, was known for his graceful poses. Only after he had retired from competition did it become known that he had dated a ballet dancer for years!

771. MORE THAN ONE?

If you develop a knack for posing, you might want to consider putting together a couple of different routines. There are two reasons for this. In a close contest, creativity will get you extra points. If you show the judges that you are very versatile and can put together more than one posing routine, chances are it will swing the contest in your favor. A second reason is that in a contest with a large number of competitors, odds are the same piece of music will be chosen by more than one person. If this person is in your weight class and is lucky enough to go onstage before you, your dramatic effect is lost. Audiences and judges are human and will get bored of listening to the same piece of music. You can avoid all this by launching into a different posing routine.

772. ROUND 4 – BODYBUILDING'S FREE FOR ALL

Although the first three rounds in a bodybuilding contest are structured, Round 4, also called the posedown, is made up on the spot. Once the top three to five competitors have been determined, they are asked to engage in a posing free-for-all for approximately one minute. If you're lucky enough to be included in the posedown, hold nothing back. Jump to the front of the stage and start hitting your best poses. If you think another competitor is the favorite, try to position yourself next to him and try to match his best shots with your best.

773. CONFRONTATION WITHIN REASON

Always be careful in the posedown about how you confront other competitors. Most will take things with good humor if you jump in front of them to hit a pose, but every contest will have an idiot who takes things personally. You'll probably have an idea of who that is from watching prior contests or through the grapevine. We are not suggesting you avoid comparing poses with such individuals, as the judges

will penalize you for it. But don't get into a shoving match. It's not worth it.

774. PRE-CONTEST EXERCISE

Besides the actual contest, posing has other benefits. No matter how much you diet and exercise, it's almost impossible to totally refine your physique. Workouts will bring out the larger muscles, but it's the smaller muscles that get you extra points. The first time you practice posing you'll be sore in spots you didn't even know existed. Many bodybuilders look their best the day or two after a contest as all the posing has brought the finer details out in their physique. If you're not convinced of the merits of posing, you should consider that most of the sport's top builders spend up to an hour a day on posing practice.

GUNTER SCHLIERKAMP

BODYBUILDING
PHOTOGRAPHY

775. Pre- and post-contest photos

776. Look at magazines

777. Background

778. Outdoor backgrounds – keep it simple

779. Let there be light – but not too much!

780. The best shutter speeds

781. The digital revolution

25

775. PRE- AND POST-CONTEST PHOTOS

If you plan on making bodybuilding a large part of your life, a photo portfolio is an absolute must. If you have the money, hire a professional photographer – preferably one who has experience shooting bodybuilders. If money is tight you can do it yourself. Nowadays most people have access to a decent camera. If possible, try to use an SLR (single-lens reflex) camera, as it will allow you to change lenses. Take a series of indoor and outdoor photos to record your physique.

776. LOOK AT MAGAZINES

If you need ideas for your photo shoot, simply buy the latest copy of MuscleMag International, REPS! or Oxygen magazines. Every monthly issue brings you the best in physique photography, from indoor studio shots and workout photos.

777. BACKGROUND

For your indoor photos, you'll need to decide on the background. Professionals have backdrops that start at the ceiling and curve out and downwards. This gives the impression that the model is within the background. A cheap way to make a backdrop is to go into a fabric store and buy some material. Even a large single-color wall will suffice (just remove anything that is hanging on the wall or any pieces of furniture, as they will detract from your physique).

778. OUTDOOR BACKGROUNDS – KEEP IT SIMPLE

You may think that the best backgrounds for outdoor photos are majestic structures like buildings and

bridges, but nothing could be further from the truth. When you look at the photos you'll see that the background overshadows your physique. Over the years photographers and bodybuilders have discovered that the best outdoor backgrounds are the sky and sea. Large mountains in the distance also work well.

DAVE DRAPER

779. LET THERE BE LIGHT – BUT NOT TOO MUCH!

The time of the day is very important. You may think the brighter the better, but this is not always the case. Bright sun directly overhead may make the physique look good, but the face will lose detail because of deep shadows in the eye-sockets and under the nose. In addition, a squinted up face does not look very attractive. The best times to shoot are about 9 in the morning and 5 in the afternoon. At these times the sun is low in the sky. While providing enough light, it won't create unwanted shadows.

780. THE BEST SHUTTER SPEEDS

You'll probably get the best photos from shutter speeds of 1/125 to 1/250. If you don't have a tripod, brace the camera on a chair, rock, or some other stationary object if your shutter speed is less than 1/125. If you are forced to shoot under poor light conditions, you should use a 400 ASA film.

781. THE DIGITAL REVOLUTION

The last decade or so has seen a virtual revolution in photography. Film-based photography, which lasted for over 125 years, is fast being replaced by digital. Instead of having to wait for your photos to be chemically developed, they are instantly available. Simply hook your camera up to a computer (or insert the memory card into a reader) and there they are. The beauty of digital photography is that you can instantly see what the photo looks like. If the angle or lighting is wrong, shoot it again.

THE BEAUTY OF **DIGITAL PHOTOGRAPHY** IS THAT YOU CAN INSTANTLY **SEE** WHAT THE **PHOTO LOOKS LIKE.** IF THE ANGLE OR LIGHTING IS WRONG, SHOOT IT AGAIN.

25 PRE-CONTEST DIETING

782. Year-round healthy eating

783. How lean?

784. How long to get in shape

785. Don't crash

786. The mathematics of fat

787. Keep a diet journal

788. Just two to three minutes

789. The AA approach

790. Avoid appetite suppressants

791. The diet doctor

792. Learn how to cook

793. Reduce fat and simple carbohydrate intake

794. Reduce or eliminate fruit juices

795. Carbohydrate loading/depleting

796. Eliminate salt

797. Reduce fluid intake

798. Try a mild herbal diuretic

799. Stay away from diuretic drugs

800. Drugs and water retention

801. Stop all anabolic steroids

802. A glass or two of wine!

803. Tryptophan for extra sleep

26

782. YEAR-ROUND HEALTHY EATING

If you've been eating clean year-round, you won't need to make drastic changes during the pre-contest season. The days of bodybuilders gaining 40 or 50 pounds during the off-season are over. Most now try to stay within 10 to 15 pounds of their contest weight (perhaps 15 to 20 pounds for the heavyweights). You should strive to do the same. Not only is regularly gaining and losing weight unhealthy, but let's face it, you'll look much better with a lower bodyfat percentage.

783. HOW LEAN?

Generally speaking, male bodybuilders will need to get their bodyfat percentage down to three to five percent, and females down to seven to nine percent. Yes, these numbers are low and unhealthy, but remember you'll only be maintaining such low bodyfat levels for a week or two.

784. HOW LONG TO GET IN SHAPE

Assuming that you have no more than 15 pounds to lose, a comfortable time period for dieting is three months, or 12 weeks. This means you lose just about one pound per week. One of the mistakes novice bodybuilders make is underestimating how long it takes to reduce fat levels. It's better to give yourself too much time than not enough.

785. DON'T CRASH

The problem with a crash diet is that much of the weight lost will be muscle. The goal is to gradually lose fat while preserving muscle. Many of bodybuilding's greatest stars have succumbed to this problem. Not only did they compete at a lighter bodyweight, but their bodyfat percentage was actually higher than previous years. The goal is to slowly lose bodyfat while preserving muscle tissue. The best way to do this is to gradually cut calories, not subject your body to a sudden 100-calorie-a-day deficit.

786. THE MATHEMATICS OF FAT

Keep in mind that what you put into your mouth is as important as how many calories – you must eat clean! However, to simplify, here is a basic math formula. Each pound of fat you need to lose contains about 3500 calories. By cutting 500 calories from your diet each day, or by doing an extra 500 calories' worth of activity, you'll lose a pound of fat each week. This means it will take you 12 weeks to lose 12 pounds of fat. If you cut your calories by 750 (or increase your calorie burning by 750 calories) it will only take you nine weeks to lose 12 pounds. Most competitive bodybuilders use a combination of cutting calories and increasing their cardio. Keep in mind experts don't recommend losing more than one to two pounds per week.

787. KEEP A DIET JOURNAL

You should already have a workout journal. Buy another one just for recording your eating habits. Write down every morsel you consumed, when you did so, and what you felt like throughout the day. Not only will this force you to be honest, it will be invaluable the next time you compete. You will be able to look back at your contest prep history and see how your diet affected your body and energy levels.

788. JUST TWO TO THREE MINUTES

With your increased cardio and decreased caloric intake you're going to suffer regular cravings for food, especially junk foods. Experts have discovered that if you can hold out for two or three minutes the cravings will subside. It seems the body gives up and leaves you in peace. When you feel one of those "I must have it!" cravings coming on, try drinking a glass of water or going for a short walk.

789. THE AA APPROACH

One of the reasons the Alcoholics Anonymous (AA) program is so successful is support. As soon as one member starts slipping, other members and councilors are ready to step in and offer support and encouragement. As soon as you decide to compete, make contact with other bodybuilders who are either doing the same thing or at least went through it before. Make a pact that as soon as one of you starts falling off the wagon, another can step in and renew your focus.

790. AVOID APPETITE SUPPRESSANTS

You may be tempted to go the "pill route" to curb your appetite, but we caution against this. Appetite suppressants not only slow your metabolism down and cause the body to store more fat, but many of the prescription forms have been linked to severe side effects.

791. THE DIET DOCTOR

If you have access to someone who is highly knowledgeable about precontest dieting, use that person as a resource. We don't mean a general nutritionist either. Such individuals are great for advising the average person, but know next to nothing about dieting for bodybuilding. In fact, they'll think what you are doing is Draconian and they'll likely try to talk you out of it!

792. LEARN HOW TO COOK

Hopefully, guys, you are not stuck in a time warp that you think the kitchen is for women only. If so you're in the wrong sport. To develop a contest-winning physique you have to become as familiar with pots and pans as you are with barbells and dumbells. Once you know how to cook you are in complete control of your nutritional destiny.

793. REDUCE FAT AND SIMPLE CARBOHYDRATE INTAKE

Although you should be keeping fats and simple sugars to a minimum year-round, this is an absolute necessity when preparing for a contest. One gram of fat contains 9 calories – over twice that of protein or carbohydrate (4 grams each). It doesn't take much fat to add an extra 500 to 1000 calories to your daily diet. Likewise, simple sugars are readily stored as fat (they also increase insulin levels, which in turn promote fat storage).

794. REDUCE OR ELIMINATE FRUIT JUICES

With one glass of orange juice containing the same amount of carbohydrate and sugars as numerous oranges, it's easy to see how drinking fruit juices can interfere with your contest preparation. Not only that, but juice is made up of simple sugars, with no fiber  to slow down the sugar rush. During the precontest season, limit your fruit consumption drastically. As the final month of contest preparation arrives, no fruit juices or sodas should be consumed.

795. CARBOHYDRATE LOADING/DEPLETING

The stored form of sugar found in muscles is glycogen. Among its many properties is its ability to hold four times its weight in water. Bodybuilders take advantage of this by depleting as much glycogen from their bodies as they can three to five days before the contest, and then "loading" in as much carbohydrate as possible 24 to 48 before the contest to replenish glycogen levels. Previously flat muscles are now bursting with water, making the skin appear paper thin and enhancing vascularity. If you decide to load/deplete, keep accurate notes. Few bodybuilders get it dead-on the first time they do it. Most look their best the day before or the day after the contest. But you've kept a journal, right? Next time you compete, simply start your loading/depleting a day earlier or later to suit your experience.

796. ELIMINATE SALT

All other things being equal, the bodybuilder who sports the most ripped physique will win. One of the ways to create that ultra-ripped look is to control the water in your body. The last thing you want on contest day is that dreaded "smooth look." For some the problem is fat, but in many cases a layer of water lies between the muscles and overlying skin. One of the easiest methods to keep water levels down is by eliminating salt from your diet. Salt promotes water retention in the body (the primary reason salt tablets are found in survival kits). One gram of salt holds 50 grams of water. Even by eliminating all visible salt from your diet you'll still be taking in more than you need. As soon as you start your pre-contest diet, eliminate all canned products that contain salt and any preserved deli meat. You shouldn't be eating any processed foods at this point anyway (not that you ever should).

797. REDUCE FLUID INTAKE

Another way to get rid of the smooth look is to restrict your water intake in the days leading up to a contest. Granted, you don't want to eliminate water entirely, but don't consume the traditional eight to ten glasses per day. If possible try to drink distilled water, as it has all the sodium removed.

798. TRY A MILD HERBAL DIURETIC

As many over-the-counter compounds like caffeine and green tea will promote water loss, you may want to experiment with them. Always pay attention to any warning signals your body may produce, however. If you suddenly find yourself developing muscle cramps, immediately stop taking the diuretic. Cramps are a sign of dehydration and electrolyte imbalance. Electrolytes are the various charged particles (called ions) that regulate many of the body's chemical reactions, including muscle contraction.

799. STAY AWAY FROM DIURETIC DRUGS

A number of competitive bodybuilders have died from diuretic overdose. Such diuretic drugs as Lasix work by interfering with the body's water-conserving hormone, aldersterone. Unfortunately, they can work far too well. They can easily cause the body to give up pounds of water in a few hours. The problem is not the water loss, but rather the electrolyte concentration. As we saw in the previous tip, electrolytes control a number of life-necessary reactions, including heart contraction. Diuretics have been linked to heart attacks and seizures.

800. DRUGS AND WATER RETENTION

If you are using any medications, check with your doctor to see which, if any, cause water retention. For example, anti-inflammatory drugs like cortisone are famous for causing severe water retention. If need be, stop the medication or switch to a different drug.

801. STOP ALL ANABOLIC STEROIDS

We are not going to preach to you about the dangers of anabolic steroids. Still, if you are using them in your contest preparations, stop at least two weeks from the contest date. Most anabolic steroids cause water retention and will give your physique a smooth look. We would be remiss if we didn't remind you that steroids have very serious side effects that will assuredly cause health problems.

802. A GLASS OR TWO OF WINE!

Believe it or not, a glass of wine on the day of the contest may actually improve your appearance. Low doses of alcohol appear to stimulate the body to release nitric oxide, which increases vascularity. There is also some evidence to suggest that one of the compounds in red wine, resveratrol, plays a role in increasing blood flow. Don't go and get corked on contest day, but drinking one four- or five-ounce glass of wine may help you start celebrating in more ways than one!

803. TRYPTOPHAN FOR EXTRA SLEEP

Given the extra stress you'll be subjecting your body to, it's imperative that you get adequate sleep as you prepare for the contest. If all the extra training and dieting interferes with your sleeping patterns, try a natural sleep aid like the amino acid tryptophan.

L-tryptophan is used in the body to produce the B-vitamin niacin. Niacin, in turn, is used to produce serotonin, a neurotransmitter that exerts a calming effect and regulates sleep.

CHRIS JALALI

PRE-CONTEST TRAINING

804. Increase your cardio

805. First thing in the morning?

806. Supersets and trisets

807. How fat am I?

808. Skin calipers

809. Bioimpedance

810. Hydrostatic testing – dunking for accuracy!

811. Stop your cardio!

812. Decrease your rest interval

27

PRE-CONTEST TRAINING

804. INCREASE YOUR CARDIO

If you're a typical male bodybuilder you are probably doing little or no cardio. That has to change. The bodybuilders with the lowest bodyfat percentage are the ones winning the contests. Increase your cardio to 30 to 45 minutes duration, four to five times per week, at least three months out from the contest.

805. FIRST THING IN THE MORNING?

For 99.9 percent of the people who work out, it doesn't really matter when cardio is performed. But if you are trying to shed every last ounce of fat from your body, try performing your cardio first thing in the morning. The brain will have used much of your glycogen (stored sugar) supplies overnight, leaving your fat reserves as the primary fuel source.

806. SUPERSETS AND TRISETS

About three months out from the contest, start doing more supersets and trisets. These advanced training techniques are a great way to both save you time and keep your heart rate elevated. If you keep your heart rate elevated you'll burn extra calories. Supersets and trisets are also safer in the precontest season, as they'll require that you use less weight.

807. HOW FAT AM I?

Measuring bodyfat percentage is not really that important for the average person (how you look and how you feel are far more important). For competitive bodybuilders, however, it is probably a good idea to measure bodyfat levels to get a good idea of where you are and how far you have to go.

808. SKIN CALIPERS

The skin caliper is the simplest method to measure bodyfat percentage. By measuring the thickness of the skin on the triceps upper arm, waist, and thigh, you can get a good idea of your bodyfat percentage, accurate to one or two percentage points. Make sure you have someone who is trained in the use of the calipers.

809. BIOIMPEDANCE

Fat and muscle conduct electricity at different rates. Scientists have used this fact to create a device that measures bodyfat percentage accurately. Called bioimpedance, this system works by sending a very low electrical current through the body. Essentially, the speed of the current determines what percentage of your body is fat.

810. HYDROSTATIC TESTING – DUNKING FOR ACCURACY!

The fact that bone, muscle, and connective tissue, collectively known as lean mass, sinks, while body fat floats, is the main principle behind hydrostatic testing. By obtaining your land weight and water weight (based on buoyancy), you can calculate your bodyfat percentage correct to within less than a percentage point. If you don't have the money to pay for the procedure, check out the phys-ed department at a university or college. They love to get guinea pigs!

811. STOP YOUR CARDIO!

As you should be in about 99 percent contest shape one to two weeks out, there is no need to be doing serious cardio training this close to the contest. In fact excessive cardio in the week or two before the show may burn away hard-earned muscle tissue. Intense cardio will also interfere with your carb loading and depletion. Most competitive bodybuilders stop all cardio about a week to ten days out. You should do the same.

812. DECREASE YOUR REST INTERVAL

During the offseason you'll be averaging 60 to 90 seconds' rest between sets. During the precontest season you should decrease this time period to 20 to 30 seconds. This will force you to use less weight (and hence give you less chance of injury) and also keep your heart rate elevated in the cardio zone.

FRANK NEZDOBA

SHAVING & LOOKING YOUR BEST ON STAGE

813. Glasses
814. Never mind Samson
815. Shaving
816. In advance
817. Where to shave
818. Electric shave
819. Water and electricity don't mix!
820. The Neet approach
821. The Neet experiment
822. Franco's way
823. The Lex Hair Removal system
824. Electrolysis – save your money
825. To wax or not to wax?
826. Your first line of defense
827. Acne – not just for teens
828. Acne – another reason to avoid the "juice."
829. Acne – it's all in the make-up

28

813. GLASSES

As there are no rules that prohibit wearing glasses onstage. Feel free to do so. However, you should keep in mind that you'll be doing a lot of sweating under the stage lights. This will mean a constant adjusting of your glasses. You'll probably have enough to worry about without your glasses sliding off your face. If you plan on competing on a regular basis you may want to invest in contact lenses.

814. NEVER MIND SAMSON

While Samson supposedly lost all his strength after his hair was removed, modern bodybuilding is the complete opposite. Your body must be completely absent of any visible body hair (with the exception of scalp hair). Not only will hairless skin help show your musculature to greater advantage, but removing body hair will allow you to acquire a better tan.

815. SHAVING

Shaving with a straight-edge is the quickest way to remove body hair. It's also the cheapest. If this is your first time shaving down the hair on your chest, back, and legs it will probably be long, so you'll need a couple of packages of razors. Also, these areas of the body are not used to having a sharp piece of metal dragged across them, so go easy and slow. You do not want visible razor-burn on contest day.

816. IN ADVANCE

Don't wait until the day before the show to shave down. Shaving an area for the first time is bound to produce cuts and nicks, not to mention the potential for a rash. We strongly suggest that you shave down a few weeks before the contest to allow any cuts and blemishes to heal. You can then do a touch-up shave a week before the show, and another just before.

817. WHERE TO SHAVE

The best place to shave off body hair is in the shower or bath. The water will make your skin soft, and the warmth will open up your pores, lessening the chance of cuts. Also, you may want to skip the shaving lotion, at least for your first shaving experience. The length of the hair plus the cream will make for an almost uncontrollable combination. Also, a thick shaving lather will obscure the various ridges and curves of your muscles. You may be familiar with the topography of your face, but how about your quads or calves?

818. ELECTRIC SHAVE

If a straight-edge is not to your liking, try an electric razor. Most electric shavers have a side attachment for trimming mustaches. This will do a better job than the regular top heads. In fact, the main cutting heads are not designed for cutting long hair and you'll probably end up yanking out more hair than you cut! You also run the risk of burning out the razor's small motor. Electric razors are quick, neat, and eliminate the risk of cuts.

819. WATER AND ELECTRICITY DON'T MIX!

Hopefully common sense, but never use an electric razor in the shower or bath. Every year hundreds of people electrocute themselves in the shower or bath while using an electric razor.

820. THE NEET APPROACH

While women are probably familiar with this approach, most males are not. If shaving (straight edge and electric) has a disadvantage, it's that even the closet shave will leave a slight stubble. Women have been getting around this for decades with hair-removal creams such as Neet. The creams work by breaking down the hair at the cellular level. Simply smear it on, wait five to ten minutes and then wash it off. The hair will be destroyed right down to just below skin level.

821. THE NEET EXPERIMENT

As hair removal creams contain various chemical compounds, we suggest you try rubbing it on a small area of skin before coating your entire chest or back with the stuff. Better to discover that you are allergic to the cream on a small area than over your entire torso!

822. FRANCO'S WAY

The masochists among you may want to try this one. According to numerous reports, former Mr Olympia Franco Columbu wasn't a big fan of shaving or lotions. Instead, in the weeks leading up to the contest, he would literally pull the hair out with his hands. By contest day his body would be hair-free. While the results may be great, we suggest sticking to less painful hair-removal techniques.

823. THE LEX HAIR REMOVAL SYSTEM

If you want the latest in hair removal creams, try the new Hair Removal System by Lex Advanced Skin Care Technologies. This three-step approach consists of two products that remove body hair and keep it from growing back, and a third product that enhances the effectiveness of the second. For more information contact Lex at www.lexskin.com.

824. ELECTROLYSIS – SAVE YOUR MONEY

It may be the rage in Hollywood for removing upper lip hair from aging actresses, but it really has no place in bodybuilding. Electrolysis involves zapping hair follicles with a volt of electricity. Unfortunately, each hair has to be targeted separately. One look at the typical male's shaggy chest highlights the drawbacks

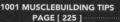
to this technique. Electrolysis is also expensive, averaging $5000 to $10,000 per session. Finally the procedure is not permanent, despite what some promoters tell you. Our advice is to skip electrolysis.

825. TO WAX OR NOT TO WAX?

Waxing is another of those hair removal techniques that men can thank women for. As the name suggests, a layer of hot, liquid wax is spread over the area and allowed to cool and solidify. The wax is then ripped off in one quick motion, bringing the hair with it. Waxing is very efficient, although a tad painful. Try it on a small area first before coating your chest or back.

826. YOUR FIRST LINE OF DEFENSE

The skin is the largest organ in the body and the first line of defense against invading germs. All those hours tanning in the sun, sweating in the gym and removing body hair take their toll. As bodybuilding success is heavily dependant on appearance, you have to give your skin the same degree of care as your muscles.

827. ACNE – NOT JUST FOR TEENS

You've seen them in gyms. The guys with small purple mountains on their backs. While not life-threatening, acne can be psychologically devastating, and it won't do your contest appearance any good either. Although the occasional skin blemish occurs for most everyone, if you develop severe acne on the back, chest, or shoulders, consult your physician immediately.

828. ACNE – ANOTHER REASON TO AVOID THE "JUICE."

The reason teenage males develop more acne than teenage females is because the higher levels of the male hormone testosterone cause the skin to produce higher amounts of acne-causing oil. As anabolic steroids are synthetic derivatives of testosterone, they'll also increase acne. In fact, heavy steroid users have some of the most severe acne around. Our advice is to avoid anabolic steroids, especially if you are susceptible to acne.

829. ACNE – IT'S ALL IN THE MAKE-UP

Many skin-care products have an oily base that only serves to clog skin pores and trap acne-causing bacteria inside. If you have acne, or had it at an earlier age, we suggest avoiding heavy skin care products. If you have to wear such products for work (i.e. acting, frequent TV appearances) be sure and remove them as soon as possible afterwards.

DARREM CHARLES

TANNING

830. Obtaining that golden look

831. Tanner beware?

832. For a tighter look

833. Tanning – the obvious advantage

834. The whole body

835. Know your SPF's

836. Two hours before

837. Five or more

838. No more than 60 minutes

839. Irregular spots

840. Are you a candidate for fake bake?

841. Try going to bed

842. Avoid the white spots

843. Can you stand it?

844. Dyeing to tan

845. Just wait a few hours

846. Beware of the jaundiced look!

847. Test first

848. The whole body!

849. Face tips

850. Hands off!

851. Combine the two

852. Get enough color!

853. Not sunscreens

854. Tanning in pill form

830. OBTAINING THAT GOLDEN LOOK

Once the symbol of lower-class peasants, the California bronze look is now sought by just about everyone. For competitive bodybuilders, a dark tan is an absolute must. Start your tanning about the same time as your pre-contest dieting. As with losing fat, you want to tan slowly and evenly, not try to do it all in a week.

831. TANNER BEWARE?

Before you start worshiping the Sun god, a few words of caution are needed. With the depletion of the earth's ozone layer, more and more of the sun's harmful rays are reaching the surface. It is estimated that a 5 percent reduction in the ozone layer produces a 10 percent increase in solar radiation, which in turn increases skin cancers by 20 percent. Ironically over the last 25 to 30 years the size of bathing suits has decreased. The end result is a dramatic increase in the rate of skin cancer. Try to limit your time in the sun and use a good sunscreen.

832. FOR A TIGHTER LOOK

One of the best reasons for spending time in the sun before your contest is that regular tanning helps tighten and "thin out" the skin. This tightening makes the muscles appear more striated and ripped. Even African American bodybuilders make tanning a regular part of their pre-contest preparations.

833. TANNING – THE OBVIOUS ADVANTAGE

The most obvious reason for tanning is that it will make you look darker and more muscular. The bodybuilder with the darker skin will usually place higher in the contest. The bright stage lights that flood down on bodybuilding contestants tend to wash out and blur muscle definition and separation. So while the lights will make you look more visible they'll also make you look smoother.

834. THE WHOLE BODY

With the exception of the naughty bits that will be covered by your posing trunks, your entire body will be on display at the contest. This means you have to approach tanning like you do cooking a turkey – baste all over! Don't spend all your tanning time lying on your stomach and back. Periodically turn over on your sides. Also, raise your arms above your head so that the area under your arms and shoulders tans. Finally, don't be afraid to lie at awkward angles to the sun. You want every inch of your body darkened by contest day.

835. KNOW YOUR SPF'S

Sunscreens are lotions that contain compounds that help block out much of the sun's harmful rays. In the 1970s the FDA came up with a numerical system to rate sunscreens. These are called sun protection factors, or SPFs. They range from 2 to at least 50, the FDA only recognizes up to an SPF of at least 15. Don't be misled by the numbers. An SPF of, say, 5, does not mean you can stay out in the sun for five hours. Instead it means that you can stay out in the sun five times longer before burning than you could if you were not wearing any sunscreen.

836. TWO HOURS BEFORE

Apply the first layer of sunscreen two hours before you go out in the sun. This gives the cream time to penetrate your skin and maximize your protection.

837. FIVE OR MORE

Most dermatologists recommend wearing a sunscreen of at least SPF 5 or 6. For fairer skin individuals, and those not accustomed to regular sun tanning they recommend an SPF of 15.

838. NO MORE THAN 60 MINUTES

No matter how dark you get, or how dark you need to get, never stay in direct sunlight for longer than 60 minutes.

839. IRREGULAR SPOTS

If at any time you notice a mole or weird-looking freckle on your skin that wasn't there before (or one that seems to have changed appearance), consult your physician immediately. Statistically it's probably nothing to be alarmed about, but why take the chance? Skin cancer is one of the most prevalent forms of cancer, and if caught early is usually curable.

840. ARE YOU A CANDIDATE FOR FAKE BAKE?

If you are very light-skinned, have a history of skin cancer in your family, or simply don't want to lie out in the sun, then you are a candidate for artificial tanning. Try using an artificial tanning bed or sunless tanning lotion to darken your skin before the big show.

841. TRY GOING TO BED

One of the primary advantages of artificial tanning beds is convenience. Most gyms and fitness centers these days have a couple of tanning beds. What better way to finish your workout than lying down for a few minutes and working on your tan. Even though the newer beds have most of the harmful rays filtered

out, too much artificial light will burn you just like the real thing, so limit your exposure.

842. AVOID THE WHITE SPOTS

One of the disadvantages of tanning beds is that they may force your skin to "bunch up." This results in a light or non-tanned area, affectionately called "white spots" by the tanning fraternity. As with lying in the sun, try to adjust your position every couple of minutes while lying on the tanning bed. It is especially useful to move your arms to different positions.

843. CAN YOU STAND IT?

In recent years the decades' old horizontal tanning beds have been receiving some serious competition in the form of stand-up models. Instead of lying down in the equivalent of a giant waffle iron, you get to stand up. No more lying in a pool of sweat. No feelings of claustrophobia.

844. DYEING TO TAN

Often called bodybuilding's equivalent of body painting, artificial tanning dyes allow you to darken the skin without the risk of sun exposure. In effect, they're a type of body paint that you brush on. One minute you're white, the next you're a golden brown. Pro-tan is the most popular product among bodybuilders.

845. JUST WAIT A FEW HOURS

Besides instant tanning dyes that you paint on, you also have the option of using products that go on as a white lotion but turn brown over a period of a few hours. The products contain compounds that react with enzymes in the skin (similar to leaving a cut apple exposed to the air).

846. BEWARE OF THE JAUNDICED LOOK!

If artificial tanners have a disadvantage, it's that their success is often dependant on your skin color to begin with. Those with extremely light skin will need many coats to achieve a really dark color. One coat often leaves the individual looking yellow and jaundiced. If you are going to go the artificial tanning route, make sure you start a week or two in advance just to see how dark these products will make your skin.

847. TEST FIRST

As with hair removal lotions, don't start out by smearing the whole body with an artificial tanning product. You may be one of those individuals who is allergic to one of the product's ingredients. Test a small area of the skin first and wait at least 24 hours. If there are no problems then by all means start coating

the body. A tanning dye should be applied with a fine brush or sponge using long strokes. After the first layer is dry, you should rinse off with warm water. When the skin is totally dried, a second layer should be added. Up to three layers should be applied to make sure there is no blotchiness.

848. THE WHOLE BODY!

It may seem unecessary to say this, but make sure you cover your whole body when you use artificial tanning products. In your haste to darken the body's more showy parts, you may forget to tan the most visible part of your body – your face! At every bodybuilding contest there is bound to be at least one contestant to walk out onstage sporting a perfect tan from the neck down but smiling at the audience with a lily-white face!

849. FACE TIPS

When you apply an artificial tanning product to your face, try to avoid the eyebrows and hairline. The skin in these areas seems to darken more than the rest of the face.

850. HANDS OFF!

As artificial tanning lotions will tan any skin they come in contact with, don't make the mistake of applying it with your bare hands. The dead skin on the palms will soak up the dye and turn your hands many shades darker than the rest of your body. This will become very obvious on any poses where your hands are open. Use a pair of latex gloves, or better yet, have someone else apply the lotion for you.

851. COMBINE THE TWO

For the darkest and most even tan possible, try a combination of both sun and tanning lotions. Use the sun to lay down a good foundation, and then a tanning dye to darken the lighter areas of your physique. Tanning dyes should be applied over a two-day period.

852. GET ENOUGH COLOR!

Contests have been lost because contestants did not tan enough. You are not trying for a natural look here. You want to get as dark as you can. The lighter your skin, the "puffier" it will appear, especially under the bright stage lights.

853. NOT SUNSCREENS

With few exceptions, artificial tanning lotions do not contain sunscreen. This means wearing them doesn't give you any extra protection from the sun. You will still need to use a good sunscreen if you decide to catch a few rays.

854. TANNING IN PILL FORM

As expected, chemistry has made available a number of pills that will supposedly darken the skin. Most work by making the skin more sensitive to sunlight. Keep in mind that few are FDA approved, and at the very least don't work. In a few individuals they may work too well and cause the skin to burn very rapidly. Or advice is to think hard before going the tanning pill route.

HAIRSTYLE

855. Hair style – creating or destroying the illusion
856. A cut above the rest
857. Hair color
858. The bald-look?

30

855. HAIR STYLE – CREATING OR DESTROYING THE ILLUSION

Most bodybuilders take great pride in how their hair looks, and so should you. Besides the personality of a good hairstyle, there are practical considerations. Having a large mass of long hair hanging down over your shoulders will make your neck and traps look much smaller and your shoulders narrower. You also have to consider all the sweating you'll be doing under the hot lights. Your previously tidy long hair will begin to look strung out and scraggly. If you prefer to wear long hair, just keep it tied up and out of the way.

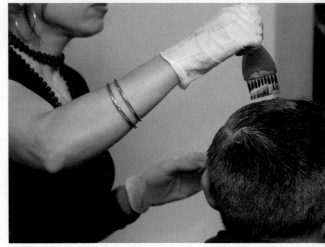

857. HAIR COLOR

A change of hair color has many advantages. For one thing it helps reflect light onstage. Also, the dye in many agents penetrates the hair fibers, swelling up the hair shaft and making it thicker and fuller. You've changed your body over the past few months, why not your hair color?

858. THE BALD-LOOK?

Receding hairline? Don't despair. Bodybuilders these days are taking a cue from athletes in many other sports. The bald look is in. Even athletes with naturally full heads of hair are taking a razor and buzzing it all off. No more having to worry about hairstyle, color, or conditioning.

856. A CUT ABOVE THE REST

The first step to an attractive hairstyle is the cut. If you have any doubt get someone else's opinion – male or female – it doesn't matter as long as it's someone you can trust. If you have the time and money go to a professional hair salon and try different styles. You might even want to get pictures taken to analyze afterwards.

STRETCH MARKS

859. Another reason not to bulk up

860. Vitamin E to the rescue

861. Hide 'em if you have 'em

31

859. ANOTHER REASON NOT TO BULK UP

Very few bodybuilders go through their careers without developing stretch marks. The areas around the pec-delt tie-in (where the chest and shoulder muscles meet) is especially susceptible. Stretch marks occur when there is a rapid gain in bodyweight. The overlying skin stretches and eventually tears. Stretch marks are more common in bodybuilders who follow the old "bulking up" philosophy of training. Even though the goal is to gain only muscle tissue, bulking up also lays down a lot of fat. The end result of all that extra bodyweight is those ugly purple scars you often see on the larger bodybuilders. Try and gain pure muscle, and never increase body weight rapidly.

STRETCH MARKS ARE MORE COMMON IN BODYBUILDERS WHO FOLLOW THE OLD "BULKING UP" PHILOSOPHY OF TRAINING.

860. VITAMIN E TO THE RESCUE

It has been scientifically proven that a diet deficient in essential nutrients, especially vitamin E, can contribute to poor skin elasticity. Odds are good that you are consuming adequate amounts of vitamin E in your diet, but you can use the essential nutrient in another manner. Go into a drug or cosmetic store and pick up a hand lotion containing vitamin E. First thing in the morning and before bed, rub a small amount over the area where your upper chest joins the front shoulder. Not only will this help prevent stretch marks from forming, it will also help promote the healing of existing stretch marks.

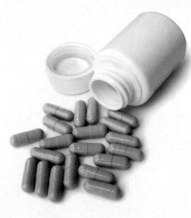

LEE LABRADA

861. HIDE 'EM IF YOU HAVE 'EM

While the judges probably won't penalize you for having stretch marks; let's face it: they look ghastly. A good artificial tanning dye will hide all but the most serious of stretch marks. By the time your skin is dark enough for a contest, your stretch marks should have disappeared.

POSING
TRUNKS

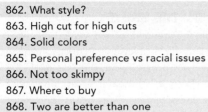

862. What style?
863. High cut for high cuts
864. Solid colors
865. Personal preference vs racial issues
866. Not too skimpy
867. Where to buy
868. Two are better than one
869. Experiment

32

862. WHAT STYLE?

Posing trunks come in two basic styles: high and low-cut. High-cut have two to three inches of material between the waist and hip and are best suited for short bodybuilders. The higher the cut (the less material) the more of the upper leg is shown, offering the illusion of increased leg length. Conversely, those with long legs can get away with low-cut posing trunks (about three to five inches between waist and upper thigh).

863. HIGH CUT FOR HIGH CUTS

Besides leg length, your condition may influence your choice of posing trunks. If you are in ultra-ripped condition and have "cuts" in your legs that run the full length of your thighs, a high-cut set of trunks will show them off to the judges.

864. SOLID COLORS

Most bodybuilding federations require competitors to wear solid-color posing trunks. This means you can't wear trunks containing stripes, lines, or dots. The rules in most federations also state that posing trunks cannot be "too shiny." Essentially this means they should absorb most of the light and not reflect it back to the audience.

865. PERSONAL PREFERENCE VS RACIAL ISSUES

While personal preference plays a major role in posing trunk's selection, a few words of caution are needed. Try to stick with darker colors. Light colors tend to make the waist appear larger than it really is. Also, African American bodybuilders should avoid black and brown colors, as they will blend in with their skin color. Stick with blues, reds, and purples.

866. NOT TOO SKIMPY

Even though the trend in recent years is to wear skimpier posing trunks, a lower limit exists. Anything much below two inches in cut and you might be accused of doing a striptease! Most federations state: "a certain percentage of the glutes appearance is permitted." If in doubt, check out the pictures in various muscle magazines such as Flex and MuscleMag International.

867. WHERE TO BUY

If you live in a large city there will probably be one or more fitness-oriented stores that carry posing trunks. If not, check out the ads in the latest copy of MuscleMag International. In fact, MuscleMag International sells posing trunks through their web site: **www.emusclemag.com**.

868. TWO ARE BETTER THAN ONE

As with your music, you should bring two pairs of posing trunks to your show. Posing oils and tanning products can sometimes stain posing trunks. It also adds a bit of variety to your routine if you can change colors between the prejudging and evening shows. Finally, competitors have been known to "steal" things back stage. Always try to have a back-up plan.

869. EXPERIMENT

If you have access to posing trunks of different colors and cuts, try them all out. Take some pictures. Have friends offer their opinion. The bottom line is that your posing trunks are like your hairstyle, they should highlight your physique, not detract from it.

STRIKING OIL

870. The great wash-out
871. Leave baby oil for babies
872. A helping hand
873. More is not better
874. Wipe down

33

870. THE GREAT WASH-OUT

For all their advantages, the bright lights used at bodybuilding contests have their drawbacks. One of these is their tendency to "wash out" the physique and make it appear flat. The old-time strongmen found that applying a light coat of oil could restore the appearance of the body's natural curves and musculature. Pick up a bottle of Pam vegetable spray to use backstage before beginning the contest. Vegetable oil works best, as it will be absorbed by the skin and then slowly surface as you sweat. The end result is a nice shine to your muscles.

871. LEAVE BABY OIL FOR BABIES

Your first instinct might be to rush out and buy a bottle of baby oil because it's the most familiar. We recommend avoiding baby oil, as mineral oils tend to lie on top of the skin rather than sinking into it. Mineral oil will make it appear as if you are wrapped in cellophane, and you'll reflect back to the audience like a mirror. Not a great image.

872. A HELPING HAND

Like a great naval fleet at sea, you should bring an "oiler" with you backstage. Granted there are other competitors backstage who could help, but bodybuilding is very competitive. Do you really want the competition applying your oil? You may find yourself going onstage with only half your back done. Unless some of the other competitors are people you can trust, ask a friend to help you out. Keep in mind though, in some contests trainers, oilers and friends are not allowed back stage.

873. MORE IS NOT BETTER

There is an art to oiling. You should practice your technique a week or two before the contest. Apply just enough oil to highlight the muscles, not drown them. In fact, too much oil will do the complete opposite of what you want; it will flatten out the muscles. After oiling do not sit down – you will lose the oil on your backside and it will look dry when you are on stage.

874. WIPE DOWN

Common courtesy demands that you wipe yourself down after coming backstage. Nothing is as off-putting as a competitor walking around backstage dripping oil all over the place. Not only is such behavior disgusting, it's downright dangerous. Oil splattered on hardwood floor is an accident waiting to happen. One competitor we know of wiped his hands on the stage drapes, leaving ugly oil stains on the felt curtains. He was sent a cleaning bill of $4800.

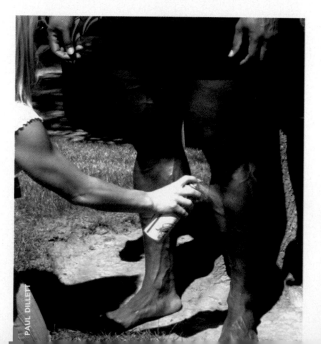

PAUL DILLETT

SHOWTIME!

875. The backstage contest kit

876. Flying and dehydration

877. Fly early

878. Play it safe – confirm!

879. Keeping warm

880. Exercise on the go

881. Check before you go

882. At least an hour

883. The check ride

884. The heavier the longer

885. Read the lights

886. No peaking now

887. The backstage pump-up

888. Don't over-pump

889. Which muscles to pump

890. Which muscles to avoid pumping

891. Pumping the deltoids

892. Pumping the lats

893. Pumping the chest and triceps

894. Pumping the thighs

895. Biceps

896. Posing for pumping

897. The five-minute warning

898. Avoid staring at the lights

899. Follow instructions

34

875. THE BACKSTAGE CONTEST KIT

Just as there are numerous training aids you use in the gym on a daily basis, so too are there items you should bring to the bodybuilding contest. Besides the previously mentioned posing trunks, oil, towel, and instant tanning lotion, we suggest a small toiletry kit containing toothbrush, shampoo, soap, small mirror, and if you need them, hair care items such as conditioner, brush, and a small hair dryer.

876. FLYING AND DEHYDRATION

Because of the dry environment inside the aircraft, you'll dehydrate very easily. Bring along extra water and sip it frequently during your trip.

877. FLY EARLY

It's also a good idea to fly in a few days before the show. This gives your body time to adjust to the new atmosphere as well as time to dry out if you consumed too much water on the plane. It also allows you time to readjust your biological clock if you have crossed a couple of time zones.

878. PLAY IT SAFE – CONFIRM!

Always confirm your flight reservation a few days before you are set to leave. As you know, anything is possible with airlines! Get to the airport at least two hours before departure time.

879. KEEPING WARM

As most amateur bodybuilding contests take place in high-school auditoriums, heat may be at a premium. Backstage at a bodybuilding contest can be a cold environment, so it's a good idea to bring along some sort of warm-up suit, robe or dressing gown.

At the very least wear a pair of shorts and T-shirt. Besides keeping you warm, the track suit has the added benefit of hiding your physique from the other competitors!

880. EXERCISE ON THE GO

As many contest promoters don't have (or allow) weights backstage, you will have to be creative with your backstage pumping up. A set of chest-expanders (strands) is small, light, and will fit in a gym bag. You can use them to work just about every muscle group.

881. CHECK BEFORE YOU GO

Make a checklist of all the items you will need backstage at the contest. Before you leave in the morning, check off every item on the list to make sure you haven't forgotten anything. In the excitement and nervousness of getting ready for the show, it's easy to overlook an important item or two.

882. AT LEAST AN HOUR

Try to arrive at the contest venue at least an hour before start-time. If instructions told you to be there sooner, follow them. Being late is no way to make friends with the judges. If you don't appear onstage with the rest of your weight class when called, you'll probably be disqualified.

883. THE CHECK RIDE

If you're in an unfamiliar town or city, memorize the shortest route to the contest venue. Don't rely on a road map come Saturday morning. Make a trial run on Friday to see how long it will take. The trip will probably take longer on Friday because of traffic, but use the time as a guide. If things go fast Saturday morning, so much the better.

884. THE HEAVIER THE LONGER

As bodybuilding contests tend to be judged in ascending weight classes (from lightweight to heavyweight), you will have extra time on your hands if you are in one of the heavier divisions. Since there will in all probability be extra seats available at the prejudging, you can sit in the audience and watch the proceedings. This may not be an option at the evening show, as it could well be sold out. Be sure and pay close attention to any PA announcements, as they'll be letting you know when the various weight classes will be judged.

885. READ THE LIGHTS

Even the best lighting professionals make mistakes. Assuming you get an opportunity to watch a couple of lighter weight classes before your own, take a close look at the lighting set up. Odds are there will be areas onstage where the lighting is poor. Try to make a mental note of this. Granted you won't be able to determine your position in the line-up (the judges and your number will determine that), but you will have control during your free-posing round and the posedown. Try to keep yourself in the best-lit areas of the stage so the judges have a good clear look at your physique.

886. NO PEAKING NOW

You may want to try one of the strategies employed by some competitors to psych-out their opponents. Keep yourself fully covered until the last possible moment before stepping onstage. Doing this keeps everyone guessing as to your contest condition. They never get a chance to analyze your strong and weak points. On the other hand, you can size up the competition and visualize what poses to hit in response to your competitors' best shots. Remember

to re-oil if you've been wearing a track suit or sitting on a couch or chair.

887. THE BACKSTAGE PUMP-UP

As muscle size and vascularity are two of the primary characteristics that you will be judged on, you want to do everything possible to highlight both. No doubt you've discovered by now that after a couple of sets of an exercise, the muscle being worked swells with blood. Most bodybuilders perform a few high-rep exercises before stepping onstage, to increase their vascularity and muscle size.

888. DON'T OVER-PUMP

You may think the goal of pumping up is to make every muscle as large as possible, but this is not the case. An over-pumped muscle is generally harder to control than an un-pumped muscle. Also, a muscle bloated with blood may lose some of its sharpness and definition.

889. WHICH MUSCLES TO PUMP

With proportion being the name of the game in bodybuilding, we suggest analyzing your physique and only pumping up your weaker muscles. If your chest and biceps are weak, it would make sense to get a good pump there before going onstage. It is always a good idea to stretch out the back by chinning or performing pulldowns.

890. WHICH MUSCLES TO AVOID PUMPING

We strongly suggest you avoid pumping up the calves and abdominals. The calves are notorious for cramping, and as you will probably be in a dehydrated state to begin with, any extra exercise may cause the calves to lock up onstage. The abdominals are probably the only muscle group that you don't want to increase in size. In addition, sending extra blood to the region may make it harder to flex them and remove some of their detail.

891. PUMPING THE DELTOIDS

As the shoulders can be seen from just about every angle, and as they can never be too large, they are the ideal muscle group to pump up. If light dumbells are available, do a few sets of front, side, and bent-over lateral raises. If there are no dumbells present, break out your chest-expander springs. You can either stretch them apart to work the front and rear delts simultaneously, or step on one handle and do one-arm raises to the front or side. At the very least, drop to the floor and do a few sets of high-rep push-ups. Besides working the chest, push-ups bring in the front and side shoulders, and the triceps.

892. PUMPING THE LATS

The lats are another muscle group that can never be too large. They give bodybuilders their classic V-shape look. If dumbells are present, do a few sets of one-arm rows. If the backstage area has open ceilings with exposed (solid) pipes, jump up and bang out a few sets of chins. Finally, you can do towel pulls. Have a willing partner hold on to one end of the towel and you pull the other end toward your mid chest.

893. PUMPING THE CHEST AND TRICEPS

One of the simplest exercises to work the chest and shoulders is the push-up. By raising or lowering your feet above or below torso level, you can target different parts of your chest (essentially, if your feet

are elevated it's more upper chest, while lowering the feet brings in more of the lower and outer chest). To hit the triceps, do dips between two chairs or benches, or perform your pushing with your hands touching each other on the floor.

894. PUMPING THE THIGHS

As the thighs need a fair amount of weight to pump up, your options are limited backstage. A few brave souls do squats with a willing partner on their back. Another option is sissy squats (grab a stationary upright with one hand, and while leaning slightly back on your heels, squat down to the floor). Beware. Pumped-up quads tend to lose their cuts and separation.

895. BICEPS

As most lat exercises also hit the biceps you probably won't have to do any direct biceps movements. A few light dumbell or spring curls (using your trusty chest expander) will give the biceps a good pump. Narrow reverse chins from an overhead pipe will also work.

896. POSING FOR PUMPING

Besides direct exercises, constantly practice your posing backstage. Not only will this distribute blood evenly to all parts of the body, it will also loosen you up before you go onstage, especially if you practice your twisting poses.

897. THE FIVE-MINUTE WARNING

In all probability you'll be given a five-minute warning before you step out onstage. When the warning comes, make a few final checks. Is the oil applied evenly to your body? Is your hair neat and tidy? Have you pinned your competition number to your posing trunks? Did you memorize the number? (The judges will call you by number, not your name.)

898. AVOID STARING AT THE LIGHTS

As soon as you walk out onstage the first thing you'll notice is the intensity (and later the heat) of the stage lights. It will take you a few minutes to get accustomed to their brightness. Try to avoid staring at the lights. Not only is doing so dangerous to your vision, but you may become dizzy and lose your balance.

899. FOLLOW INSTRUCTIONS

Once the judging starts simply follow the directions of the head judge. When your number is called out, step forward and take the requested position. When a particular pose is requested, immediately go into it and hold it until the judge indicates the next pose or calls for you to "break" position.

BOTTOM (LEFT TO RIGHT): ROBERT HATCH, RODNEY DAVIS, MIKE ERGAS, OMAR DECKARD

POST PREJUDGING

900. Replacing lost fluids

901. Oiling down

902. Final checks before you leave

903. Eat sparingly

904. Take a nap

905. Don't forget the alarm clock!

906. Visuallze

907. Two-hour warning

908. Be ready for similarities and differences

909. Sportsmanship

910. Ask about it

911. Take it to heart

912. I was robbed!

913. Take a rest!

900. REPLACING LOST FLUIDS

As soon as the prejudging has ended, your first task is to replace lost fluids. After three rounds of posing, you'll be dehydrated. The instant you get backstage take a few sips of water. Don't gulp all at once as it may give you cramps or gas. Try consuming the water over an hour or two.

901. OILING DOWN

Before putting on your clothes, remove as much of the oil from your body as possible. Oil stains are very difficult to remove from clothes. If shower facilities are available, use them. If not, you can remove the oil with a towel and rubbing alcohol.

902. FINAL CHECKS BEFORE YOU LEAVE

Before leaving the contest venue, check with someone to find out what time contestants should return. In most cases it will be an hour before curtain time. Remember that there will be a bigger crowd in the evening, so parking may be an issue. You don't want to have to do a mini cardio session by walking to the venue. Finally, make sure you have some sort of identification to confirm you are a competitor (hopefully your physical appearance should be all that's required). You don't want to be accused of trying to sneak in. But be aware that even the contest promoters themselves get refused admission at times if they don't have the right ID.

903. EAT SPARINGLY

Most competitors go for a small meal between the prejudging and evening show. Nothing major mind you. Just a few carbs to bring your energy levels back up. In the event that your muscles were not fully carb-loaded, this will give them a fuller appearance. Don't make the mistake of eating a large meal, as it will make controlling your abdominal muscles more difficult as well as increase the risk of getting cramps. Continue eating clean food from your cooler rather than eating at a restaurant. Even the smallest amount of salt can cause physique-damaging water retention.

904. TAKE A NAP

No doubt nervousness has prevented you from sleeping regularly in the days leading up to the contest. After you have your small meal, take a one- to two-hour nap. Try not to crash for three hours or more, or the body will go into a deep-sleep mode and you'll need a couple of hours just to fully wake up again. The idea is to sleep long enough to recharge your batteries but not long enough to shut you down for the day.

905. DON'T FORGET THE ALARM CLOCK!

If you are excessively tired you may crash as soon as your head hits the pillow. You may not be heard from until the next morning! Either have a trusted friend call you, or set an alarm clock (if you're staying at a hotel, arrange for a wake-up call).

906. VISUALIZE

As soon as you wake up from your nap, don't rush to put on your clothes. Take a few minutes and visualize the morning's proceedings. By now you have a pretty good idea who the top competitors are in your weight division. Visualize their weak points and your strong points. Decide which poses you'll hit when they strike their best shots. Try to anticipate how the posedown will develop. Granted there's no way to plan it out pose for pose, but at least you'll have a strategy.

907. TWO-HOUR WARNING

Give yourself a minimum of two hour's preparation before the evening show – an hour to wake up and get dressed and an hour to get there. The checklist you followed in the morning also applies in the evening. Check it yourself and then have someone else confirm things for you.

908. BE READY FOR SIMILARITIES AND DIFFERENCES

The evening show may or may not resemble the prejudging. The free-posing and posedown rounds will be much the same, but the comparison rounds may be different. This is especially true if the quality of competitors is very high.

909. SPORTSMANSHIP

After the winners are announced, accept the results unreservedly. This will be no problem if you place first. But if you placed out of the top three when you felt you should have placed higher, don't create a scene. In the vast majority of contests the judges do rank the competitors fairly. It's not what you want to hear but it's a fact of life.

910. ASK ABOUT IT

The best way to find out why you placed in a certain position is to ask the judges. They are usually more than happy to let you know, especially if you treat them with respect.

911. TAKE IT TO HEART

The best bodybuilders work very hard to consistently improve and bring up their weak points. Take what the judges (and others) say, and apply it to your training over the next while to be better prepared for the next event.

912. I WAS ROBBED!

What do you do if you (and the majority of the audience) feel you were robbed? Simply smile, strike a few of your best poses, and congratulate those who placed above you. Don't curse, throw your trophy, or give the judges the finger (they'll probably be judging again next year, and they have great memories for wayward fingers!). Channel your frustration into preparing for next year's contest and working on your weak points.

913. TAKE A REST!

The first thing you do after the contest is nothing. That's right. Take two or three weeks and avoid the gym completely. No matter how much fun you may have had over the past few weeks and months, preparing for a bodybuilding contest places a tremendous amount of stress on the body. Don't worry about "losing" muscle mass, as precontest bodybuilding is for the most part a state of overtraining. You may actually gain muscle mass during your two or three-week hiatus.

COMMUNICATION SKILLS

914. I'd love to!

915. Learn to relax

916. Slow and controlled

917. Keep it clean

918. Listen to yourself

919. Learn from your tape

920. What's "uh" your "ah" problem?

921. Use familiar language

922. Don't blame the judges

923. Those who do it well

924. Help from the business world

COMMUNICATION SKILLS

914. I'D LOVE TO!

If you plan on making bodybuilding a major part of your life, then we suggest you get comfortable doing interviews. This is especially true if you start winning contests on a regular basis. Most sports receive regular TV coverage, even sports as obscure as bodybuilding. If you win or place high in a contest, sooner or later you'll be asked to do an interview. Your response should be a whole-hearted yes! You can't beat TV interviews to further your bodybuilding career. Your next competition may be hundreds of miles away, and if the judges have seen your face on TV you have an advantage over a competitor who has never received media coverage.

915. LEARN TO RELAX

Public speaking is like most things in life – you'll do a much better job if you are relaxed. Remaining calm often solves many of the problems of public speaking. If you let yourself get uptight at the first sign of a microphone, your nerves are probably going to have a major effect on what you say and how you say it.

916. SLOW AND CONTROLLED

No matter how excited you are, try to speak slowly and carefully. Don't race along trying to put as many words as possible into one sentence. Reporters usually ask enough questions to allow almost anyone to say what's on his or her mind.

917. KEEP IT CLEAN

There are enough foul-mouthed people around without you becoming one of them. If you have a habit of tossing in the occasional curse word during your day-to day-speech, you'll have to show restraint during an interview. Vulgarity may be accepted among your peers but it's a definite no-no on TV.

918. LISTEN TO YOURSELF

It's probably a good idea to tape record yourself at some point just to see how you sound. You can even get a friend to play the part of the interviewer. If this is the first time hearing yourself on tape the results may surprise you. Most people don't realize how their voice sounds to others. In fact you may not even recognize it the first time you play it back!

919. LEARN FROM YOUR TAPE

After recording yourself a couple of times, play it back and analyze how you sound. Pay attention to how fast you speak and how you pronounce each word. If you have an accent or dialect, you may want to consider changing it. Not that dialects or accents are wrong, but you want your interview to be clear and concise. Both Arnold Schwarzenegger and Lou Ferrigno spent years working on their public speaking (Arnold because of his native Austrian dialect and Lou because of a hearing loss suffered from an ear infection in childhood). Now both are among the sport's best public speakers.

920. WHAT'S "UH" YOUR "AH" PROBLEM?

Another thing to avoid is the use of "uhs" and "ahs". Make a conscious effort not to string sentences together with such idiosyncratic grunts. Finish one sentence and then start the next. If you have nothing more to add, don't say anything. Don't leave the interviewer hanging with an "uh" or "ah".

921. USE FAMILIAR LANGUAGE

Nothing sounds as stupid as someone trying to imitate a thesaurus. It's so obvious that he or she has no idea the meaning of the words being used. Keep it straightforward and be yourself. Simple words are better than long or uncommon words.

922. DON'T BLAME THE JUDGES

If the reporter asks you to comment on your low placing, don't dump on the judges. Instead of being negative, show good sportsmanship by saying how you underestimated the competition, and how the whole show was a great learning experience.

923. THOSE WHO DO IT WELL

Most of the sport's superstars are very professional when it comes to giving interviews. Go through your video or DVD collection and see how they do it. In fact many are so proficient at giving interviews that they are frequently called on to MC shows and do color commentary on TV.

924. HELP FROM THE BUSINESS WORLD

If you feel you have a great future in bodybuilding but are still nervous about public speaking, give serious thought to doing a public speaking course. Such courses will give you the skills to master public speaking and presentation. Not only will this help your bodybuilding career immensely, but good public-speaking skills are an asset in most facets of life.

LEE PRIEST

THE BUSINESS OF BODYBUILDING

925. Don't just sit there and wait – promote yourself
926. Guest posing – be in shape
927. Be on time
928. More than just two minutes
929. Seminars – two in one
930. The big three
931. Take notes
932. Photos
933. Videos
934. Don't skimp on production.
935. Dressed to kill – make money!
936. Dressed to kill – get to know your friendly neighborhood tailor
937. Mail-order courses
938. Write articles
939. Take a writing course
940. The training article
941. Books
942. A chicken and egg situation
943. Sample chapters
944. Ghost writing
945. Supplement promotion

925. DON'T JUST SIT THERE AND WAIT – PROMOTE YOURSELF

Unlike his counterpart 30 years ago, the modern bodybuilder can look forward to receiving more than a handshake or trophy after winning a major title. But for every Arnold Schwarzenegger or Ronnie Coleman, there are hundreds, if not thousands, of bodybuilders out there just waiting for something to happen. Unfortunately it doesn't work that way. You have to take the bull by the horns, so to speak, and promote yourself. You have to be an agent and marketer all rolled into one.

926. GUEST POSING – BE IN SHAPE

Thanks to Arnold Schwarzenegger and Franco Columbu, today's bodybuilders can earn hundreds of thousands of dollars a year displaying their physiques. Of course there are thousands of bodybuilders offering their services, and reputation is a big factor in determining who lands the posing contracts. If you normally compete at say, 220-pounds, and start showing up to guest pose at 250+ pounds, your guest-posing career is over. With the exception of a few "massiveness nuts," most in the audience want to see guest posers in or near contest shape. This means keeping your weight within 10 to 15 pounds of your contest weight year-round.

927. BE ON TIME

Bodybuilding contests are like most sports in that there are schedules to keep. Arriving five minutes before you are to guest pose will give contest promoters ulcers. You even run the risk of having the audience turn against you. If you are late for a couple of shows, or worse, don't show at all, your name will be mud within the small bodybuilding fraternity and you'll be lucky to get asked to guest pose ever again – word gets around quickly.

928. MORE THAN JUST TWO MINUTES

If you really want to enhance your reputation as a great guest poser, don't limit your appearance to your two-minutes onstage. Arrive at the show early and mingle with the audience and competitors. Take time to answer questions and sign autographs. All these little extras will have promoters lining up for your services.

929. SEMINARS – TWO IN ONE

Most guest posers also give seminars on the weekend of the contest. If it's a big show there may be three seminars: Friday after the weigh-in, Saturday afternoon between the pre-judging and evening show, and Sunday afternoon. For most amateur contests the seminar will be Saturday afternoon. At $10 to $20 a seminar, it doesn't take long for your income to grow considerably. Now you see why public speaking is such an asset to bodybuilders.

930. THE BIG THREE

Most bodybuilders divide their seminars into three broad categories: training, diet, and nutrition. How much time you spend on each will depend on the audience and the questions they ask. Even though there will be questions during the seminar, always leave room at the end for additional comments and questions. Give the audience their money's worth. Give them more than they were expecting.

931. TAKE NOTES

If you are attending a seminar, treat it like a college course – take notes. Even if you are a novice bodybuilder and competition is still a few years away, jot down anything related to contest preparation.

You can't beat the first-hand advice that seasoned competitive bodybuilders can give when it's time to step onstage.

932. PHOTOS

As soon as you start winning top amateur contests, have a series of 8 x 10 glossy photos produced. Get them done in both black and white and color, and take them with you to seminars and posing exhibitions. If you decide to sell them, the average price is $5 to $10. Many of the pros charge $20 or more and have discounts available if people buy a set. Bodybuilding photos not only bring you in additional income, but you can't beat that kind of exposure. Fans will talk about and show off your signed 8 x 10 for years!

933. VIDEOS

Besides contests, there is nothing as inspirational as watching a top pro bodybuilder going through a real workout. If you start winning major titles you should seriously consider releasing both posing and training tapes and DVDs.

934. DON'T SKIMP ON PRODUCTION.

The video industry is like the photo industry – you get what you pay for. Invest the extra dollars and have a professional videographer do it right. Not only will your fans appreciate it, but word will get around. Develop a reputation for mediocrity and your business dreams will end up the same.

935. DRESSED TO KILL – MAKE MONEY!

It was only a matter of time before bodybuilders joined the fashion set. Many pro bodybuilders have turned their talents to marketing gym wear. If you or someone you know has a talent for clothing design, you may want to seriously investigate coming out with your own line of workout wear.

936. DRESSED TO KILL – GET TO KNOW YOUR FRIENDLY NEIGHBORHOOD TAILOR

If not already the case, it won't be long before most off-the-rack clothes won't fit you properly. Sure you'll find a 48 or 50-inch shirt, but it will come with a 40+-inch waist. When you reach the point that store-bought clothes start looking sloppy on you, consult a tailor. A professional tailor can make you pants, shirts, and sports jackets that will hug your physique. Not only will you feel better, you'll make a much more professional impression as you promote yourself.

937. MAIL-ORDER COURSES

Although replaced in recent years by training videos, mail-order courses are still a viable way to make extra income with your bodybuilding expertise. Mail-order courses were first popularized by Charles Atlas. (Remember the skinny guy on the beach getting sand kicked in his face?). Since then most of the top bodybuilders have printed training courses and placed ads in the various muscle magazines. If you decide to produce your own, have someone with good writing and layout skills design them for you. Don't simply scribble a few items on paper and photocopy them. Remember, being professional will bring you a professional-level income.

938. WRITE ARTICLES

Every month there are scores of bodybuilding and fitness-related magazines hitting the newsstands. While most have their own writers, much of the content is submitted by freelancers. If you have a talent for writing, start putting pen to paper and make submissions. You may have to let your first couple go as freebies, but once you develop a reputation for quality writing, the magazines will be offering you top dollar for your work.

939. TAKE A WRITING COURSE

Ron Harris is a good example of someone who makes his entire income (and a pretty good one, too) from writing bodybuilding articles. But that wouldn't be the case if he didn't have the skill. Magazines will clean up your article a bit if you know what you're talking about, but if you want to make a living, go to your local college and take a writers' course.

940. THE TRAINING ARTICLE

If you have access to a top bodybuilder, pro or amateur, you have the basis for one or more training articles. Ask the individual if you can interview him about his training methods. Most will be only too happy to oblige, as it's free advertising for them. Take the person's comments and build a training article around them. If you're handy with a camera, take a few training shots to accompany the article. Send it to **MuscleMag International** .You could have a whole new career just waiting for you!

941. BOOKS

If you have a real gift for writing, the logical step up from writing articles is a book. Many of bodybuilding's biggest names have released autobiography and training books.

942. A CHICKEN AND EGG SITUATION

If you decide to write a book you may run into the chicken and egg situation. Most publishers will only want you if you've already written a book that was a success, but to get a book published you'll need a publisher! It's the old "I need experience to get a job to get experience" circle. Don't get discouraged. Few authors get their book published by the first publisher they approach.

943. SAMPLE CHAPTERS

Rather than complete a whole book before you land a publisher, write a couple of sample chapters. Together with the book outline, try submitting them to numerous publishers. It doesn't make sense to invest months if not years of your time on a project if there is no light at the end of the tunnel. In addition, submitting an outline plus sample chapters will give a potential publisher a chance to offer suggestions on other topics to include in the book.

944. GHOST WRITING

Writers have been doing it for years. There is even speculation that the works of William Shakespeare were produced by another person. Many of bodybuilding's greatest publications are not the work of the person whose name appears on the cover. Instead the pro bodybuilder will hire a writer to produce the work for him. The late Bill Reynolds wrote books for dozens of the sport's top bodybuilders. There is an old saying "nothing ventured nothing gained." Try submitting ghost-writing proposals to a number of top bodybuilders who don't have a training book released yet. Your first book might only be a postage stamp away.

945. SUPPLEMENT PROMOTION

By far the biggest industry in the bodybuilding world is the food-supplement business. Each year such companies such as MuscleTech, Twin Lab, Pro Lab and EAS gross billions of dollars. You can grab a big piece of this action once you reach the top amateur or pro level of bodybuilding. Bodybuilders have been endorsing supplements for decades. It started with protein powder but now includes the full spectrum of the supplement industry. Don't be surprised if a supplement manufacturer approaches you at a contest and offers you a contract to endorse their products.

DON'T BE SURPRISED IF A SUPPLEMENT MANUFACTURER APPROACHES YOU AT A CONTEST AND OFFERS YOU A CONTRACT TO ENDORSE THEIR PRODUCTS.

TITO RAYMOND

CONTEST PROMOTION

946. After winning them, promote them
947. Try the apprenticeship route first
948. Getting affiliated
949. The lowest bidder
950. Those who know best
951. Never too many contacts
952. Contest venue
953. The all-important lighting
954. Let there be light
955. The guest poser
956. The MC
957. Promotion
958. Go where they hang out
959. The upcoming events section
960. A TV or newspaper spot
961. The paid advertisement
962. Tickets
963. Two sets
964. The all-important ushers
965. Lodging & transportation
966. Delegate
967. Keep notes

946. AFTER WINNING THEM, PROMOTE THEM

Just as many actors decide to become directors, so too do many bodybuilders throw their hat into the contest promotion ring. The most famous is Arnold Schwarzenegger with his Arnold Classic in Columbus, Ohio, each year. If you decide to start promoting contests you must become familiar with such topics as venue selection, marketing, and sponsor recruitment.

947. TRY THE APPRENTICESHIP ROUTE FIRST

Before you decide to promote your first contest we encourage you to learn the ropes by volunteering at other promoters' shows. Offer to help out with such tasks as ushering, ticket collecting, and being a stagehand. The more you learn now the easier things will be when you start promoting contests on your own.

948. GETTING AFFILIATED

As a future contest promoter you don't just decide to hold a contest, you first must become affiliated with a major bodybuilding federation. You then have to follow the rules and regulations of that federation. This gets more complicated as you work your way up the contest hierarchy. At the local level, there may only be one federation to choose from.

949. THE LOWEST BIDDER

If the previous promoter has retired and the contest has been successful the last couple of years, odds are more then one person will come forward to continue the tradition. This means you may have competition in your quest to promote the contest. All the prospective promoters will be asked to submit a bid, and just like a business tender, the lowest bidder usually wins.

950. THOSE WHO KNOW BEST

Although not necessary, your first step in contest promotion should be to interview previous promoters. If they are friendly types, and promotion has not left a sour taste in their mouths, they'll probably be only too happy to help you out. During the course of your interviews you may find that most contests in the area lose money. If this is the case, and it often is, you might want to reconsider the whole venture.

951. NEVER TOO MANY CONTACTS

One thing you should obtain from previous promoters is a list of contacts. A couple of phone calls can save you a lot of time and effort. People with prior experience can give you a run-down on all the little problems that will pop up.

952. CONTEST VENUE

One of your first steps in contest promotion is to acquire a venue. For a small, local show you could probably get by with a high school gym, but as you work up the contest ladder, the audience and competitors will expect better facilities. Of course the better the facility the higher the cost and the farther in advance you'll need to book. Don't expect to phone up the local arts or concert theater and book two weeks before your date. You may have to phone months, if not years, in advance.

953. THE ALL-IMPORTANT LIGHTING

Many potential great contests have been ruined by amateurish lighting. While most facilities will have their own lights, keep in mind that lighting a bodybuilding show is different from lighting a play or rock concert. You don't need fancy colors, either. In fact plain white light works best. What is important is how the lights are positioned. Once you book your contest venue, check the lights out. If there is any doubt, spend the extra money and hire a lighting contractor.

954. LET THERE BE LIGHT

Always test out the lighting situation a day or two before the contest. Get a couple of willing volunteers to shed their clothes and hop up onstage. Position the lights so that your "competitors" are well lit from every angle. Also make sure that the competitors on the ends are just as visible as those in the middle of a line-up. In many contests the unevenness of the lighting gives those in the center of the stage an unfair advantage over those on the periphery.

955. THE GUEST POSER

There is nothing like the presence of one of the sport's superstars to boost ticket sales. If fans know that Ronnie Coleman, Jay Cutler or Markus Ruhl will be in attendance, you won't have to worry about unsold seats. In fact, your biggest concern may be scalpers! As most of the sport's top pros have excellent reputations, you probably can't go wrong booking any of them. Still there are a few pros that have developed reputations for being difficult to work with or arriving in pitiful shape. If there is any doubt, check with promoters who have booked guest posers before.

956. THE MC

One extremely important choice is the MC, or master of ceremonies. This can be anyone from a local celebrity to a highly respected bodybuilding personality. One piece of advice though: don't rely on the services of someone who is not a fan of bodybuilding. Many such individuals have a habit of belittling the sport. Nothing is as demeaning as some wisecracking comedian using the show as an occasion to try out his new musclehead jokes.

957. PROMOTION

Once you have your contest venue booked, your next step is to let everyone know about it. Bodybuilders need a minimum of three months to prepare for a contest. In fact, you may want to start promoting five or six months in advance as this will give potential competitors time to make up their minds.

958. GO WHERE THEY HANG OUT

The most logical places to start your promoting are local gyms. This is where your competitors train. Have a series of professional-looking flyers printed, then go to each gym and ask the owner to place one on their public notice board. As most gym owners support bodybuilding, you should have no problem getting support.

959. THE UPCOMING EVENTS SECTION

Most of the major bodybuilding magazines have an upcoming contests section. Send in a brief description of your contest (title, date, place, etc) and they'll print it free of charge. You can send yours to *MuscleMag International* at 5775 McLaughlin Rd., Mississauga, ON, L5R 3P7 Canada.

960. A TV OR NEWSPAPER SPOT

Many sports reporters are tired of reporting the same sports over and over. They are always on the look out for something different. If you have a contact at the local paper or TV station, give them a call about possibly doing a story on your upcoming contest. Not

only does this give them a story with a slightly different angle, but more important, you get free advertising!

961. THE PAID ADVERTISEMENT

If you don't have a contact at a local media outlet, you'll have to dig into your pockets for a paid advertisement. If you have the cash, TV is the way to go. Nothing beats the appeal of actually seeing what's being advertised. A cheaper alternative would be to check out the local cable TV station. Most have free (or relatively cheap) community events spots during the day. With the rate at which people channel surf these days, odds are many potential competitors or audience members will see your ad. Radio is probably the cheapest route for advertising.

962. TICKETS

Unlike the airlines, don't sell more tickets than your venue holds. Bodybuilding spectators are a very loyal bunch and will show up. The last thing you want on contest night is a couple of hundred large and angry bodybuilders being turned away at the door. Print only as many tickets as your seating capacity. Additional tickets will have to be identified as "standing room only."

963. TWO SETS

Keep in mind that you are really running two shows – prejudging and evening. This means that'll you need two sets of tickets. If the auditorium has numbered seats, the numbers should appear on the tickets. This is probably not a big deal for the prejudging when the numbers will be much lower, but it will make things run much more smoothly at the evening show where all seats could be sold out.

964. THE ALL-IMPORTANT USHERS

If the contest venue you booked includes ushers within the rental cost, take advantage of them. If not, hire your own (odds are you'll be able to get volunteers). There is nothing like the confusion of 1000 people all trying to find their numbered seats at the same time.

965. LODGING & TRANSPORTATION

If most of your judges are from out of town, you may have to supply transportation and lodging. Now this usually only applies to pro events, but you should be aware of it just the same. The one person you will most definitely need to look after is the guest poser. Have someone designated to pick them up at the airport and shuttle him from the hotel to the contest venue (and anywhere else he or she might want to go). Make sure the hotel the guest poser is booked into has a decent restaurant.

966. DELEGATE

One of the signs of a great leader is being able to delegate responsibility. There is no way one individual can run a bodybuilding contest. As soon as you land the job of promoting the contest, recruit a couple of trustworthy individuals to help you out. Put one in charge of venue, another for lighting, another for tickets, another for marketing, etc. Your role should be more of overseer than hands on.

967. KEEP NOTES

Keep detailed notes of every aspect of planning. This will make running next year's show that much easier. With time comes experience and a reputation for quality. Don't be shocked if down the road you are asked to run a national or international show. Most of the sport's top organizers got their start at the local level.

MR. OLYMPIA 2006, JAY CUTLER

ACTING

968. Try being heavy at home first
969. Concentrate on bodybuilding first
970. Acting lessons
971. Acting as sideline
972. Be professional
973. Stuntman

968. TRY BEING HEAVY AT HOME FIRST

Most movies these days have a "heavy" or two. These are the big (but not so intelligent) character actors who usually get their butts kicked by the star of the show. If you have an inkling for acting, check out auditions in your area to see what's open. Don't hop on a plane for Los Angeles thinking you will be the next Arnold. Every year thousands do just that, and the vast majority end up broke and lost in the crowd.

969. CONCENTRATE ON BODYBUILDING FIRST

With few exceptions, all the bodybuilders who made it in acting achieved considerable bodybuilding success first. From Steve Reeves, Dave Draper and Reg Park to Arnold, Lou Ferrigno and Mickey Hargitay, all won major titles before they stepped in front of a TV or movie camera. In fact it was their bodybuilding success that brought them to the attention of TV and movie producers. It's virtually impossible for an unknown to jet off to Hollywood and land an acting job.

970. ACTING LESSONS

If you are still determined to be an actor, we suggest taking acting lessons. If you are still in high school, check out your school's drama club. At first the other students may think it strange that a jock wants to act, but you'll soon win them over. If you are finished school, check out the local theater companies. Most offer lessons and small roles to newcomers. Finally, if you live in a bigger area, you'll probably have access to a college or university that offer full-fledged programs in acting. Taking acting lessons does two things; it gives you the skills necessary to be competitive, and it gives you as taste for the acting profession. Acting sounds glamorous, but it's not all fun.

971. ACTING AS SIDELINE

There are a hundred times more actors available than roles for then to play. Does this mean you won't be a success? No. You will be a success if you have the talent, the dedication and the will. However, every actor has lean times, and those lean times can go on for months – even years. You will have the most fun (and ironically, the most success) as an actor if you don't take it too seriously.

972. BE PROFESSIONAL

Not taking it too seriously doesn't mean not caring about it at all. Of course, you should show up on time, be in the right frame of mind, work hard, and do your job to the best of your abilities.

973. STUNTMAN

The acting profession gives bodybuilders another option besides starring in the movie. With movie stars making millions of dollars per picture the last thing the stars (and their agents!) want is for accidents to happen while shooting an action scene. Odds are the next time you see some action star jumping from a moving vehicle or falling off a horse, it's a stuntman doing the work. If you are the acrobatic type and have a knack for falling on your face, give stunting a try. As with acting, approach your local film industry first before heading to Hollywood.

THE GYM
BUSINESS

974. Starting your own

975. The private gym

976. The franchise or licensed gym

977. The business plan

978. What's in the plan

979. Personal preference versus making money

980. Buying

981. Leasing

982. Making your own

983. Buying second hand

984. Membership for salaries

985. Who must be qualified?

986. First Aid and CPR

987. Maintenance

988. A pro shop?

989. Business is business

40

974. STARTING YOUR OWN

Sooner or later most people who lift weights toy with the idea of opening their own gym. Most quickly drop the idea, but you may give it some serious thought. Operating your own gym has numerous advantages. For starters you are your own boss. You also have full control over what training equipment to include in your gym. Finally, if you work hard at it and have a certain amount of luck, you may actually make a comfortable living at it.

975. THE PRIVATE GYM

If you decide to venture into the gym business the simplest type of gym to open is a private training gym. By this we mean everything about it is yours and yours alone. No forking out big bucks for name rights, no listening to someone else dictate how you are running things.

976. THE FRANCHISE OR LICENSED GYM

Such names as Gold's, World, and Powerhouse are fixtures in the bodybuilding world. All started out as one location and with time and success, multiplied. The advantage to opening a franchise gym is that you'll have name recognition from day one. You'll also receive backing from head office, as the owners don't like to see their gym name go down in flames. In addition, you will have access to knowledge that has been gained from many, many years in the business.

977. THE BUSINESS PLAN

Your first step in opening a gym is developing a business plan. Before you approach a bank, investors, or Gold's or World, you'll need to organize things on paper to show people that you are both serious and more important, viable. Even if you have your own money, you want to think seriously about your business implications. Owning a business can be an easy way to turn a big fortune into a double-digit bank account if you don't think strategically. If your town of 5000 people already has two or three gyms, forget it. With only about 10 percent of the population working out you just won't get the numbers to keep your gym afloat.

978. WHAT'S IN THE PLAN

In your business plan you'll need to outline such topics as location, anticipated demand, start-up and maintenance costs, and type of facility (hardcore bodybuilding, fitness facility, health spa, private training).

979. PERSONAL PREFERENCE VERSUS MAKING MONEY

Unless you live in a large population center, our advice is to open a general fitness facility. Hardcore bodybuilding gyms will only attract serious bodybuilders. Even though you may be one yourself, guys doing heavy deadlifts and squats will frighten everyone else away. At the other extreme, health spas only attract executive types. Again a small number of the population to begin with. A general fitness facility will attract the most people and give you a fighting chance of success.

980. BUYING

The advantage of buying equipment is that once it's paid off you own it. No more payments. Of course, while strength equipment will last forever, the average life of a cardio machine is about five years. Maintaining your older equipment can be prohibitively expensive. Another disadvantage of buying is the up-front cost. Unless you have a good, long-term credit rating, equipment manufacturers will want you to pay the cost up front in full. They may give you some sort of payment plan, but odds are you'll need to pay off the equipment in a short period of time.

981. LEASING

The advantage of leasing equipment is that you are not committed to keeping it. After the terms of the lease are up, you can send it all back for new gear. This is very beneficial for cardio machines, which can wear out and become outdated rather quickly. Of course if you decide to keep the equipment you'll have most of the cost already paid off.

982. MAKING YOUR OWN

Making your own equipment is a dangerous practice. On one hand the cost may be lower than buying or leasing. On the other hand, very few people know how to design and build strength-training equipment. You also have the risk of a lawsuit if a piece of your homemade equipment collapses. It's unlikely that you would even be able to get insurance with homemade equipment. Our advice is to let the machine manufacturers do their job.

983. BUYING SECOND HAND

The advantage of buying second-hand equipment is that it is cheaper and was built by a commercial manufacturer. The disadvantage is that there will be wear and tear. You can't go wrong with second-hand free weights like barbells and dumbells. Even racks are fairly risk-free. But be careful about buying anything with wheels, pulleys, and cables. Treat buying second-hand gym equipment like buying a used car. Bring someone with you who knows what to look for. If there is any doubt give it a pass.

984. MEMBERSHIP FOR SALARIES

As there is no way you can run your gym by yourself, you'll need to hire staff. One way to cut down on salaries is to trade a gym membership for work. You will still need to pay any full-time employees, but it is fairly easy to get part-time staff to volunteer their services in exchange for a free membership.

985. WHO MUST BE QUALIFIED?

While your front desk receptionist doesn't need any special certification, your gym instructors do. All it takes is one bad piece of advice from an unqualified instructor and you're in serious trouble. Make sure all your gym instructors have certification from a recognized strength and conditioning, or personal training, organization. You don't want a lawsuit because some unqualified instructor showed a new client the wrong way to perform squats.

986. FIRST AID AND CPR

Depending where you live CPR may or may not be mandatory for staff. But it's always a good idea. If someone collapses in your gym and no one is certified in CPR or first aid, the situation could be dire. At the very least try to have it so at least one person certified in CPR and first aid is on duty at all times.

987. MAINTENANCE

Maintenance is one of those gray areas you must be aware of. Although fixing a cable or bolt is not that big a deal, repairing the latest cardio machine presents many challenges. Even if you have someone on staff who is handy at that sort of thing, the issue of legal liability may rear its ugly head. What happens if your uncertified staff member fixes a machine and then an hour later someone hurts himself on the exact same machine? In court a piece of paper from a certified technician will carry more weight, and the odds are good to excellent that he or his company will carry insurance.

988. A PRO SHOP?

One way to maximize your odds of staying in business is to have a pro shop within your gym. Just like golf clubhouses, which have pro shops to sell clubs, clothes, and golf balls, you can fill your bodybuilding pro shop with a wide assortment of items. Include the latest in supplements such as whey protein, creatine, and glutamine. Have a couple of racks of stylish workout clothes. Finally, have a couple of coolers containing energy drinks. Many gyms will even mix up a protein shake for you for a couple of dollars.

989. BUSINESS IS BUSINESS

To run a successful business you must be a successful businessperson. You can be the best house builder in the world but you may not run a successful construction business. Similarly, you may be the best bodybuilder in the world, but not run a successful gym. If you do not have good business acumen, it's best to work for someone else.

DAVE PALUMBO

FINAL
THOUGHTS

990. Eat your vegetables

991. Right equipment

992. Sleep!

993. Rest

994. Use your noggin

995. The artistic sport

996. We are sculptors

997. A long time coming

998. Get a life

999. Stay in shape

1000. Dedication and drive

1001. Set your goals today

FINAL THOUGHTS

990. EAT YOUR VEGETABLES

Yes, bodybuilders need extra protein. But too many live on chicken, tuna and rice and neglect what should be making up half their food volume. Vegetables help prevent cancer and heart disease and keep your digestive system working properly. And if you eat as much protein as you should be, you're going to need an efficient digestive system!

991. RIGHT EQUIPMENT

No, I don't mean barbells and dumbells. I mean that you need amino acids, protein, and plenty of vitamins and minerals to allow muscle to be created.

992. SLEEP!

Muscle is built while you sleep. Not only that, but your hormone levels are also controlled while you sleep. And hormones control such things as metabolism, growth and appetite, so you, as a bodybuilder, definitely don't want your hormone levels to go out of whack!

993. REST

If you can't get a full eight hours a night, at least grab a nap in the afternoon. And try not to expend too much energy in the rest of your life. Top bodybuilders are notorious for doing little but eating, sleeping, and working out.

994. USE YOUR NOGGIN

The very best bodybuilders use their brains as much as their brawn. In fact, Arnold stated repeatedly that what he had over the other bodybuilders of his day was the consciousness to use his brain power – both to build muscle and to win.

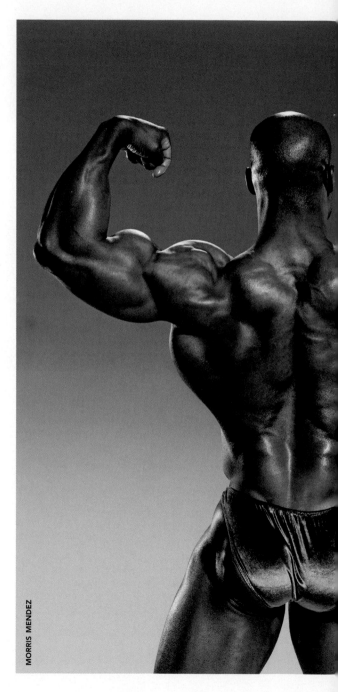

MORRIS MENDEZ

995. THE ARTISTIC SPORT

Some think of bodybuilding as an art, some as a sport. But regardless of which way you think of it, you will need an artistic eye to become the best you can be.

996. WE ARE SCULPTORS

Just as Michelangelo carved David from marble, so you carve your body from weights and food. And you must pay just as close attention to proportion, detail, and all three dimensions.

997. A LONG TIME COMING

The planning and execution of the carving of David took 40 years. That masterpiece didn't happen overnight and neither will yours. However, as long as you are consistently moving in the right direction, your work of art will come.

998. GET A LIFE

There is no question that bodybuilders tend to be an obsessed lot. But try to give your life some balance. At the end of the day all the trophies are meaningless if you end up alone because you can't talk about anything but anabolism and growth hormone.

999. STAY IN SHAPE

It's ironic that so many people who spend so much of their time in the gym end up in rotten shape. Sure, they may have muscles, but can they walk a block? Tie their shoes? Go upstairs without huffing and puffing? You don't have to do an hour a day of cardio, but your heart needs exercise, too. Exercise it at least three times a week for half an hour.

1000. DEDICATION AND DRIVE

There will be times you don't seem to be making any progress. Likewise, there will be days when you would rather drink beer and play pool with your buddies than get under a bar and squat till you want to puke. You won't get the body you desire unless you make it a priority.

1001. SET YOUR GOALS TODAY

Write down some very short-term goals, some mid-range goals and some long term goals. Look at them every day. You might state: "This week I will train four days, and concentrate on every single rep. By next month I will have added 10 percent more weight to every lift. By next year I will have gained 10 pounds of muscle." These are realistic goals that will keep you on track and keep you progressing.

GOOD LUCK!

"THIS WEEK I WILL **TRAIN** FOUR DAYS, AND **CONCENTRATE** ON EVERY SINGLE REP. BY NEXT MONTH I WILL HAVE ADDED **10 PERCENT** MORE WEIGHT TO EVERY LIFT. BY NEXT YEAR I WILL HAVE **GAINED 10 POUNDS OF MUSCLE.**"

CREDITS

NOTES

NOTES

NOTES